SMITHSONIAN INSTITUTION
BUREAU OF AMERICAN ETHNOLOGY
BULLETIN 190

An Ethnography of the Huron Indians, 1615-1649

By ELISABETH TOOKER

U.S. GOVERNMENT PRINTING OFFICE
WASHINGTON : 1964

For sale by the Superintendent of Documents, U.S. Government Printing Office
Washington D.C., 20402 - Price $1.00 (Paper)

LETTER OF TRANSMITTAL

SMITHSONIAN INSTITUTION,
BUREAU OF AMERICAN ETHNOLOGY,
Washington, D.C., DECEMBER 28, 1962.

SIR: I have the honor to submit the accompanying manuscript, entitled "An Ethnography of the Huron Indians, 1615–1649," by Elisabeth Tooker, and to recommend that it be published as a bulletin of the Bureau of American Ethnology.

Very respectfully yours,

FRANK H. H. ROBERTS, Jr.,
Director

Dr. LEONARD CARMICHAEL,
Secretary, Smithsonian Institution.

II

CONTENTS

	PAGE
Preface	1
Introduction	3
The Huron League	9
Neighboring tribes	12
The Tobacco League	12
The Neutral League	13
Other Iroquoian groups	16
The Iroquois League	17
The Algonquin	19
Dress	20
Travel	22
Intertribal relations	25
Trade and war	25
Torture of prisoners	31
The village	39
Government	42
Chiefs	42
Councils	48
Crime	52
Suicide	56
Etiquette	57
Subsistence	58
Division of labor	58
Agriculture	60
Gathering	62
Fishing	62
Hunting	65
Meals and their preparation	67
Seasonal cycle	71
Religion	72
Feasts	72
Dancing	76
Eclipse	79
Ceremony of the Marriage of Two Virgins to the Seine	79
Spirits	80
Types of illness	82
Cure of natural illnesses	84
Dreams and the desires	86
Medicine men	91
Acquisition of power	97
Curing ceremonies	101
Games	114
Witchcraft	117
Charms	120

PAGE

Life cycle_____ 122
    Birth and childhood_____ 122
    Youth_____ 124
    Marriage_____ 125
    Descent_____ 128
    Kinship terms_____ 128
    Death_____ 128
        Burial_____ 130
        Mourning_____ 133
        Feast of the Dead_____ 134
        The afterlife_____ 140
Mythology_____ 143
    Land of the dead_____ 143
    Creation myths_____ 145
Appendix 1. Names and probable tribal affiliations of Huron villages____ 149
Appendix 2. The Iroquoian origin myth cycle_____ 151
Appendix 3. Additional Huron words and phrases_____ 156
Appendix 4. Authors of the documents contained in "The Jesuit Relations
    and Allied Documents"_____ 160
References_____ 161
Index_____ 169

PREFACE

In the first half of the 17th century, the Iroquoian-speaking Huron lived in an area at the southern end of Georgian Bay in the present Province of Ontario, Canada. It was there that the French visited them, some recording what they saw and thus providing much of what we know of Huron culture—for in 1649 the Huron were driven from their homeland by the Iroquois and dispersed.

The body of this work, a compilation of the ethnographic data contained in 17th-century descriptions, is intended to be a more convenient general introduction and index to Huron culture than is presently available. It is also to be hoped that it will prove useful to students of Iroquoian culture change, for this body of data offers an almost unique vantage point from which to view such change. Temporally close to the archeological data, it affords both a point from which to look backward in time and, close to pre-Columbian times, a view of an Iroquoian culture little affected by Western civilization and a point from which to look forward in time.

The ethnography may be read either with or without reference to the notes which, in addition to serving their usual function as a vehicle for editorial comment (both mine and that which various students of the Iroquoians have previously made), also serve as a vehicle for indicating the cultural similarities and differences between the Huron and other Northern Iroquoian cultures, particularly those of the 19th- and 20th-century Wyandot and Iroquois cultures, and for indicating evidence of culture change. A brief history of the Huron after their defeat also is included.

For these notes, much, but by no means all, of the important materials on the Iroquoians published in the 19th and 20th centuries was consulted. Unfortunately, while the material on the Iroquois is quite full, that on the descendants of the 17th-century Huron is, at best, spotty. As a result, not all the comparisons that ought to be made can be. Although a few references that occur in the later literature have been included, the 18th-century data was not consulted and is probably best considered separately.

An American Indian would say that *four* things are necessary for the successful completion of a task. In this case, the four are the following individuals: Marian E. White, Wallace L. Chafe, William

1

N. Fenton, and William C. Sturtevant. All have made important suggestions as to what the content, specific and general, of this study should be, have corrected errors in the drafts, and have indicated their interest in the project at those times I most needed such reassurance. For all this, I am grateful. In spite of their best efforts, errors and inadequacies remain and for these, the responsibility is mine.

AN ETHNOGRAPHY OF THE HURON INDIANS, 1615–1649

By Elisabeth Tooker

INTRODUCTION

Our knowledge of the Huron for the period beginning with their first extensively described contact with the French and ending with their defeat and dispersal by the Iroquois in 1649–50 rests on three primary documents: Samuel de Champlain's account of the winter (1615–16) he spent in Huronia; Gabriel Sagard's account of his winter visit in 1623–24; and the yearly Relations of the Jesuits who began intensive work among the Huron in 1634. These accounts, however, are not the earliest on an Iroquoian group: Jacques Cartier in 1535 had met some Iroquoian speakers living along the St. Lawrence, a group which perhaps joined the Huron between the time of Cartier's visit and that of Champlain.[1]

---

[1] The two Huron tribes, Arendahronon and Tohontaenrat, which joined the Huron about 1590 and 1610, respectively, may have been the Laurentian Iroquois, the Iroquoian-speaking peoples Cartier found living along the St. Lawrence in an area Champlain later found to be inhabited only by Algonquian tribes (Hewitt 1907 c: 585; Wilson 1885: 58–60). Other students of the Iroquoians, however, have suggested that the Laurentian Iroquois in whole (Bailey 1933: 97–102) or in part (see Fenton 1940 d: 167–177; cf. Morgan 1901(2): 188–191) joined the Iroquois. It also is possible that the St. Lawrence valley was occupied by the Iroquois after the Laurentian Iroquois had left (Hale 1894: 10).

Various reasons have been suggested for the migration of the Laurentian Iroquois out of the St. Lawrence valley. Wars with the Huron (Lighthall 1899: 207), the Iroquois (Hale 1894: 10–11; Hewitt 1907 c: 584; Connelley 1899 c: 95), or the eastern Algonquians (Fenton 1940 d: 174) have been cited as the cause for the abandonment of the valley. Another suggestion is that Iroquoian agriculture was hazardous at best in the St. Lawrence valley (the northern limit for maize agriculture) and that climatic conditions forced the Laurentian Iroquois to move south, to an area where the growing season was longer (Barbeau 1949: 228–229). European-introduced diseases and abandonment of hilltop strongholds for more vulnerable positions near the river, after first contact, have also been suggested as factors contributing to the disappearance of the Laurentian Iroquois (Fenton 1940 d: 175).

The migration of these Iroquoian peoples out of the St. Lawrence valley and the wars that were the cause of these migrations may have led to the formation, or at least the strengthening, of the Huron and Iroquois Leagues. The addition of two tribes, perhaps the Laurentian Iroquois from the St. Lawrence, to the Huron League about 1590 and 1610 probably influenced the character of that league and may have been the actual time of its founding. The Iroquois League also may have been founded about the same time. Although both Morgan (1871: 151; 1881: 26; 1901(1): 7; 1901(2): 190) and Hale (1881: 5; 1883: 178–180) thought that the Iroquois League was founded about 1460 or not later than 1459, Hewitt (1894: 67; 1944: 80; cf. Morgan 1901(2): 189–190) disagreed and

(Footnote continued at bottom of next page.)

These descriptions picture a Northern Iroquoian group relatively unaffected by European civilization (probably the Huron even at this early date had been affected by French trade, as Europeans had been trading with Indians to the east for some years previously). French traders probably had met Hurons and knew a little of their customs, but such material is fairly inaccessible, if available. The interest of merchants often precludes an interest in writing of the common customs of a people. It is rather the professional explorers and missionaries who write of strange lands and peoples for publication at home.

The most extensive data on the Huron is that contained in the Jesuit Relations. Each year the Jesuit missionaries working in New France sent back to their Superior in France a report, or relation, of their activities, and each year these reports were edited and printed in France with the intent of gaining support for the missions. Similarly, Sagard's account was written and published to obtain support for the Recollets, a reformed Franciscan order. Champlain, who worked closely with the missionaries, asking them to aid him in New France, wrote to justify his explorations. Such motivations should not blind us to the value of these documents, as one is impressed with the amount of ethnographic detail in them and the extent to which the data are consistent, both internally and with what is known of other Iroquoian and North American Indian cultures.

There are available two shorter works based on these documents, but neither is completely satisfactory for anthropological purposes. Kenton (1927) republished only extracts of the Relations, and, although Kinietz (1940) uses some of the material in the Jesuit Relations and in Champlain's and Sagard's accounts, he omits much that is of interest to anthropologists.

---

suggested, on the basis of a tradition recorded by Pyrlaeus, that the league was formed between 1559 and 1570. Using this statement of the Mohawks to Pyrlaeus, a similar statement of the Onondagas to Ephraim Webster (both to the effect that the Iroquois League was founded a length of a man's life before the Europeans came to trade in the country), and the statement of some Senecas that the league was formed about 4 years before Hudson's voyage up the river named after him, Beauchamp (1891 a: 297–298) concluded that the probable date for the founding of the league was about 1600. Fenton (1961: 271) agrees with Beauchamp, and ends his discussion, "Let us fashionably say, 1600 plus or minus 30 years!"

Although confederations of Indian tribes were common in post-contact times, they do not seem to have been a feature of pre-Columbian North American cultures. Most of the Indian confederacies were formed to combat the superior strength of European intrusions through greater numbers. A similar reaction may have strengthened the Iroquoian leagues, but their formation prior to first contact with Europeans requires another explanation. The Indians along the Atlantic coast who were trading with the Europeans in the 16th century may have formed a kind of alliance with them and caused the more interior tribes, the Iroquoians, to confederate to gain superiority and thus take part in this trade. Further, as alliances serve to make communication easy and to facilitate trade between their members, the various Indian confederacies directed the trade that became important. These considerations support the suggestion that the Iroquoian confederacies were founded (or at least strengthened) in the latter part of the 16th century rather than at an earlier date.

In its original form, the ethnographic data in the documents is scattered through many volumes and understandably few have read through the sources. This is particularly obvious in the case of the Jesuit Relations. One deterrent to the use of the Jesuit Relations in archeological and ethnographic research is the initial shock of seeing over 70 volumes on a library shelf although only certain of these documents pertain to the Huron. For this compendium, volumes 7 through 34 of the Thwaites edition, which cover the years 1634 (the beginning of intensive Jesuit proselytizing) to 1649 (the defeat of the Huron by the Iroquois) were used. Of these, Brébeuf's Relation of 1636 is perhaps the most important, but the other Relations, also quite long and detailed, contain valuable ethnographic information sandwiched in between accounts of baptisms, deaths, conversions, and hardships of life in foreign lands. The material in Bressani's Relation (JR 38–40)[2] that repeats data contained in the preceding Relations has not been included; the principal new ethnographic material in this Relation, that referring to hair styles, painting, and tattooing (JR 38:249–253), and death customs (JR 39:29–33), is included.

Although the period of intensive Jesuit missionizing in Huronia, 1634–50, produced the most extensive collection of material on the Huron, Champlain's and Sagard's shorter accounts, both of which relate to earlier and brief expeditions, contain valuable information. The first such expedition began in the summer of 1615 when Champlain and Joseph Le Caron, a Recollet, left for Huronia with different groups of Huron traders; they returned in the summer of 1616. (The Huron made their trips to Three Rivers and Quebec to trade during the summer when the rivers were open; as the French obtained passage with the Indian traders, they also left and returned during the summer months.) At times during the winter of 1615–16, Champlain and Le Caron met and both made a visit to the Tobacco League. Although Le Caron's memoirs are not preserved, Champlain's are, thus providing an important source of information about the Huron.

No missionaries went to Huronia from the summer of 1616 until the summer of 1623, when Le Caron returned accompanied by two other Recollets, Father Nicolas Viel and lay Brother Gabriel Sagard-Théodat. In the summer of 1624, Le Caron and Sagard returned to Quebec. Viel remained in Huronia for another winter and left for Quebec in the summer of 1625, but drowned on the way. This second expedition was reported by Sagard.

In the summer of 1626, the Recollets were joined by the Jesuits in their activities, and three priests, a Recollet, Joseph de la Roche d'Aillon, and two Jesuits, Jean de Brébeuf and Anne de Noüe, went

---

[2] For explanation of citation abbreviations, see text, p. 8.

to Huronia. Brébeuf and d'Aillon had arrived in Quebec in 1625 but probably postponed leaving for Huronia because the news of Viel's death implied native hostility. De Noüe returned to Quebec in 1627, d'Aillon in 1628, and Brébeuf in 1629. This expedition produced no significant account of Huron culture.

After the French had surrendered Quebec to the English in July of 1629, missionary activity ceased until Canada was ceded back to France in 1632. In 1634, the Jesuits resumed their missionary work among the Huron when Brébeuf, accompanied by two other priests and other Frenchmen, returned.

The characteristics of the writers on the Huron are most easily discussed in terms of familiar stereotypes. In the Jesuit Relations, the Jesuits applied their almost intuitive devotion to scholarship to the study of the Huron, as in other writings they applied it to Western culture. In contrast, Champlain, the explorer, and Sagard, the lay brother and member of the reformed Franciscan order, were less scholarly but not necessarily less accurate. These differences in style have present advantages. The Jesuits, consistent with their devotion to religion, give extensive accounts of Huron religion (a difficult subject at best) but treat in a more cursory manner other aspects of Huron culture. In contrast, Champlain's and Sagard's accounts of religion are grossly inadequate, but as both deal extensively with aspects of Huron culture slighted by the Jesuits (particularly the life cycle, descent, and subsistence techniques), they provide an important supplement to the latter's documents.

Although both Champlain and Sagard were interested in the life of the ordinary person, Sagard perhaps resembled most closely the modern anthropologist. Unlike Champlain, he did not seek to lead men or change their destinies, but rather recounted only what he saw and did. Champlain, who saw himself as a man among men, went on a war expedition with the Huron against the Iroquois, hunted big game with the Indians and later wrote of his exploits—an early version of Theodore Roosevelt. Sagard, a follower of St. Francis who loved the plants, animals, and people of the new country, did not hunt or fight. He was a participant-observer who joined a Huron fishing expedition to better understand religious practices.

As is apparent in his account, Sagard was learned, but not scholarly. This is substantiated by the fact that he based a sizable amount of his description on that of Champlain. The reader of both recognizes, even in translation, sentences and paragraphs which Sagard has taken from Champlain. (In the compendium below, the number of references to both Sagard and Champlain and not to the Jesuit Relations reflects the extent to which Sagard has used Champlain as a guide.) This copying was not simple plagiarism: Sagard probably omitted those data he did not observe, expanding, contracting, and rearranging the text to suit his purpose. He was learned, he knew the source and used it to his advantage; but he was not scholarly, he did not engage in arguments on the validity of Champlain's data.

The Jesuits ignored these earlier accounts, apparently preferring to make their own more extensive study of Huron culture. Their scholarly attention is apparent not in the use of such sources as Champlain and Sagard (the Jesuits were in a position to learn more than either of these men) but in the treatment of the data they received, for they often carefully noted the source of each item of information, and whether it was actually observed or was hearsay. (This can be noted in the number of examples that are given to illustrate a general statement.) Sagard and Champlain were not as careful. In the most striking instance, Sagard implies that the Huron medicine man isolates a sick person (S 198) and later says that he observed this among the Algonquin (S 263). This should not lead us to question too seriously the validity of Sagard's statements. For example, the distinction Sagard made between the "wandering" and "sedentary" tribes (i.e., between the Algonquian- and Iroquoian-speaking groups) resembles the kind of distinction a modern student of North American Indians would make and indicates his knowledge of what he writes.

Although these documents should not be read uncritically, the cautions are few. By omitting the obvious biases of the writers (for example, their tendency to see the hand of the devil in the beliefs of the Indians) and by not reading the descriptions so literally that the reading is at variance with what one would expect in such a North American culture, a probably quite accurate picture of Huron culture is obtained. (The Jesuits, Sagard, and Champlain are akin to informants whose descriptions must be weighed against the ethnographer's knowledge of anthropology.) The footnotes, which were compiled after the ethnography was written, indicate the effectiveness of this method in obtaining an accurate picture of Huron culture. With few exceptions, they confirm the probable accuracy of the descriptions.

The authors of the various Relations are listed in Appendix 4.

With few exceptions, I have omitted statements that refer specifically to the behavior of Indians toward the French priests: There is no way of ascertaining whether such behavior was the customary Huron behavior toward other Huron or an appropriate modification of such behavior for use with the French. Similarly, behavior of the French which is obviously not within French culture but derived from Huron culture is omitted: There is no way of ascertaining the degree, if any, the Huron cultural adjustments were modified to fit the French needs. In a sense, then, this is a conservative reading and more information could be gleaned from these documents.

The generally recognized definitive sources were used in compiling this ethnography. Each of these contains both the French text and the English translation, a convenience for those who wish to check the original.   In general, the indexes in these sources are inadequate. To compensate for this deficiency and to increase the usefulness of this compendium, the source citations are extensive and may serve as an index.   The sources and the abbreviations used in the citations are as follows:

C=H. P. Biggar (ed.), *The Works of Samuel de Champlain*. Vol. 3. (Toronto: The Champlain Society, 1929.)
S=G. M. Wrong (ed.), Father Gabriel Sagard, *The Long Journey to the Country of the Hurons*. (Toronto: The Champlain Society, 1939.)
JR=Reuben Gold Thwaites (ed.), *The Jesuit Relations and Allied Documents*. (73 vols.; Cleveland: Burrows Bros., 1896–1901.)

Each citation in the text refers to the material between it and the preceding citation in the same paragraph.   Because with few exceptions a section in the documents is cited only once, similar material may occasionally be found in other parts of the text.

For readibility I have paraphrased the statements in these documents and have used direct quotes only (1) when I wished to indicate that an awkward or obscure phrase has not been paraphrased or (2) to set off material that was recorded as actual Indian discourse.   These latter statements have been reworded so that they are not direct quotes from the sources.   I have left them as quotations for the same reason that the original authors did: to give vividness to the description. Parentheses in a statement which the citation attributes to Sagard indicate additions which he made to "Histoire du Canada" (1636), a later edition of "Le Grand Voyage du Pays des Hurons" ("The Long Journey to the Country of the Hurons") (1632).   Brackets indicate my additions.

Throughout, certain consistent changes in wording have been made. For example, "chief" has been used in place of "captain"; "wampum," for "porcelain"; "house," for "cabin"; "spirit," for "demon" and "devil"; and "you," for "thee."   The current names of the Iroquois tribes have been used, not those the French give.   The spelling of certain Huron words in some accounts has been changed for the sake of consistency.   For linguistic purposes, the alternate spellings and references to these are cited when the Huron word is first used.

The orthography of the word "Algonquin" has not been changed, except to alter "Algonquain" spellings to "Algonquin."   The term probably usually refers to a number of politically independent groups which spoke the same language or very closely related languages, including such peoples as the Nipissing and Ottawa (all of whom lived near the Huron), and perhaps also occasionally to such others as the Potawatomi.   The word probably does not usually refer to speakers of other Algonquian languages, as, for example, the Montagnais.

A discussion of the Huron language has been omitted; the chapter on language (JR 10: 117–123), two interlinear translations (JR 10: 69–73 and JR 21: 251–265), and a brief comment on the Huron language (JR 15: 155–157) are located easily in the Relations. I have embodied transcriptions (including alternate spellings) of Huron words and phrases for the benefit of linguists. References for alternate spellings are included for all words except tribal names, for which only the earliest reference is given. A list of words and phrases that could not easily be included in the body of the description is given in Appendix 3.

THE HURON LEAGUE

The Huron, or *Wendat* [3] as they called themselves, were a league of four nations [tribes] sharing a common language, but each retaining its own traditions. These nations, the Attignawantan [Attignaouentan (JR 19: 125), Atignaouantan (JR 23: 43), Atinniawentan (JR 26: 217), Atinniaoenten (JR 34: 131), Attigouautan (C 55), Atingyahointan (S 91), Nation of the Bear (JR 34: 131; S 91)], the Attigneenongnahac [Atignenonghac (JR 13: 37), Atignenongach (JR 13: 125), Attigueenongnahac (JR 15: 57), Attinguenongnahac (JR 19: 125), Attingueenongnahak (JR 21: 169; 23: 117), Atingueennonniahak (JR 26: 259), Atigagnongueha (S 91)], the Arendahronon [Arendarhonons (JR 8: 71), Arendarrhonons (JR 13: 37), Ahrendaronons (JR 19: 125), Arendaronnons (JR 27: 29), Arendaenronnons (JR 33: 81), Henarhonon (S 91)], and the Tohontaenrat

[3] Hewitt (1907 c: 584) has suggested "Wendat," the Huron name for themselves, means "the Islanders" or "Dwellers on a Peninsula."

The Huron were defeated and dispersed by the Iroquois in 1649–50. It was probably the desire of the Iroquois to control the fur trade, as Hunt (1940) has ably suggested, or at least to control the areas in which the fur-bearing animals were to be found, as Trelease (1960: 120) suggests, that motivated the Iroquois to go to war against the Huron and other Indians (see note 17, p. 16). The beaver in Iroquois territory had been exhausted by 1640 and the Iroquois were forced to look elsewhere, to the north and east, in order to continue their trade with the Dutch (Hunt 1940: 34–37). By this time, the Huron were firmly entrenched as the important middlemen between the French and the Algonquian tribes to the west and north. (The Huron acceptance of the French priests into their country probably was to cement this relationship.) The Huron controlled this trade to the extent that the Petun (the Tobacco Nation) and the Neutral provided them with corn, tobacco, and hemp, products that the Huron themselves could and did produce. (Hunt 1940: 59 and passim probably overemphasizes the amount of hemp traded by the Petun to the Huron.) The Huron reaped a profit from these transactions (see also note 12, p. 13).

After some years of trade, the two important Iroquoian leagues, the Huron and the Iroquois, found themselves in similar positions. Both had to obtain furs from sources outside their own territories by trade and both had the same goods, corn and tobacco, to trade to the Algonquian for these furs. Wars ensued in which the Iroquois destroyed first the Huron and then the other Iroquoian nations. In these wars, the Iroquois were aided by the guns they had obtained from the Dutch in trade. The Huron probably had far fewer weapons, which gave the Iroquois the advantage.

Other factors may have contributed to the destruction of the Huron League. Trigger (1959) suggests that the Iroquois, left in relative isolation from the Europeans, were able to develop into a stronger military and political power than the Huron, who were

(Footnote continued at bottom of next page.)

[Tohontaenras (JR 13: 55), Tahontaenrat (JR 26: 293)],[4] were united by their common interests and by their common enemies. [Later in the Relations another group, the Ataronchronons (JR 19: 125) [Ataconchronons (JR 13: 61)] [5] is mentioned.] The Attignawantan and Attigneenongnahac, who called each other "brother" and "sister," [6] were the most important, largest, and oldest nations of this league, having lived in the region for more than two hundred years. The two others were recent arrivals: the Arendahronon joined the

beset by the division between Christian converts and pagans and by their dependence on the French.

After their defeat, many Hurons were either killed outright or died from starvation and disease in their flight from the Iroquois. Many became captives of the Iroquois. Others fled to other Iroquoian tribes, the Neutral, the Petun, and the Erie and some to the French. The Tohontaenrat (the village of Scanonaerat) and some Arendahronons were given the privilege of founding a separate town (called Gandougarse) among the Seneca. For some Hurons their flight to other tribes only postponed their eventual captivity; with the destruction of the Erie and Neutral, these Huron refugees among them were also taken prisoner. Those who had retreated to Orleans Island were forced by the Iroquois to either fight or migrate to Iroquois country. Of this group, the Bear (Attignawantan) joined the Mohawk, the Rock (Arendahronon) joined the Onondaga, and the Cord (Attigneenongnahac) remained with the French.

Those Hurons who joined the Tobacco Nation, although driven from the area, retained their identity. This group of Hurons and Petuns came to be known as the Wyandot, a corruption of the term *Wendat* (Hale 1888 : 177; 1894: 6). Most of this group fled west, becoming involved in the complex history of the Upper Great Lakes area. After the peace of 1815, they were given land in Ohio and Michigan. In 1819, they sold much of this land, but retained some near Upper Sandusky in Ohio and some near Detroit. Later, these tracts were also sold and most of these Wyandots moved to Kansas and then to Oklahoma, where they are still found. Some remained in the vicinity of Detroit. The present Wyandot are considered more Petun than Huron.

The Hurons who had settled on Orleans Island moved near Quebec in 1656 and, although several successive villages were built, they have remained in this area. The remnants of this group are the present Huron of Lorette. They have lost their old culture. (For a detailed description of this group in 1899, see Gérin 1900; for the history of the Huron after their defeat, see Clarke 1870; Connelley 1899 c: 92–96; Hale 1888: 177; 1894: 4–5; Hewitt 1907 c: 585–590; Jones 1909: 447 ff.; 1910: 577–582; Kinietz 1940: 1–4.)

[4] Hewitt (1907 c: 584) and Jones (1909: 72) identified the Attigneenongnahac as the "Cord People" and the Arendahronon as the "Rock People." Hewitt (1907 c: 584) suggests Tohontaerat means "White-eared" or "Deer People"; Jones (1909: 181) suggests the name means "People of One Single White Lodge." The Attignawantan are the Bear people.

[5] The Ataronchronon were one of several groups of Indians which had moved to near the mission of Ste. Marie (Jones 1909 : 447; 1910 : 578; Fenton 1940 d : 184). The meaning of the name, Ataronchronon, has been suggested as "People who Dwelt beyond the Fens, Morass, or Silted Lake" (Jones 1909 : 314; 1910 : 578) or "People on the Fens" (Fenton 1940 d : 181).

[6] Similarly, the Iroquois League was divided into two sisterhoods, the Mohawk, Onondaga, and Seneca forming one sisterhood of tribes and the Oneida and Cayuga, the other. The tribes of one sisterhood addressed each other as "brother" and tribes of the other sisterhood as "our cousins." In another, and ritualistic, form of address, the Oneida and Cayuga called the Mohawk, Onondaga, and Seneca sisterhood "my or our father's clansmen" and the Mohawk, Onondaga, and Seneca called the Oneida and Cayuga, "my or our offspring" (Hewitt 1916: 164; 1917: 325–326; 1944: 83–84; Hewitt and Fenton 1945: 305; Goldenweiser 1913: 464; Morgan 1901(1): 79, 91–92; Shimony 1961 a: 117–118). There is also a tripartite division of the tribes in the Iroquois League (Hewitt and Fenton 1945: 305).

Also compare the Wyandot (and Iroquois) custom: the members of the clans of one moiety call each other "brothers" and call members of clans of the opposite moiety "cousins" (Connelley 1899 b: 27).

League about 1590 and the Tohontaenrat about 1610.[7] Families might affiliate themselves with another nation by being adopted into it and sometimes a group of families left a nation to become one in their own right. The Attignawantan and Attigneenongnahac nations were the largest as they, over a period of time, adopted more families. These adopted families remained distinct little nations, retaining the names and memories of their founders, a general name [for themselves], and a war chief and a council chief (JR 16: 227–229).[8]

Of the four nations of the League, the Arendahronon were the easternmost (JR 20: 19; 33: 81) and the group that the French first met (JR 20: 19), but the Attignawantan were the most receptive to Christianity (JR 10: 31).

Champlain found 18 villages, 6 of which were palisaded, inhabited by 2,000 warriors and perhaps 30,000 people (C 122). Sagard said there were about 25 villages, 30,000 to 40,000 people and 2,000 to 3,000 warriors (S 91–92). When the Jesuits arrived, they found 30,000 Hurons (JR 7: 225; 8: 115; 10: 313) located in 20 villages (JR 8: 115; 10: 313; 11: 7).[9] By 1640, however, the population had been reduced to 10,000 (JR 17: 221–223, 227; 19: 77, 127). The Attignawantan were the most numerous; they accounted for half of the Hurons (JR 10: 77) and the most (14) villages (JR 15: 39). [Later, after the Jesuit-introduced disease in the village of Ihonatiria so reduced the population that it was abandoned, they had 13 villages (JR 17: 11, 59, 115).] The other nations had fewer villages: the Attigneenongnahac, 2 [this figure is based on a comparison of JR 19: 183–185 and 17: 87–89; cf. also JR 19: 125, 167, 209; 20: 21, 43]; the Arendahronon, 3 (JR 20: 21); the Tohontaenrat, 1 (the village of Scanonaerat) (JR 17: 87).[10]

The country of the Huron was not large; at its greatest extent, it could be traversed in 3 or 4 days (JR 8: 115). Its length, east and west, was no longer than 20 or 25 leagues and its width, north and south, was in many places very slight, nowhere exceeding 7 or 8 leagues (JR 7: 225; 16: 225). [The earlier estimate of an east-west

---

[7] See footnote 1, p. 3.

[8] The Iroquois also adopted individuals, families, and tribes into their confederacy.

[9] The differences in number of Huron villages given by Champlain, Sagard, and the Jesuits is quite understandable, and may not be due to error in counting. An Iroquoian village may combine with another village to form a larger single village or one village may split into two or three separate villages. Further, there were hamlets; settlements that were not villages proper, but small residential units that were politically attached to the village proper. Thus, the difference between Champlain's figure of 18 Huron villages and the Jesuits' figure of 20 may indicate the splitting of a single village unit and the difference between Sagard's figure of 25 and those given by Champlain and the Jesuits may only mean that Sagard included some hamlets in his total.

[10] See Appendix 1. "Names and probable tribal affiliations of Huron villages" (p. 149).

length of 230 leagues would appear to be a typographical error for 20 or 30 leagues. A breadth of 10 leagues given in the earlier accounts agrees satisfactorily with that of the Jesuits' 7 or 8 leagues (C 121–123; S 90).] Its latitude in the central part was 44.5 degrees (JR 33: 61; C 121; S 90; cf. JR 15: 175; 16: 225). It had the shape of Brittany and was similarly situated, almost surrounded by the Freshwater Sea [Lake Huron] (C 122).

The greater part of Huronia was cleared (C 122) and consisted of plains surrounded and intersected by a number of lakes (JR 8: 115) and streams (C 50). The country was "full of fine hills, open fields, very beautiful broad meadows bearing much excellent hay" and in many places there was "much uncultivated wheat, which has an ear like rye and grains like oats" (S 90). There were forests containing oaks, beeches, maples, cedars, spruces, yews, elms, and other types of trees (S 91; C 51) and, in the interior, forests of fir (C 51). The country was warmer and more beautiful and the soil richer and better, the farther south one went (S 91). Although the soil of the country was quite sandy, it produced a quantity of corn (JR 8: 115).

NEIGHBORING TRIBES

THE TOBACCO LEAGUE

About 12 or 15 leagues to the west (JR 20: 43) or west-southwest (JR 33: 61) of the Huron lived a group which spoke the same language (JR 20: 43). They were called the Khionontaterrhonons (JR 8: 115) [Khionontaterons (JR 17: 165), Khionontateronons (JR 19: 125), Kionontatehronon (JR 23: 179)], "the Nation of the Tobacco" (JR 20: 43) and by the French Petun [Tobacco] Nation (C 95) because of the abundance of tobacco that grew there (JR 20: 43). The Tobacco Nation was a confederacy of two separate groups, the Nation of the Wolves and the Nation of the Deer (JR 33: 143),[11] and had at least nine villages (JR 20: 43). The largest of these villages, Ehwae, was burned by the Iroquois in 1640 resulting in the deaths of many by starvation, cold, smallpox, and drowning, and in the capture of others by the enemy (JR 21: 181). Algonquins lived among the Tobacco people as they did among the Huron: one missionary found two villages in which Algonquin was spoken (JR 21: 125, 185).

The Tobacco confederacy had been an enemy of the Huron confederacy, and the two peoples waged cruel wars against each other. Not long before the Jesuits arrived in Huronia, however, the two leagues

---

[11] The names of these two tribes, Wolves and Deer, are names of clans among the present Iroquois and Wyandot. Perhaps in this case the Jesuits have recorded the names of clans rather than tribes. [Mooney (1910: 755) calls them clans.]

entered into an alliance and formed a new confederation against their common enemies (JR 20:43).[12]

The Tobacco Nation did not trade with the French, as the Huron controlled this trade (JR 21: 177). They lived like the Huron and had the same customs. Like them, they planted corn and had a fixed abode (C 95–96).

THE NEUTRAL LEAGUE

To the south and a little toward the west lived another Iroquoian-speaking neighbor of the Huron, the Neutral Nation (JR 33: 61–63). The Neutral [Atiouandaronks (JR 8: 115), Attiwandarons (JR 17: 165), Attiouandarons (JR 20: 49), Attiwandaronk (JR 21: 193), Attiouendaronk (JR 23: 179), Atiouendaronk (JR 27: 21), Attiuoïn-daron (S 151)] were called in the Huron language "peoples of slightly different language." (Peoples speaking an entirely different language were called *Akwanake*, 'strangers.') Conversely, the Neutral called the Huron by the same term as that used by the Huron to refer to the Neutral, *Attiwandaronk*. Probably not long ago, the Jesuits thought, the Huron, Iroquois, and Neutral were one people who over the course of time had become separated from one another to a greater or lesser extent. As a result, some became enemies; some neutral; and some maintained a special connection and means of communication (JR 21: 193–195).

The French named this group "the Neutrals" because they were at peace with both the Iroquois and the Huron (JR 21: 193–195; C 99–100). The term "Neutral" originally had been used to refer to many separate tribes, all groups south and southwest of the Huron, but later the French applied the name to only the one nation or confederacy (JR 21: 191–193; cf. C 99; S 157–158). Perhaps because of their position, the French made journeys to the Neutral country to trade for furs and other items (JR 21: 203). The Neutrals felt free to visit the Huron (JR 27: 25) and to seek refuge in Huronia in time of famine (JR 20:47–49; cf. JR 20:69).

About 40 villages and hamlets comprised this nation (JR 20: 95, 105; 21: 189) of at least 1,200 individuals (JR 21: 191). The Jesuits estimated about 500 fires and 3,000 persons in 10 villages visited on one trip (JR 21:223).

---

[12] The alliance of the Huron League with the Tobacco League proved to be a lasting one. After the defeat of the Huron, a number of them joined the Petun and their histories became linked, the combined group becoming the present Wyandot. At the time of the Jesuits, the close relationship between the two leagues may have been based on trade: as the Huron controlled the trade with the French, the Tobacco League may have found it advantageous to have the Huron as friends. The Huron probably found it advantageous to have access to the tobacco that grew in abundance in Petun country. Apparently, both groups wished to maintain this partnership, for both effectively prevented the French from establishing missions in Tobacco country, an act that would have indicated an alliance between the Petun and the French independent of the Huron (Hunt 1940: 56). The geographic position of the Petun, west of Huronia, may have fostered their dependency on the Huron.

The western edge of the confederacy was located a 4- or 5-day journey (about 30 or 40 leagues) directly south of Huronia, at about the latitude of 42.5 degrees (calculated from Ste. Marie at about 44°25'') (JR 20 : 95; 21 : 189, 205–207; 33 : 61–63; S 158). From the westernmost Neutral villages to the mouth of the river of the country that emptied into Lake Ontario [Lake St. Louys (JR 33 : 63)] was a 4-day journey south or southeast. In this area were most of the Neutral villages, although three or four were east of the [Niagara] river (Onguiaahra), ranging from east to west, toward the Nation of the Cat (JR 21 : 189–191). The extent of the country mentioned above was 40 or 50 leagues (JR 33 : 63).

The tribe of Neutrals nearest the Huron was the Aondironnons, a great many of whom were killed in 1647 by the Seneca (JR 33 : 81–83).

One of the associate nations of the Neutral, the Wenrôhronon [Ahouenrochrhonons (JR 8: 115), Weanohronons (JR 16: 253), Wenroronons (JR 17: 37), Awenrehronon (JR 21: 233)] [13], was located near the boundary with the Iroquois and joined the Huron about 1638 (JR 16: 253; 17: 25). This occurred after the Neutral had severed their relationship with the Wenrôhronon leaving them prey to their enemies. As they would have been exterminated if they had remained, the Wenrôhronon sent a delegation to the Huron to ask if they might join them. The Huron agreed to this, knowing the Wenrôhronon would help defend the Huron country. As a result of these negotiations, over 600 people, most of whom were women and children, made the journey of more than 80 leagues to Huronia assisted by the Huron, who escorted them, helped carry their household goods and children, and defended them against their enemies. In spite of this, many Wenrôhronons died on the way and nearly all of the remainder were sick either when they arrived or shortly thereafter. The newcomers were distributed in the principal villages of Huronia, most of them remaining in the village in which the Jesuits lived, one of the largest in the country. In all these villages, they were given the best places in the houses and corn from the granaries (JR 17 : 25–29). Five years later the chief of these people led a band of 300 warriors (JR 26 : 273).

Although the Neutrals were neutral in respect to the Iroquois and Huron, they had their bitter enemies, especially the Nation of Fire [Atsistaehronons (JR 20: 61), Athistaëronnon (JR 30: 89), Assitagueronon, *assista-* meaning 'fire' in Huron and *-eronon* meaning 'tribe' (S 67)] (JR 20: 61; 21: 195; S 157–158). The Fire Nation people were speakers of an Algonquian language, not an Iroquoian one (JR 21 : 125; 27 : 27) and were a large group, larger than all the Neu-

---

[13] Although it would seem likely on the basis of the material in the Jesuit Relations that the Wenrôhronon was a tribe in the Neutral League, Hewitt (1907 b : 430–431) thought that it was either an independent tribe or confederated with the Erie.

trals, Hurons, and Iroquois combined (JR 27: 27). The extent of the animosity between the Neutral and the Fire Nation is indicated by their battles. About 1640 the Neutral took 100 prisoners; in the following year, with an army of 2,000, they took over 170 prisoners (JR 21: 195); in 1642, they attacked a palisaded village of the Fire Nation with an army of 2,000 (JR 27: 25).

The Neutral practiced the same kind of cruelties on their prisoners as did the Huron. But, unlike the latter who either spared the women or, having knocked them down in the heat of battle, took a piece of their bodies, the Neutral burned women prisoners as well as men (JR 21: 195).

The dress of the Neutral was like that of the Huron. So also was their food. The Neutral grew corn, beans, and squash; their fishing was equal to that of the Huron; and they hunted "stags, cows, wild-cats, wolves, black beasts, beaver, and other animals" for their skins and meat. Flocks of wild turkeys roamed the fields and woods of their country. Wild fruits were to be found, chestnuts and wild apples being possibly more abundant than in Huronia (JR 21: 195–197). Deer were also more plentiful in this country than in any other (S 225). They grew a large quantity of very good tobacco, which they traded to their neighbors (S 158).

As among the Hurons, the basic Neutral garment was a skin. According to the Jesuits, the Neutral men were less modest than the Huron: many did not use the breechcloth and others used it "in such a way that with great difficulty is that concealed which should not be seen." The women were ordinarily clothed from at least the waist to at least the knees. The skins were dressed with much care and skill and decorated in many ways. Like their clothing, their bodies might be decorated; in this case with tattooing (JR 21: 197) which, common among both the Tobacco and Neutral tribes, was done by perforating the skin on the face, neck, breast, or some other part of the body with a needle, sharp awl, or thorn to make an eagle, snake, or other figure. Powdered charcoal or other black coloring matter was then traced over the figure, indelibly imprinting the designs (JR 38: 251) with which some of them were covered from head to foot (JR 21: 197).

The Neutral disposed of their dead in a manner different from the Huron. The latter buried their dead immediately after death and reinterred them at the Feast of the Dead. The Neutral took their dead to the burying ground only at the latest possible time, when decomposition made the bodies insupportable. Thus, the dead bodies often remained in their houses for the entire winter. After the corpse had finally been put outside on a scaffold and after the flesh had decayed, the bones were taken and put here and there in the houses until the Feast of the Dead. As these bones were constant reminders of loss, the Neutral women frequently cried and made "most lugubrious lamentations" in song (JR 21: 199). The Neutral also enacted the Resurrections of the Dead (S 209–210).

OTHER IROQUOIAN GROUPS

The Huron knew of other Iroquoian-speaking groups. One was the Nation of the Cat [Rhiierrhonons (JR 8: 115), Erieehronons (JR 21: 191][14] who had been forced to move inland to escape their enemies who lived farther west. This nation had a number of stationary villages, as they, too, were agricultural (JR 33: 63). Sagard thought that they were called the Cat tribe after the wildcats or leopards (*tiron*) found in their territory and from the skins of which were made robes or blankets with a number of animals' tails around the edge and at the top of the back (S 224).

Another Iroquoian-speaking group, the Andastoerrhonons (JR 8: 115) [Andastoerhonon (JR 14: 9), Andastoëronnons (JR 30: 85), Andastoeronnons (JR 33: 123), people of Anastohé (JR 30: 253) or Andastoé (JR 33: 129)][15] had been allies of the Huron (JR 30: 253; 33: 63, 73, 129) and, in fact, some resided in Huronia (JR 30: 253). The Jesuits thought that they lived in or near Virginia where the English traded (JR 14: 9; 30: 85, 253) or in New Sweden (JR 33: 63, 73) where various people, mostly Dutch and English, had placed themselves under the protection of the King of Sweden (JR 33: 137). Their country was 150 leagues distant and beyond the Neutrals to the south and a little toward the east (JR 33: 63, 129). In a single village they had 1,300 men capable of bearing arms (JR 33: 129). Champlain placed this group about 7 days' journey from where the Dutch, who aided them, went to trade on the 40th degree (C 54).

There were once Iroquoian-speaking groups along the St. Lawrence (JR 9: 159).[16] The village of Ochelaga [Hochelaga] Cartier found at Montreal was designated *minitik outen entagougiban*, 'the island on which stood a town or village' [an Algonquian name]. War led to its abandonment (JR 22: 205–207).

Two other Iroquoian-speaking groups are mentioned in the Relations, the Conkhandeenrhonons and Scahentoarrhonons (JR 8: 115), but no other information is given.[17]

---

[14] The Cat Nation also is referred to now as the Erie.

[15] The Andastoerrhonon now usually are called the Susquehanna or the Conestoga (Hewitt 1907 a; Fenton 1940 d: 232).

[16] These peoples were the Laurentian Iroquois (see note 1, p. 3).

[17] Beauchamp's (JR 8: 302) suggestion that the Scahentoarrhonons may have been the Skenchiohronons, and the Conkhandeenrhonons, the Carantouans or part of the Seneca seems unlikely. The Scahentoarrhonons may have been part of the Andastoerrhonon or a separate group living on the Susquehanna (Hewitt 1907 a: 336; 1910 d: 653–659; Fenton 1940 d: 232–233). It does not seem impossible to suppose that the Conkhandeenrhonon was one of the tribes of the Neutral League; as probably the Neutrals were

(Footnote continued at bottom of next page.)

THE IROQUOIS LEAGUE[18]

The Huron were on friendly terms with all Iroquoian-speaking groups except the Iroquois (JR 8: 115). The Iroquois, also enemies of the Algonquin, Montagnais, and French, were a confederacy of six (JR 21: 21)[19] or five (JR 17: 77; 21: 201; 33: 65, 71) nations.

Seventy leagues south-southeast of Huronia (JR 33: 65) and a day's journey from the last Neutral villages on the east side of the Onguia-ahra [Niagara] River, in an area also called by that name (JR 21: 209–211) (for a mention of Niagara Falls see JR 33: 63), lived the nearest and most-feared Iroquois nation, the Seneca [Sonontrerrhon-ons (JR 8: 69), Senontouerhonons (JR 17: 111), Sonontwehronons (JR 21: 209), Santweronons (JR 24: 271), Sonontwaëronons (JR 28:275), Sonnontoueronnons (JR 33: 65), its chief town being Sonon-toen (JR 8: 117), Sonontoüan (JR 14: 39), Sonnontouan (JR 29: 253; 33: 95)].

The antagonism between the Huron and Seneca continued for the period that the Jesuits lived in Huronia. In the spring of 1634 before the Jesuits arrived, the Huron suffered great losses and defeat at the hands of the Seneca (JR 8: 69, 115). Representatives of the Huron went to Sonontoen [chief town of the Seneca] to confirm the peace, a treaty in which the other four nations of the Iroquois league also wished to participate (JR 8: 117). The Seneca were equal or slightly greater in number than the Huron[20] and although for a time the Huron had the upper hand, this nation of Iroquois finally gained superiority in both number and strength (JR 7: 225; 24: 271).

---

a confederacy of several tribes and as only one or two of these tribes are mentioned by the Jesuits, it is possible that this is the name of a Huron tribe.

The history and culture of the Neutrals, Eries, Susquehannas, and their possibly allied tribes is not well known. The Europeans did not have much contact with them and, after the defeat of the Huron, when they threatened to form an alliance (Fenton 1940 d: 188), the Iroquois systematically conquered them. The Iroquois first attacked the Neutrals, defeating them in 1651; then, the Erie, subjugating them in a series of attacks beginning in 1654 and lasting for 2 more years; and finally, the Susquehanna, defeating them in 1675. (Hewitt, 1910 d: 657–658, says that the Scahentoarrhonons were destroyed by the Iroquois in 1652.) The geographic position of the Susquehanna, which permitted them to trade with the Europeans on the Delaware Bay, probably allowed them to hold off the Iroquois for a longer time than could the other Iroquoians, for they obtained firearms from the Swedes and Dutch (Fenton 1940 d: 237).

[18] The Jesuits accurately portray, as this section indicates, the Iroquois League as composed of five tribes extending across much of the present upstate New York: from west to east, these tribes were the Seneca, Cayuga, Onondaga, Oneida, and Mohawk. The Iroquois characterization of their league as a longhouse indicates the roles of the several tribes in its organization. The Mohawk kept the eastern door of the league and were important in dealing with the Dutch, and later the English, at Albany. The Seneca, keepers of the western door, were important in quelling the aspirations of groups to the west who wished to establish their own empires. The Onondaga, between the Mohawk and Oneida on the east and the Seneca and Cayuga on the west, served as lawmakers and arbitrators. The two tribes between these three, the Oneida sandwiched between the Mohawk and Onondaga and the Cayuga between the Seneca and Onondaga, had lesser importance in the League.

[19] The statement that the Iroquois League was a confederacy of six tribes is probably an error.

[20] The Jesuits probably exaggerated the number of Seneca.

About 25 leagues from the Sonnontoueronnons were the Cayuga [Onoiochrhonons (JR 8: 115), Oniontcheronons (JR 28: 275), Ouionenronnons (JR 33: 65)].

Ten or twelve leagues farther down [i.e., farther east] from the Cayuga were the Onondaga [Onontaerrhonons (JR 8: 115), Onontagueronons (JR 28: 275), Onnontaeronnons (JR 33: 65), Onontaé (JR 23: 155), Onnontaé (JR 33: 119, 133)], most warlike of the Five Nations (JR 33: 117).

The Oneida [Oüioenrhonons (JR 8: 115), Oneiouchronons (JR 17: 65), Oneiochronons (JR 21: 201), Onneiochronnons (JR 33: 65)] were 7 or 8 leagues from the Onondaga (JR 33: 65). They were said by the Neutral to have a peculiar form of government: the men and women administered alternately, so that if a man who had been chief died, his successor was a woman, who, upon her death, was succeeded by a man (JR 21: 201).[21]

The Mohawk (Agnierrhonons (JR 8: 115), Agniehenon (JR 14: 9), Agnietironons (JR 14: 45), Agnierhonon (JR 17: 77), Agnieeronons (JR 21: 21), Agneronons (JR 24: 271), Agnierronons (JR 27: 297), Annierronnons (JR 28: 275), Annieronnons (JR 33: 65), Agnée (JR 23: 155) lived 25 or 30 leagues from the Oneida and were the farthest east from the Huron (JR 33: 65). These people lived between Three Rivers and the Upper Iroquois and had only three villages (JR 24: 271) located rather near each other on three little mountains (JR 21: 21; 28: 301).[22]

One village, Ononjoté (JR 27: 297) [Onnieoute (JR 28: 281), i.e., Oneida], the men from which were killed by the Huron (JR 27: 297) or by the Upper Algonquin (JR 28: 281), was repeopled by the Mohawk men in order that the tribe might not become extinct. For this reason, the Mohawk called the village their child or their daughter (JR 27: 297; 28: 281–283).[23]

---

[21] The statement of the Neutral that the Oneida had a peculiar form of government would seem to be in error. The Neutral apparently misinterpreted the common Iroquois custom, that after a chief has died, the clan mother appoints (with the advice of others in the clan) his successor (see note 62, p. 46) and construed the role of the clan mother in this election as that of chief rather than as the person who appoints the chief.

[22] The number and location of the Mohawk villages is confirmed in other sources. For example, Fenton (1940 d: 201) says that the Mohawk "protohistoric sites were fortified on the hilltops overlooking tributaries north of their historic valley" and that about the year 1600 there were three such sites.

[23] On the basis of its name, this village can be identified as the Oneida village. (Beauchamp, 1900: 84–85, also accepts this Jesuit statement as referring to the Oneida.) This piece of history may also help account for the designation of the Oneida (along with the Cayuga) as "offspring" by the other three Iroquois tribes (see note 6, p. 10), for the present Oneida are truly the offspring of Mohawk men. At least, this is the reason suggested by the Jesuits. A relationship similar to that between the Mohawk and Oneida may have existed between the Onondaga and the Cayuga: the Cayuga are said to be an offshoot of the Onondaga (Hale 1883: 27).

The migration of Mohawk men to the Oneida village probably strengthened an older connection, for the Mohawk would not have gone there if ties had been absent. The similarity of Mohawk and Oneida clan organization seems to confirm the suggestion that the relationship between the two was closer than that between other tribes of the Iroquois League, and that, as Fenton (1940 d: 218) suggests, the two tribes were probably one people before they settled in their present locations.

THE ALGONQUIN [24]

Algonquin were scattered on all sides, both to the north and south of Lake Huron (JR 16: 253). On the south shore of Lake Huron lived the Ouachaskesouek, Nigouaouichirinik, Outaouasinagouek, Kichkagoneiak, and Ontaanak—allies of the Huron. Farther toward the west lived the Ouchaouanag, who were part of the Nation of Fire, and the Ondatouatandy and the Ouinipegong, who were part of the Nation of the Puants (JR 33: 151). On the eastern and northern shores of Lake Huron lived the Algonquin tribes—Outaouakamigouek, Sakahiganiriouik, Aouasanik, Atchougue, Amikouek, Achirigouans, Nikikouek, Michisaguek, and Paouitagoung (JR 33: 149).

The Nipissiriniens [called by the Huron, Askikwanehronons (JR 21: 239)] lived 70 or 80 leagues from the Huron, on a small lake of about 80 leagues in circumference on the route to Quebec (JR 33: 153).

Various Algonquin groups were allies of the Huron. Some of these Algonquins wintered with the Huron (JR 13: 191; 14: 7; 20: 39–41, 97; 21: 143; 23: 19; 26: 301; 27: 53–55; 33: 153) and they seem to have come in numbers. In April of 1637, the Bissiriniers returned to their country after the ice had broken and the lake was opened, carrying with them in seven canoes the 70 bodies of those who had died while wintering among the Huron (JR 14: 37; cf. JR 13: 211). In the winter of 1623–24, the Epicerinys ["Sorcerers," so named because of their many medicine men who talked with spirits "in little round towers isolated and apart" which they built in order to receive oracles [probably a reference to "shaking tents"] (S 64)] camped in Huronia. They knew the Huron language although the Huron did not know theirs. They told the Recollets that they traded once a year with a nation a month's or 6 weeks' journey by land, lake, and river. Certain other people, having no beard or hair on their head, also traded with them, coming by sea in great wooden ships laden with such goods as "axes shaped like the tail of a partridge, leggings with shoes attached but as flexible as a glove, and many other things, which they exchanged for furs" (S 86–87).

As did other Huron allies, the Algonquin felt free to join the Huron in times of trouble; for example, one group of Algonquin came to live near the Huron when forced to abandon its country on the banks of the river (JR 27: 37). In at least one case, an Algonquin was raised from infancy among the Huron (JR 13: 139). The latter also might go to live with the Algonquin, as in the case in which some Hurons took refuge with some Algonquins to escape the Iroquois (JR 30: 87).

---

[24] Only the material that pertains to the relationship between the Algonquin and the Huron has been included here. There is, of course, much ethnographic material on the Algonquin in the Jesuit Relations.

DRESS

The Indians wore little apparel and often painted, oiled, and greased their bodies and hair (JR 15: 155; S 228). For clothing, the Huron used dressed and well-prepared deer and beaver skins which they obtained from the animals they took or from trade with other Indians (C 53, 85, 131–132). The basic garment was a single beaver skin worn over the shoulders or back as a mantle and, in winter, "shoes" and leggings of skin (JR 15:155; 17:39). A tobacco pouch hung behind the back (JR 15:155). Their breeches [breechclout] were made of a moderately large deer skin and their leggings, which reached as high as the waist and had many folds, were made of another piece of skin. Moccasins were made of the skins of deer, bear, and beaver. A robe was worn as a cloak and sleeves were attached with a cord behind. When they went into the fields, they girded up their robes about their bodies; when in the village, their robes were ungirded and they left off the sleeves (C 131– 132). This rather simple dress had its advantages: when a canoe containing two Indians overturned, a Huron convert dressed in the conventional French manner drowned, whereas his Algonquin companion threw off his robe and saved himself by swimming to safety (JR 16: 177–179).

The trimmings for their clothes consisted of pale bands made of glue and the scrapings of skins alternating with bands of red and brown paint (C 132–133). On their robes they [it is not clear if the Huron are being referred to here] put bands of porcupine quills dyed a fine scarlet color. These bands were highly valued and might be detached and put on other robes, or used to decorate the face (C 133). Some of the men put feathers in their hair and some made little ruffs of down to wear around their necks (S 145). Some had frontlets made of the longest snake skins, the tails of which hung behind as long as two French ells or a yard or more (S 145, 235).

The women dressed as the men, except that they always bound up their robes, which extended to the knee (C 134). A small piece of leather was girded around their loins and hung down to mid-thigh (S 66). Women were not ashamed to expose their bodies from the waist up and from the mid-thigh down (C 134).[25]

Around their necks and arms, the Huron wore bead necklaces and bracelets of wampum. Beads were also worn from their ears and in their hair (JR 15:155). Some wampum was strung to make neck-

---

[25] Iroquois ornamentation, dress, and hair styles were similar to those of the Huron and remained so for at least two centuries after European contact. The major changes during this period were the substitution of cloth for skins, the addition of a shirt to the men's usual costume and an overblouse to the women's, and the addition of new types of ornaments, most notably, silverwork, to the costume (see Jackson 1830 b: 14–15; Morgan 1850: 69–70, 87–94; 1852: 88–97, 110–111; 1901(1): 252–257; 1901(2): 11–13, 38–39, 46–56; Shimony 1961 a: 160).

laces three or four fingers wide and about 3½ feet in circumference. The women wore as many of them on their necks as their means and wealth allowed (S 144). Some wampum was strung "like our rosaries" and fastened to their ears so that they hung down. Chains made of wampum as large as walnuts were fastened to both hips and arranged in front in a slant over their thighs or the girdles they wore. Some women wore bracelets on their arms, and great circular (and square) plates in front over the stomach and others behind hanging from their hair plaits (S 144; C 134). The plates which hung on the back were a foot square and covered with wampum (C 134–135). The girls appeared at dances and feasts loaded with wampum and adorned with the best and most costly things they possessed (C 134–135, 164). Some women also had belts and other finery made of porcupine quills dyed red and neatly interwoven (S 144). There was no lack of feathers and paint (S 144–145).

The wampum (*onocoirota*) was made from the ribs of large seashells like periwinkles, called vignols. These were cut into a thousand pieces, then polished on sandstone; a hole was pierced in them, and necklaces and bracelets made of them. This took great trouble and labor because of the hardness of these ribs (S 146).[26]

Both men and women painted themselves (S 144–145). Most adorned their faces in black and red (JR 15: 155; 38: 249; C 133) or in various colors (JR 38: 249). They decorated their bodies as well as their faces with black, green, red, and violet paints, and in many other ways. Others, primarily those of the Tobacco Nation, had their bodies and faces tattooed with representations of snakes, lizards, and squirrels. A few women were also tattooed (S 145). The black usually was obtained from the bottom of pots; the other colors from various earths or from certain roots which yielded a fine scarlet color (JR 38: 251). These colors were mixed with sunflower seed oil, bear's fat, or other animal fats (C 133, cf. JR 38: 251). They also painted pictures of men, animals, birds, and other objects on stones, wood, and similar materials as well as on their bodies. These pictures served simply as ornament for their pipes and for the fronts of their houses (S 98).[27]

Both men and women oiled their hair (S 144–145) with oil made from the seed of sunflowers (C 50). The women and girls always

[26] Although the use of wampum was an aboriginal culture trait, it increased in availability and use after Europeans came to the continent because European metal tools made the manufacture of wampum easier and because trade increased and beaver skins were exchanged for wampum (Beauchamp 1898: 3–4; 1901 b: 329, 342, 354). There is some evidence that the wampum "collars" of the Huron were not the wampum "belts" of the Iroquois (Beauchamp 1901 b: 342–343, 384–387).

[27] The pictures painted on the houses were probably clan symbols (Barbeau 1917: 402 n.; Beauchamp 1905: 108–109, 132; Fenton 1951 b: 51; Goldenweiser 1913: 467; Morgan 1881: 64; 1901(1): 309). Some face painting also may have indicated clan affiliation: Powell (1881: 64) says that each Wyandot clan had its distinctive method of painting the face.

wore their hair in a uniform style (C 134): one braid (JR 38: 249) or tress which hung down the back and was tied up with leather thongs (S 143). When they went to a dance, their tresses were carefully combed, dyed, and oiled, with a tuft of hair tied up behind with eel skin as a band (C 134). The men also dyed their hair. Some wore their hair long, others short, and still others on one side only (C 133–134). The men wore their hair above their ears in one or two great rolls "like moustaches," which they often twisted and corded with feathers and other articles. The rest of the hair was kept short, cut in sections, with a ruff like that outside the tonsure, or in any other manner they pleased (S 143). The men cut their hair in different ways: some wore it in ridges, a ridge of hair one or two fingers wide on the crown of their heads and on either side the same amount shaved off and then another ridge of hair; others shaved one side of their heads and on the other left the hair long, so that it reached to their shoulders. Most commonly, the men allowed their hair to grow very long. Some said that the French name for these Indians came from these hair styles: their heads reminded a French sailor or soldier of boars (*hures*) and he called them Hurons (JR 16: 229–231; 38: 249).[28]

In order to remove lice from skins and furs, two sticks, one on each side, were placed in the ground in front of the fire and the skins spread over them, the side without hair being next to the fire. The vermin, feeling the heat, came out of the hair and remained on the surface, where the women caught them without trouble and ate them (S 228).

Women also ate the lice from their own bodies and from those of their children (S 88).

TRAVEL

Travel within Huronia and to other tribes was by foot and by canoe.

Their largest canoes were from 8 to 9 paces long and a pace or pace and a half wide at the middle, tapering off at both ends; others were smaller (S 100). The largest canoes held five, six (S 56), or three men and the smallest, two (S 246). The size varied as to the use to which the canoe was put (S 100), the smaller vessels being used if the route had rapids, difficult channels, portages, etc. (S 246). A canoe could carry the weight of a hogshead (S 101). They were made of birchbark, strengthened with small hoops [ribs] of white cedar, light enough to merely skim over the water and to be easily

---

[28] The frequency with which this etymology has been cited in the secondary sources reflects the writers' interest in etymology, not the accuracy of the statement; it is suggested only tentatively by the Jesuits. It is quite possible that even by this early date it was a folk etymology.

carried by one man on his head or shoulders (JR 15: 151, 161; S 101).[29] If they wished, the Indians could, under favorable conditions, travel 25 or 30 leagues a day (S 101).

The Huron also traveled by land and would walk 10, 20, 30, and 40 leagues without carrying provisions and taking only tobacco and steel and bow and quiver (S 98–99). Little reed mats, on which to sleep, were customarily carried with them (S 62). If they had no water and were thirsty, they sucked it from trees, particularly the beech tree, which had a sweet and pleasant liquid when in sap (S 98–99).

In winter, a kind of sledge (*arocha*) was made of long boards of white cedar on which were put the loads (S 93) to transport them over the ice (C 93). Snowshoes, called *agnonra* (S 84), strung with animal gut (S 98), were used after the snow had fallen (S 83–84, 93). The Neutral using these ran after deer to catch them (S 227).[30]

The shelter made by those traveling by canoe, and arranged to slope over its occupants, consisted of two pieces of birchbark laid against four small poles stuck into the ground (S 57). A site was selected on the bank of a river or other place where dry wood could be found. While one man collected the wood, another put up the shelter and found the stick on which to hang the kettle over the fire. A third sought two flat stones with which to crush the corn. After the crushing, which was done over a skin spread on the ground, the corn was put into the kettle to boil. When boiled "quite clear," this *sagamité* was served in bowls of birchbark that each man carried with him together with a large spoon. *Sagamité* was eaten twice a day, after pitching camp in the evening and before leaving in the morning. If two groups occupied the same shelter, each boiled its own corn and then all ate together, using the contents of both kettles. [Commenting on the hardships of this journey Sagard remarked that "the bowls could hardly have a pleasant smell, for when they were under the necessity of making water in their canoe they usually used the bowl for the purpose; but on land they used to stoop down in some place apart with a decency and modesty that were anything but savage" (S 59–60).] Sometimes the corn was cooked uncrushed, but it was

---

[29] During this period the Huron and Algonquin made their canoes of birchbark and the Iroquois made theirs of the bark of the red or slippery elm or of butternut hickory. The Iroquois were forced to use these inferior materials, as birch trees did not grow in their country. Later, however, they did make them out of birchbark. They also used dugout canoes. (Beauchamp 1905: 139–146; Fenton and Dodge 1949; Morgan 1852: 105–106; 1901(2): 25–27.)

[30] It is possible that the Iroquois did not use the sled; at least, Beauchamp (1905: 163) found no mention of the sled in New York State. The Iroquois did, however, use snowshoes (Beauchamp 1905: 161–162; Jackson 1830 b: 22; Morgan 1850: 79–80; 1901(2): 34–35).

Jackson (1830 b: 22) also mentions that an Iroquois hunter without a weapon would sometimes catch a deer by running it down while wearing snowshoes.

always very hard because of the difficulty in cooking it thoroughly.
Occasionally, by dragging hebind the canoe a line and frog's-skin-
baited hook, fish were caught and added to the kettle. Or, if not
pressed for time after making camp, the Indians would set nets in the
river to catch fish (S 59-60). Corn was cached along the way in little
bags of birchbark. Every second day on the return trip, these caches
would be sought out although, occasionally, they were missed or not
found (S 60; JR 8:77; 19:253). The Indians smoked often during
the day, deadening their hunger between the two meals (S 62).

In order to make a fire, the Huron used two sticks of willow, lime,
or other dry, light wood. The first stick, cut an ell or a little less in
length by an inch wide, was slightly hollowed on one side. With a
beaver's tooth or the point of a knife, into this hollowed, broad side
was cut a little pit and then, beside it, a small notch into which was
put the end of a cotton match or other easily inflammable material.
The second stick, made of the same wood as the first and as thick as
a little finger, bore a pointed end which was inserted in the pit of the
broader stick. Kneeling on the end of the first, or broader, stick, the
Indian twisted the second between his hands so rapidly that the wood
was set on fire and the end of the cotton match ignited. If fire-making
proved difficult, he crumbled a little charcoal or some powdery dry
wood taken from a stump into the pit. If a broad stick was lacking,
a substitute was made by tying two round sticks together and placing
the point of a third between them (S 61).[31]

Each town or village of the Huron had its special coat of arms which
the travelers erected along the route when they wished it known that
they had passed there. In one case, the coat of arms of the town of
Quieunonascaran were painted on a piece of birchbark as large as a
sheet of paper. They consisted of a roughly outlined canoe and drawn
in it as many black strokes as there were men on the trip. To indicate
that Sagard was with them, the Indians roughly drew a man in the middle above the strokes. At the bottom of the piece of bark, they tied
with a shred of bark a piece of dry wood about half a foot long and
three fingers thick. Then this coat of arms was hung on the top of a
pole stuck in the ground so that it leaned over a little (S 251-252).[32]

---

[31] This method of making fire is only one of the methods known to the Iroquois (Beauchamp 1905: 91-93; Waugh 1916: 50-53). It seems likely that the Huron also knew
of these methods.

[32] Jackson (1830 b: 33) describes a similar Iroquois custom: "In their travelling excur-
sions, they frequently describe on the bark of trees, by certain emblems or characters
which they understand, the time they have been from home, the number of persons in
company, the ensign of the tribe they belong to, the course they are going, and the number
of deer or other animals they have killed."

The Iroquois also recorded their war records by paintings on bark (Fenton 1953: 106).

INTERTRIBAL RELATIONS

TRADE AND WAR

There was trade between the Indian groups in furs, pigments, wampum, and other articles (S 66–67).

Corn, fishing nets, wampum, and other objects were traded to the Algonquin for fish and for animal skins (JR 13: 249; 27: 27; 31: 209; 33: 67; C 53, 131). This trade made Huronia "the granary of most of the Algonquins" (JR 8: 115). After the ice on Lake Huron was strong enough, the Huron took corn to the Algonquin to trade for fish (JR 13: 249; cf. JR 27: 27). Other Algonquin came to the Huron. For example, the Nipissirinien left their homes in the middle of the fall and started for Huronia. On the way they caught as many fish as possible and dried them. When they arrived in Huronia to spend the winter, they traded the fish for corn (JR 21: 239). [These Indians did cultivate a little land in the summer (JR 21: 239–241).][33]

The Huron began trading with the French about 1600. They had learned of this trade when occasionally, while going to war, they encountered a place where the French were so engaged (JR 16: 229).

By the time the Jesuits arrived, beaver had already been exterminated in Huronia (JR 8: 57). To obtain skins of beaver, deer, elk, and other animals, the Huron and some nearby Algonquin traded with the other, more northerly, Algonquin tribes (JR 31: 209; 33: 67; C 53). Many of these furs were then taken to Quebec (JR 13: 215–217; 22: 307; cf. JR 28: 45). This trade was important: if the Huron had not been able to go to Quebec to trade they would have found themselves in such a plight they would have considered themselves fortunate to join the Algonquin (JR 13: 215–217).

The Indians did not wish the French traders to learn the source of their fur supply: the Montagnais and Huron were not willing to take them to the Saguenay because they feared revealing their most profitable source; neither were the Epicerinys willing to take the French traders on their journeys (S 87).

Several families had private rights to trade. The first to discover a line of trade was considered the master of such. Children shared the rights of their parents to this trade, as did those who bore the same name. No one else entered it without permission, which was granted only in consideration of presents. A man who had rights to trade could have as many or as few associates as he wished. Inasmuch as most of the riches of the country were obtained by trade, if he had a

---

[33] Apparently this trade between the Algonquin and the Huron rested not on Algonquin lack of knowledge of agriculture or on Huron lack of knowledge of hunting and fishing, but rather on the amount each could conveniently practice.

good supply of merchandise it was to his advantage to divide it with few companions, as he thus secured all that he desired. If a man engaged in trade without permission from the master of that trade, he might conduct a good business in secret. But if he was surprised returning with his goods, he was treated as a thief: unless he was well accompanied all his possessions were taken from him. If, however, he returned with his baggage, safe, there were only complaints about his actions, but no prosecution (JR 10: 223–225).

Indians from neighboring villages came to Quieunonascaran (St. Joseph) seeking permission of Onorotandi, brother of the great chief Auoindaon, to go to the Saguenay, for he was the master and overlord of the roads and rivers that led there, up to the limits of the Huron country. Similarly, the Indians had to get permission from Auoindaon to go to Quebec. As each brother wished to be master in his own country, no one of another tribe of Indians was allowed to pass through his respective country to go trading unless each was recognized as master and his favor secured by a present (S 99).

According to the laws of the country, the trade with the French belonged to the Arendahronons, as they were the first Huron nation to meet the French. They could have enjoyed the privilege of being sole traders with the French, but they shared it with the other nations, retaining the special character of allies with the French (JR 20: 19).

From one point of view, the priests were also traders in Huron country. As gifts and for their food, wood, houses, and other necessities, they gave the Huron little beads or tubes of glass or wampum (plain and colored), knives, awls, needles, fishhooks, iron arrow points, blankets, kettles, hatchets, rings, earrings, and similar items (JR 7: 223; 8: 97, 105–107, 145, 149; 10: 249; 12: 119–121; 15: 159, 163; 18: 19; S 84, 87, 245), and tobacco (JR 13: 141, 171, 219; S 85). The wooden plates used by the Jesuits were expensive; they cost one beaver robe worth a hundred francs (JR 15: 159). The Jesuits also gave the converted Indians rosaries to wear around their necks as a sign of their faith (JR 26: 287).

Other Indians wanting to control trade with the French forced the Huron to travel the longer way, a distance of 300 instead of 200 leagues, to Quebec. This route, which went by way of the River des Prairies, was also the more difficult one as it had more falls and rapids—some, 2 or 3 leagues long—on it (JR 8: 75; 15: 151; 16: 227; 18: 15; 33: 65). The route had more than 60 falls around which canoes and baggage had to be carried (JR 33: 65) or had 35 portages and at least 50 places where the canoe had to be dragged (JR 8: 77). When these rapids or strong currents were reached, the men in the canoes landed and carried the canoes and the baggage on their shoulders around these unnavigable sections. This entailed some work: a number of portages were 1, 2, or 3 leagues long and several trips had to be made for each. Where the rapids were not too swift, the Indians got into the water (sometimes it came to their necks) and hauled and guided their canoes by hand, a procedure that could be dangerous (JR 8: 77–79; cf. S 58, 62–63). The trip took at least 3 or 4 weeks (JR 8: 89; 10: 89; 15: 161; 16: 231; 18: 11, 17).

Even this route was not without its hazards: the tribes along the rivers might cause difficulties. The Island Indians, Algonquin and other tribes between Quebec and Huronia did not want the Huron to trade with the French as they themselves wished to be the intermediaries (JR 6: 19; 9: 275; cf. JR 10: 77). Each year, for example, the inhabitants of an island 150 leagues above Three Rivers blocked the passage of the Huron, who usually gave them gifts in order to continue (JR 9: 275). The Honqueronons [Kichesperini, an Algonquin band] did not allow passage of one canoe alone or two together during the trading season. In order to get corn and flour cheaper, for which they bartered furs, they made them wait for other canoes and pass as a fleet (S 255). Further, on at least one trip, some Montagnais a league or two from Quebec tried to get the Indians to give them a portion of corn and meal for passage and entry into their territory (S 268). On such trips, the Huron also traded with groups along the way (S 63–66).

Iroquois could also be expected to ambush the Huron on this trip (JR 18: 33; 22: 307; 23: 35, 247; 24: 271–273; 25: 21, 25; 26: 31 ff.; 27: 37, 63; 28: 45; 29: 247; 33: 69; S 261). In the summer of 1647, the Huron did not go to Quebec because they feared Iroquois would attack them along the way (JR 33: 69).

The allies of the French, the Huron and their allies, were at a disadvantage in this struggle, as the French did not trade guns for furs as did other Europeans (JR 24: 271–273; cf. JR 10: 51). [The French did however give guns to their neophytes—a policy that at least won converts (JR 25: 27).] The Dutch did trade guns [as well as axes, kettles, and blankets (JR 26: 183)] to the Iroquois, particularly to the Mohawk (JR 21: 119; 22: 307; 24: 271; 26: 183; 34: 123; cf. JR 21: 269–271; 27: 71). By about 1643, the Iroquois had 300 guns (JR 24: 271). In contrast, by 1649, the Huron had very few (JR 34: 137).[34] The English and Flemish were also accused by the Jesuits of inciting some Indians against the Huron and the French (JR 17: 121–123, 223). The Seneca Iroquois eventually defeated the Huron forcing them, in 1649, to flee to the woods, lakes, rivers, and islands and compelling many to take refuge with neighboring nations, particularly the Tobacco Nation (JR 34: 197, 203, 223). (The account of this defeat is given in JR 34.) [It might have been that the Iroquois wished to control

---

[34] The Jesuits may have underestimated the French trade in guns and overestimated the Dutch trade to the Iroquois (Hunt 1940 : 165–175).

the fur trade with the Europeans and that furs were already scarce in Iroquois country: in some peace negotiations between the Huron and the Onondaga, the Onondaga gave presents of wampum collars, while the Huron gave furs, which were of great value to their enemies (JR 33: 121).]

Wars between the various tribes were not undertaken without cause. The most common reason was the refusal of a group, after they had killed a member of another nation, to give the necessary presents, the restitution required by their agreements. This failure was interpreted as a hostile act, and the entire country, particularly the relatives of the deceased, felt obligated to raise a war party to avenge the death (JR 10: 225; 17: 111).[35] A band of young men also might avenge some private quarrel or the death of a friend (JR 10: 227).

Relations between the various Indian groups were not always simple. For example, about 1636, the Island Savages [Kichespirini], wishing to avenge the death of 23 people the Iroquois had massacred, collected 23 collars of wampum. They went to the Huron and Algonquin, but neither listened to them and both refused the presents. The Bissirinien also refused to listen because they demanded tribute when the Bissirinien went down the river to trade. The Huron also were annoyed at the Island Savages because they did not invite the Nation of the Bear, did not offer them presents, and even forbade others to tell them of the matter (JR 10: 75–77).

The Huron maintained pensioners among the people with whom they were neutral and among their enemies so that they might be secretly warned of all plots (JR 10: 229; 22: 309). The person who gave the information had to send a gift of some value to vouch for the truth of what he said (JR 22: 311).[36] As the Huron were circumspect about their own war plans, they allowed people with whom they had not broken entirely to come and go in the country, but assigned them to special houses to which they had to retire; if they

---

[35] Although the Huron and the Iroquois gave as their reason for going to war the obligation to avenge a death, some of these wars probably also involved economic motives. Goods probably were offered as restitution if the people wished for other reasons to maintain friendly relations with the tribe of the murdered person; they probably were not offered if for other reasons they wished for war with the tribe. So important was the idea that recompense be given if tribes were to remain friendly that when the Iroquois League was established to secure peace among the five tribes, the amount to be given to the family of the murdered person also was established (see note 79, p. 53).

Not only were single murders by enemies avenged by warfare, but also, in general, those captives taken in war were given to families who had lost a member in war. These captives were either adopted into the family or were tortured to death (Connelley 1899 b: 34–35; Powell 1881: 68; Hewitt 1918: 533–534; 1932: 479–480, 486; Morgan 1901(1): 331–335; see also "Torture of Prisoners," p. 31).

[36] Similarly, among the Iroquois all important messages are accompanied by wampum (see Beauchamp 1901 b: 344–347 for a summary of such uses of wampum).

were found elsewhere, they would do them grievous harm (JR 10: 229).

Every year rumors circulated among the Huron that the enemy was raising an army, either to attack them while they were away trading or as they were going down to Quebec. It was said that the old and the influential men often authored these rumors in order to keep a number of young men and those capable of bearing arms in the villages and to prevent them from all leaving at the same time to do their trading (JR 14:39).

Every year in the spring and summer, five or six hundred young Huron men, or more, went to Iroquois territory and scattered there in groups of five or six. There they lay flat on their bellies in the fields and woods and along the main paths and at night prowled about and even entered the villages to capture a man, woman, or child. If they took them alive, they carried them back to their own country and put them to death over a slow fire. Or, having clubbed them or shot them to death with arrows, they carried off the heads. If too much encumbered with these, they took the scalps with the hair on them [which they called *onontsira* (S 153)], tanned them and put them away for trophies. In time of war, the scalps were fastened to the end of a long pole and set on the palisades or walls of their town (S 152–153).

When they went to war, two or three of the older or more daring chiefs who undertook to lead them on this occasion went from village to village to explain their plans, giving presents in some of the villages in order to persuade them and procure their aid and support in the war. These chiefs had the authority not only to choose the places to which to go, to assign quarters, and to form battalions, but also to dispose of the prisoners taken and to settle everything else of great consequence (C 159; S 151).

In one case, a young man before going on the warpath, proposed to give the war feast himself on the day of the general assembly and to defray the expenses of all his comrades. The feast required six large kettles with many large smoked fish, and meal and oil for basting them—a large outlay for him and he was accordingly much praised and honored. The kettles were put on the fire before daylight in one of the largest houses in the village. When the council was over and the votes for war taken, they all came to the feast, during which they performed the same military exercises, one after another. When the kettles were empty and the compliments and acknowledgments made, the Indians left to invade the enemy's country. There they captured about 60 of the enemy, most of whom were killed on the spot and the rest brought back alive, put to death, and then eaten at a feast (S 151–152).

When they went on the warpath into the enemy's country, the Huron carried on their backs a bag full of cornmeal that had been roasted and scorched in the ashes. They ate this just as it was, without soaking or even softening it in water. [37] Thus they did not have to make a fire in order to prepare their food, although they sometimes did. In this case it was made in the depths of the forest to prevent it from being seen. The cornmeal lasted from 6 weeks to 2 months, after which they had to return to their village. Some then set out for war again with another supply of food (S 153).

For weapons they used a wooden club (S 98, 154) and bow and arrow. The arrows were made with a knife or a sharp-edged stone, if the maker had no knife. They were fletched with the tail and wing feathers of eagles, as these were strong and flew well. But lacking eagle feathers, others might be used. Points of sharp-pointed stones or bones or iron heads were attached to the arrows with strong fish glue (S 98, 154). A quiver of tanned dog skin was worn like a scarf (S 154). Animals' guts were used to make bow strings (S 98).[38]

They also wore a sort of armor and cuirass, which they called *aquientor*, on their back, legs, and other parts of the body for protection against arrows. Although it provided protection against arrows tipped with stone points, it was ineffectual against those with iron points. The cuirasses were made of white rods cut the same length and pressed against one another, very tightly sewn and interlaced with little cords. They also used a shield (S 154). Some shields (of cedar) covered almost the whole body (and smaller ones of boiled leather were also made) (S 98).[39]

An ensign or flag, a round piece of tree bark painted with the armorial bearings of the town or province and fastened to the end of a long stick, was used (S 154).

On days of important business and rejoicing, as well as when they went on the warpath, the Indians wore a kind of plume, most of them around the head standing up like a crown and others sloping down like a moustache, made of the long hair of the moose dyed a scarlet red glued to a leather band 3 fingers wide and long enough to go around the head (S 155). [40]

---

[37] Corn is still prepared in this way (see footnote 10, p. 69).

[38] The Iroquois had similar weapons (Beauchamp 1905: 122–126; Morgan 1850: 70–74; 1852: 105, 108; 1901(2): 13–16), but it has been suggested that the spear may not have been an aboriginal weapon (Morgan 1852: 105; see also Beauchamp 1905: 120–121).

[39] The Iroquois also had similar armor and shields (Beauchamp 1905: 127–128).

[40] The wearing of special dress on the warpath and on certain other occasions survives today in two Iroquois dances in which costumes are worn. One of these dances, the Thanksgiving Dance, is now remembered as having once been a war dance. Although the costumes usually now worn for these dances are of a Plains type (or what Whites think Indians should wear), the older headdress, a twirling feather attached to a cap (see Morgan 1901(1): 253–254), bears a resemblance to the Huron headdress described by Sagard.

Warfare between the Indians was so intense that the women, especially on the frontiers, could not till the ground and raise corn unless they had with them at all times a man with weapons to protect them (S 164). The Iroquois, however, did not usually come to make war on the Huron except when the trees were covered with leaves. At this time of year they could conceal themselves more easily, especially as there was much forest in the country, most of it near the villages (S 162).

When war was declared, all the villages near the frontiers were destroyed if they were incapable of holding back the enemy. To prevent this, some villages were fortified, each man going to such a place and building new houses with the help of the inhabitants of the village. The chiefs, assisted by the members of their council, worked without ceasing to make the place capable of being held. If any additions to the fortifications were deemed necessary, they had them made. They had every house swept and all the soot and spiders cleaned out for fear of fire which the enemy might cause by means of certain devices learned from some other nation. They got stones and water carried to the watch towers. Many dug holes in which they put their most precious possessions. Some warriors were sent out to ascertain the whereabouts of the enemy while others were encouraged to make weapons and otherwise prepare themselves to defend the village. Each village made similar preparations until it became obvious what villages the enemy was going to attack. Then, if there was no necessity for a large army, a number of warriors in the other neighboring villages went at night with little noise to give them aid, shutting themselves into the besieged town to help defend it (S 155–156).

TORTURE OF PRISONERS

The Huron took prisoners in war to burn and then eat (JR 19: 81). Such captives might be distributed to different villages or nations (JR 15: 171; 17: 73; 23: 33) and given to those who had lost relatives to the enemy (JR 17: 101; 23: 33). A prisoner might be given to a distant tribe (JR 17: 111). They seldom put to death women and children, but kept some for themselves or made presents of them to those who had previously lost some of their own in war. They made much of these substitutes, as if they were actually their own children. When the captives grew up, they went to war against their own parents and men of their nation as bravely as if they had been born enemies of their own country. If the warriors were unable to carry off the women and children they had captured, they put them to death and carried off the heads or the hairy scalp. It happened, but rarely, that after they had been carried back, they were tortured to death. The tears of these tortured women did not move the torturers; men did not weep, for fear of being thought effeminate and lacking in courage (S 159).[41]

Sometimes an enemy would escape. To distract the pursuer, he would throw his wampum necklaces far behind him so that a pursuer, by picking them up, gave the prisoner a head start. Sagard thought that this was why the Indians usually wore all their finest necklaces and paintings on the warpath (S 160).

When they came upon an enemy, they said *sakien,* "sit down," and the captive did so unless he preferred being knocked over on the spot or dying in defense of himself. He surrendered, hoping to escape later. In one case, two or three Hurons, each desiring to be credited with taking an Iroquois prisoner, could not agree, and made the captive decide. He used the opportunity to say that "So and so took me and I am his prisoner," but purposely told a falsehood so that the man who really took him captive would be dissatisfied. That man did speak to the prisoner in secret the following night, saying "You have given and adjudged yourself to another instead of to me who had taken you, and for this reason I would rather set you free than that he should have the honor due to me" and then untied his hands and made him secretly escape (S 160–161).

When the Huron captured an enemy, they made a speech about the cruelties he and his people practiced toward them and said that he must make up his mind to endure as much. They told him to sing, if he had enough courage, during the whole course of their journey home. He did this, singing a song that was often very sad and mournful. While awaiting the hour of his death, they feasted him continually "in order to fatten him and give him more strength and vigor, that he may the better endure injuries and slow torture, and not out of kindness and pity" (S 158–159).

One of the first acts after a prisoner had been taken was to tear out his nails or cut off his fingers (JR 17: 101; 18: 31; 33: 93). They also cut his shoulders and back with a knife, bound him tightly and, mocking him, led him to the village where he was to be tortured (JR 18: 31). In one case, the people went out to meet the prisoners at 500 paces from the village. Armed with clubs, thorns, knives, and firebrands, they formed two lines and struck the prisoners until they reached the platform where they were to be tortured. Each captive was bound, both arms and feet, and was naked except for a wampum

---

[41] Huron and Iroquois prisoners were either adopted into the tribe or tortured to death (see footnote 35, p. 28). As is apparent in the following description, the torture was a religious ceremonial. Knowles (1940 : 215, 219) has suggested that this rite was similar to the Mexican one, both having a cardiac emphasis, death by knife, eating of victims, use of a platform, and sacrifice to the sun or war god. A white dog may have been substituted in more recent times (in the 18th and 19th centuries) for the human sacrifice (Knowles 1940 : 214).

collar around his head which designated him as a victim (JR 15:185–187).

After the captive had arrived at the village he was adopted by someone who had lost his son in war. This adopted parent was charged with "caressing" [torturing] the prisoner (JR 18:31).

The torture of the prisoner might last 5 or 6 days (JR 10:227), but, although the length of time varied, it was essential that one night be devoted to the torture (JR 17:75). The torture consisted of cutting the legs, thighs, arms, and most of the fleshy parts of the body and thrusting glowing brands or red-hot hatchets into the wounds (JR 10:227; 15:173, 187; 17:65, 109). His hands and feet might be pierced with a heated iron (JR 17:75). His fingers were cut off or crushed (JR 15:173, 187), or the nails torn out and the three fingers used in drawing the bow cut off. They stripped off all the skin of the head with hair and applied fire and hot ashes to it or dropped a certain melted gum on it. They might make him walk naked through a great number of fires kindled from one end to the other of a large house while all the people of the village stood on two sides and applied a burning brand to his body as he passed (S 161). Sometimes, while the prisoner was being tortured he was forced to sing and dance (JR 10:227; 15:173, 187; 17:65, 109). He was tied to a stake and with a hot iron, they gave him, as it were, garters around his legs, and with red-hot tomahawks they rubbed his thighs from the top down and thus little by little burned him. Sometimes to add to his sufferings they dashed water over his back and applied fire to the tip of his fingers and of his private parts. Then they pierced his arms near the wrist and drew out the nerves with sticks or if they could not get them out in that manner, they cut them (S 161). The adopted father might approach the captive with a necklace in the form of a hot iron and say, "See here, my son; you love, I am sure, to be adorned, to appear beautiful." While saying this, he burned him from the soles of his feet to the top of his head with firebrands and hot cinders and pierced his feet and hands with reeds or sharp irons (JR 18:31). The prisoner was tortured in the hope that he would cry out; if he did not, he brought misfortune on his torturers (JR 17:65), and, if he did not, the torturers were furious (JR 17:109). If he had the courage to do it, he cursed those who tormented him (JR 10:227; S 161–162).

The prisoner might be tortured first at the platform and then taken to a house to rest so that he might be more cruelly tortured by fire at night (JR 15:187). Later, in the largest house in the village, all the people gathered to torment him (JR 15:173). He was made to walk over the fires and, if he could not walk over them, he was taken by the hands and feet and carried over them (JR 15:173; 18:31). Everyone tormented the prisoner as he wished (JR 15:173).

Sometimes the prisoners escaped, especially at night when they were made to walk over the fires. As they ran over them, they scattered the coals with their feet and kicked aside the brands, ashes, and burning coals. This produced such a darkness from the ashes and smoke that the people could not recognize one another and all were forced out the door. The prisoner might get into the crowd and hence flee. If he could not do this immediately, he hid in an out-of-the-way corner until an opportunity came to escape (S 163).

In the morning, the prisoner was taken outside to the platform where he was tortured again (JR 15: 173, 187; 17: 109; 18: 31) when he was about to die (S 162). He was fastened to a stake on this platform, and firebrands and glowing irons applied to his body again (JR 17: 65). The people underneath the scaffold thrust firebrands through the open places (JR 17: 69). If he fainted, he was given water to revive him. In one case, at least, they bit off pieces of his ears and forced him to eat them (JR 15: 173). While being tortured, he was invited to sing, and he sang in order not to be thought a coward (JR 18: 31; cf. JR 10: 227). His scalp might be removed (JR 17: 67; 18: 31; 29: 253) and preserved as a very precious object (JR 17: 67).[42] Finally, when he died, they cut off his head (JR 15: 187; 17: 71; S 162). Then his belly was opened and all the little children there got some small fragment of bowel, which they hung on the end of a stick and carried in triumph through the village as a symbol of victory (S 162).

The following is an account of the torture of one prisoner. The Huron had come upon 25 or 30 Iroquois fishing at the Lake of the Iroquois [Lake Ontario]. They captured 8 and the rest fled. Of the 8, they brought back to Huronia only 7; the other's head only was kept. When they were beyond the reach of the enemy, the band assembled and held a council. It was decided that 6 should be given to the Attigneenonghac and the Arendahronon and the seventh to the place where the Jesuits were [among the Attignawantan]; the prisoners were divided among these three nations since it was these three that had composed the war party. When the prisoners arrived in Huronia, the old men, to whom the young men on returning from war gave their spoils to be distributed, held another council to decide on which villages the prisoners should be bestowed. It was customary to give a notable person who had lost one of his relatives in war an enemy captive "to dry his tears" and to partly assuage his grief (JR 13: 37–39).

When the Jesuits arrived at the village to which the prisoner was being brought, they saw him coming from a distance, singing in the midst of 30 or 40 Indians who were escorting him. He was dressed

---

[42] The scalp, either the entire scalp or a piece of it, was also regarded by many other North American Indians as an object having supernatural power.

in a beautiful beaver robe and had one string of wampum beads around his neck and another, in the form of a crown, around his head. A large crowd was present for his arrival. The captive was made to sit down at the entrance of the village while it was decided who would make him sing. He had already been roughly handled; one of his hands was badly bruised by a stone, one finger had been violently wrenched away, the thumb and forefinger of his other hand had been nearly taken off by a hatchet blow, one arm joint had a deep cut, and both were badly burned. Meanwhile, they brought him food. From time to time he was commanded to sing; he sang with much vigor, especially in view of the fact that he was over 50 years old and had done nothing else day and night since his capture. Meanwhile, the chief addressed him, "My nephew, you have good reason to sing, for no one is doing you any harm; behold yourself now among your kindred and friends" (JR 13: 39–41).

In all the places through which the prisoner had passed, he had been given something with which to make a feast. The same courtesy was extended in this village: a dog was put into a kettle, and, while it was cooking, the captive was brought into the house where the people were to gather for the feast. As soon as the dog was cooked, the prisoner was made to eat a large piece of it; it was put into his mouth as he was unable to use his hands. He also shared it with those who were near him. His hands caused him so much pain that he asked to go outside the house to get a little air. His request was granted. His hand were unwrapped and some fresh water was brought to refresh them. They were half putrefied, swarming with worms, and had an almost unbearable smell. He asked that the worms be removed, and they were. Meanwhile, he sang from time to time and the people at the feast continued to give him something to eat (JR 13 : 43–47).

During a good part of the night, the old men of the village and some chiefs who were guarding him talked with the prisoner about his capture and the affairs of his country. The next day he went well escorted and singing as usual to another village a league distant. At this village in the evening he made a feast and sang and danced for most of the night (JR 13: 49–51).

The next day the people of the village were still awaiting the return of the chief, who had gone trading, to fix the day and place, as this captive was entirely at his disposal. When the chief arrived, he had a talk with the prisoner. In summary he said—

My nephew, you must know that when I first received news that you were at my disposal, I was wonderfully pleased, fancying that he whom I lost in war had been, as it were, brought back to life, and was returning to his country. At the same time, I resolved to give you your life; I was already thinking of preparing you a place in my house, and thought that you would pass the rest of your days pleasantly with me. But now that I see you in this condition, your fingers gone and your hands half rotten, I change my mind. I am sure that you yourself would now regret to live longer. I shall do you a greater kindness to tell you that you must prepare to die. Is that not so? It is the Tohontaenrats who have treated you so ill, and who also cause your death. Come then, my nephew, be of good courage; prepare yourself for this evening, and do not allow yourself to be cast down through fear of the tortures.

The captive then asked the chief how he would be tortured and the chief replied that he would die by fire. While the chief was talking, a sister of the deceased Huron whom the captive replaced by adoption brought the prisoner food. She showed great solicitude for him and treated him almost as if he were her own son. Her face was very sad and her eyes were full of tears. The chief often put his own pipe into the prisoner's mouth, wiped the sweat from his face, and fanned him with a feather fan (JR 13:53–55).

About noon the captive made his *athataion*, his farewell feast.[43] Everyone was free to come and people were there in crowds. Before the feast began, the prisoner walked through the middle of the house and said in a loud and confident voice, "My brothers, I am going to die; amuse yourselves boldly around me; I fear neither tortures nor death." Then he began to sing and dance through the entire length of the house and some others also sang and danced in their turn. Next, food was given to those who had plates while those who had none watched the others eat. The feasts over, the captive was taken back to the village to which he had been originally brought to die (JR 13: 55–57).

The torture took place in the house of the war chief, the house where all war councils were held. About 8 o'clock in the evening 11 fires were lighted along the house, about 1 brasse [44] from each other. The people gathered immediately, the old men taking places above, on a sort of platform that extended along both sides of the house. The young men were below; it was so crowded that there was hardly a passage along the fires. Cries of joy resounded on all sides. Each provided himself with a firebrand or a piece of bark with which to burn the prisoner. Before he was brought in, a chief encouraged all to do their duty and told them of the importance of this act which was viewed by the sun and by the god of war. He ordered that at first they should burn only his legs, so that he might hold out until daybreak. He also said that for this night they were not to go and amuse themselves in the woods. Shortly after he had finished speaking, the captive entered. The cries redoubled at his arrival. He was made to sit down upon a mat and his hands were bound. Then he rose and made a tour of the house, singing and dancing. After he had returned to his place, the war

---

[43] This farewell feast was similar to that given by any man before he thought he was to die (see below, "Feasts" and "Death").

[44] A brasse was about 5.3 feet (Kinietz 1940: 40).

chief took his robe and said that a particular chief would despoil him of the robe which he held. He added, "The Ataronchronons will cut off his head, which will be given to Ondessone, with one arm and the liver to make a feast." After this, each armed himself with a brand or a piece of burning bark and, as the captive ran around the fires, each attempted to burn him as he passed. He shrieked and the whole crowd imitated his cries, or rather smothered them with shouts. They often stopped him at one end of the house; some broke the bones of his hands, others pierced his ears with sticks which they left in them, others roughly bound his wrists with cords and pulled each end with all their might. After he had made each round and could pause to catch his breath, he was made to rest on hot ashes and burning coals. On the seventh round, his strength failed him. After he had rested a short time on the embers, they tried to make him rise as usual, but he did not move. One Indian applied a brand to his loins and he fainted. The chiefs ordered them to cease torturing him, saying that it was important that he live until daybreak. He was put on a mat, most of the fires were extinguished, and many people left. After an hour he began to revive a little, and was commanded to sing. At first, he did so in a broken and dying voice, but finally he sang so loudly that he could be heard outside the house. The youth assembled and began torturing him again. As they took turns, they had leisure in which to devise other methods to make him feel the fire more keenly. He was scarcely burned anywhere except on his legs, but the flesh on them was in shreds. Some applied burning brands to them and did not withdraw them until he cried out. As soon as he stopped shrieking, they burned him again, repeating this seven or eight times, often reviving the fire by blowing on it. Others bound cords around him and then set them on fire, thus slowly burning him. Some made him put his feet on red-hot hatchets and then pressed down on them. They struck him with clubs on the head, passed small sticks through his ears, broke the rest of his fingers, and stirred up the fire around his feet. As they burned him, they made various remarks. One said, "Here, uncle, I must burn you," and later another called the prisoner a canoe, "Come, let me calk and pitch my canoe, it is a beautiful new canoe which I lately traded for; I must stop all the water holes well," meanwhile passing the brand all along his legs. Another asked him, "Come, uncle, where do you prefer that I should burn you?" and the captive had to indicate some particular place. Someone else said, "For my part, I do not know anything about burning; it is a trade that I never practiced"; meanwhile, he performed tortures more cruel than those of the others. Some tried to make him believe he was cold. Said one, "Ah, it is not right that my uncle should be cold; I must warm you," and another added, "Now as my uncle has kindly deigned to come and die among the Hurons, I must give him a present; I must give him a hatchet," and with that he applied a red-hot hatchet to his feet. Another made him a pair of stockings from old rags which he then set on fire. Often, after having made him utter loud cries, he asked him, "And now, uncle, have you had enough?" and when he replied, *onna chouatan, onna,* "Yes, nephew, it is enough, it is enough," they replied, "No, it is not enough" and continued to burn him at intervals, demanding of him every time if it was enough. From time to time they gave him something to eat and poured water into his mouth so that he would last until morning. At the fire, there might be green ears of corn roasting at the same time as the red-hot hatchets were heated and sometimes while they were giving him ears to eat, they were putting hatchets on his feet. If he refused to eat, they said, "Indeed, do you think you are master here?" and so added, "For my part, I believe you were the only chief in your country. But let us see, were you not very cruel to prisoners? Now just tell us, did you not enjoy burning them? You did not think you were to be treated in the same way, but perhaps you did think you had killed all the Hurons?" (JR 13: 59–71).

As the day began to break, fires were lighted outside the village in order to display the cruelties to the sun. The victim was led to this place. Two Indians took hold of him and made him mount a scaffold 6 or 7 feet high. Three or four followed him. They tied him to a tree which passed across the scaffold in such a way that he was free to turn around. Then they began to burn him more severely than ever, leaving no part of his body untouched by fire. When he tried to avoid one torturer, he fell into the hands of another. From time to time, the torturers were supplied with new brands, which they thrust down his throat, and even forced them into his fundament. They burned his eyes; they applied red-hot hatchets to his shoulders; they hung some around his neck, putting them first on his back, then on his breast, according to the position he took to avoid their weight. If he tried to sit or crouch down, someone thrust a brand from under the scaffolding which made him arise. They so harassed him that they finally put him out of breath. Then they poured water into his mouth to strengthen his heart and the chiefs said he should take a little breath. But he remained still. Fearing that he would die other than by the knife, one cut off a foot, another a hand, and, almost at the same time, a third cut off his head. The head was thrown to the crowd, where someone caught it and took it to the village chief to whom it had been promised [see above] so that he could make a feast. The trunk remained in the village where he had been killed and a feast was made of it the same day (JR 13: 77–79).

If the prisoner had been particularly brave before he died, the Indians would eat his heart, blood, and roasted flesh in order to be courageous also (JR 10:227; cf. JR 17:75). Sometimes a man made an incision in the upper part of his neck and let the blood of the tortured prisoner run into it: since the enemy's blood had mingled with his own, he would never be surprised by the enemy, no matter how secret that knowledge might be (JR 10:227–229). The dead prisoner might be cut up and put piece by piece into a kettle to be cooked. At other feasts the head of the animal—bear, dog, deer, or large fish— was given to the chief; [45] but at this feast it was given to the lowest person in the company. Some ate of the prisoner with horror, others with relish (JR 10:229; cf. JR 15:173; 17:99; 18:31–33; S 162). [See the martyrdom of Brébeuf and Lallemant (JR 34:27–35, 141–149) for further accounts of torture of prisoners.]

The war song (JR 33:183) was sung on other occasions in addition to the farewell feast and the torture. The "doleful chant" the Jesuits mention the Indians singing when they despair of their lives (as before going to war or while in the midst of a storm on the lake) was probably this song (JR 23:173–175).[46]

After sunset on the day the captive was tortured to death, his soul was expelled from the houses by making a "horrible and universal noise." Souls of enemies who died in other ways and those of friends and relatives were not feared (JR 39:29).

THE VILLAGE

Some of the villages, the principal ones, were enclosed by strong wooden palisades (JR 10:51, 229; 11:7; 22:305; 23:57; 34:125–127; S 91).[47] One such stockade was made of pine trees from 15 to 16 feet high and had a deep ditch (JR 34:123–125). In general, these palisades were made in three rows, interlaced into one another and reinforced within by large thick pieces of bark to a height of 8 or 9 feet. At the bottom were placed lengthwise large tree trunks that rested on strong short forks made from tree trunks. Above the palisades were galleries or watch towers [called *ondaqua* (S 91)], which in war time were stocked with stones to hurl upon the enemy and

[45] See below, "Feasts." The head of the animal, now often that of a pig, still has a special importance in the feasts of some medicine societies (see note 24, p. 73).

[46] See "Death" (p. 129), for singing of this song at the farewell feast. By Iroquoian custom, each man has a personal chant (adónwe') which belongs either to his father or to his maternal line and which was and is sung on certain occasions. It was the last song sung by an Iroquois warrior before his death and was the song sung by a warrior while boasting during the war feasts. It is currently sung as a part of certain Iroquois ceremonials, as Midwinter, and is one of the Four Sacred Ceremonies of the Iroquois, ceremonies thought to have been given in the creation and confirmed by Handsome Lake. Its war connotations are no longer important and its purpose is now to return thanks to the Creator (Fenton 1936: 16; 1941 b: 106 n ; 1942 b: 18–19; 1953: 103; Speck 1949: 135–137).

[47] The Iroquois village often also was stockaded (see Beauchamp 1905: 110–116 and Morgan 1852: 113–114 for descriptions of these stockades).

water to put out the fire that might be made against the palisades. Ladders were used to ascend to them (S 91–92; C 122).

The towns on the frontiers and nearer to the enemies were the best fortified in respect to the enclosing walls, which were about 2 lances high, to the gates and entrances, which were closed with bars and built so one had to turn sideways and could not stride straight in, and location. The site adjoined some good stream. It was on a place slightly elevated and surrounded by a natural moat if possible and, although the walls were rounded and the village compact, had enough space vacant between the houses and the walls to defend itself against the enemies' attacks (S 92).

In villages that were not fortified, the inhabitants could only flee when attacked (JR 10: 51, 95). In the summer, the people could escape to an island or hide in the forest. In the winter, they did not know where to hide: they could not hide on an island as the ice served as a bridge for the enemy; they could not hide in the forests as the leaves had fallen from the trees and, in the winter, the tracks made in the snow gave away their location (JR 10: 51). The indefensibility of these villages led the Jesuits to advise the Huron to construct square forts with four little towers at the four corners so that four Frenchmen with guns could easily defend the entire village (JR 10: 53).

Longhouses comprised the Huron winter village. A village might have as many as 50, 60, or 100 of these houses and might contain as many as 300 or 400 families (JR 10: 211; cf. JR 15: 153; 35: 87). The chief town once contained 200 houses, but it was divided into 2 villages and rebuilt in a new locality (S 92).

In each house were from 4 to 5 fires, usually 2 or 3 paces apart (JR 15: 153; 16: 243; 17: 177). As 2 families used each fire, 1 on each side, 8 to 10 families (60 to 80 people) occupied 1 longhouse (JR 15: 153; 16: 243; 35: 87; S 94). Some houses had 8, 10, or 12 fires (or 24 families); others, fewer, depending on their length (S 94; C 123–124). One house in which there was one fire and one family is mentioned (JR 17: 91). A hole in the top of the house permitted the smoke to escape (JR 8: 107; C 124; S 80, 95). The houses were filled with fire, smoke, naked bodies, and dogs (JR 17: 13).

The dwellings were made of large sheets of cedar [by common consensus and usage, the best (cf. JR 14: 43–45)], ash, elm, fir, or spruce bark and had the shape of a bower or garden arbor. These houses [called *ganonchia* (S 93)] were of various lengths; some were 2, others 20, 30, or 40 brasses and often 25 or 30 fathoms long and were usually 4 brasses or 6 fathoms wide and high (JR 8: 105–107; C 122–123; S 93). Some of these houses were 70 feet long (JR 15: 153). Inside, along both long walls, sheets of bark were placed on the ground to make a bed and over this, placed on poles laid and suspended down the whole length of the house, a kind of bench 4 or 5 feet high of other sheets of bark, making a sort of canopy for the bed (JR 17: 203–205; S 93). These benches were called *andichons* (JR 17: 203) [*endicha* (JR 8: 107), *garihagueu* and *eindichaguet* (S 94)]. In the summer, the Indians slept on this bench to escape the fleas [mosquitoes?]; in the winter, they slept on the ground below on mats near the fire and close to one another (C 123; S 93). The children slept in the warmest and highest place and the parents next with no space between them or at the foot or head (S 93). When going to sleep, they simply lay down and muffled their heads in their robes (S 93–94). A sleeping mat was used (S 72). In the space beneath these benches was kept wood to burn in winter (JR 8: 109; C 123; S 94). Inside the door there was a storeroom for provisions (JR 8:107). These enclosed porches at each end were used principally to hold large vats or casks of tree bark in which were stored well dried and shelled corn (C 123; S 95). The logs, called *aneincuny*, used for keeping the fire in by being lifted a little at one end, were piled in front of the house or stored on the porches (*aque*) (S 94). In the middle of the house were suspended two big poles [*ouaronta* (S 95)] from which pots were hung and on which clothing, provisions, and other articles were placed to keep them dry and away from mice (C 123; S 95). Smoked fish were stored in casks of tree bark (*acha*) except *leinchataon*, a fish which the Indians did not clean but hung with cords in the roof of the house; if these fish were packed in a cask, they would smell too badly and would become rotten at once (S 95).[48]

As the houses were made of bark that dried out and burned easily, destruction of the village by fire was a constant threat (JR 8: 95, 105; 10: 35, 65, 145, 169; 14: 43–45). Thus, the most precious possessions were put in casks and buried in deep holes outside the houses. Such

---

[48] The Iroquois lived in longhouses similar to those of the Huron as late as 1700. One hundred years later, bark houses were still made, but they were considerably shorter and most houses were made of logs rather than bark (Jackson 1830 b: 15–16; Morgan 1852: 114; 1881: 65). In the early part of the 19th century very little was remembered of the form of the old longhouses and of life in them (Morgan 1881: 122). (Descriptions of Iroquois houses may be found in Morgan 1852: 112–115; 1881: 119–121; 1901(1): 308–310; 1901(2): 287–300; Beauchamp 1905: 97–109.)

The change in Iroquois houses from the 17th century to the present can be summarized as both a change in materials used and size. Houses in the 17th century were made of bark, a material replaced in the 18th century by logs, a material which was subsequently replaced in the 19th and 20th centuries by frame construction. As Morgan found few bark houses in the 19th century, so there are few log houses now being used by the Iroquois. The change in size of the houses—from a longhouse occupied by many nuclear families to that occupied by a single family—occurred during the 18th century. The first step in this change was that to a bark house of shorter length than the old longhouse, but otherwise constructed in the same manner.

The families who occupied the old type of longhouse probably formed an economic unit: the provisions were common property and what was taken in the hunt and raised by agriculture was for the common benefit of the residents of the longhouse, although probably in practice these products were owned by individuals or individual families and when one family exhausted its supply, they were given food by others (Morgan 1881: 64–67, 121).

caches were protected from thieves as well as fires (S 95). To prevent the spread of fire, the houses were separated from each other by 3 or 4 paces (C 125).

In each village, one longhouse was built larger than the others so that the people could gather in it for ceremonials and meetings.[49] Sometimes this house was as much as 25 or 30 brasses long (JR 10: 181).

When one of the villagers had no house to live in, all the people built one for him, either completely or to the extent that the occupants could finish it easily themselves. The decision to build the house was made in full council and each day the summons to work was cried through the village so that all could gather at the appointed hour (S 79). These houses were probably built during the season of the year when the bark used for the covering was suitable (S 81).

The villages were moved and rebuilt every 8 to 12 years as the land became exhausted and firewood scarce (JR 10: 275; 11: 7; 15: 153; 19: 133; cf. JR 8: 89–91; S 92–93) or, in certain districts, every 10, 15, or 30 years (C 124; S 92).[50] They were moved a distance of 1, 2, or 3 leagues, but if forced to move as a result of enemy attacks, the distance was greater, as when the Onondaga moved some 40 or 50 leagues (C 124–125). In at least one instance, the village was relocated in the spring (JR 8: 101).

GOVERNMENT

CHIEFS

The "old men" in a village decided all matters within the village and their advice was tantamount to an order (JR 10: 15).[51] One 50-year-old Huron man, after he had been told that he could not go to the seminary, emphasized this attitude in his reply to the Jesuits. He told them:

It seems to me that you are not right to prefer children to grown men. Young people are not listened to in our country; if they should relate wonders, they would not be believed. But men speak; they have solid understanding, and

---

[49] The houses of the Iroquois chiefs also generally were longer than those of others (Beauchamp 1905: 104–105; 1907: 426). For example, Cornplanter's house in the settlement where he was chief was somewhat larger than the others (Jackson 1830 a: 29).

This practice of gathering in a large building for purely religious ceremonies and for ceremonies that have political implications still survives among the Iroquois: they still gather in what is called a "Longhouse" to perform their ceremonies, a building that serves the followers of Handsome Lake as a church. Like the old longhouse, it is rectangular in plan with benches for the congregation along both long walls.

[50] In general, Iroquoian villages were moved frequently (see, for example, Fenton 1940 d). Fenton (1951 b : 42) suggests that the movement of the Iroquois villages was due to depletion of game as well as exhaustion of the soil and scarcity of firewood; Randle (1951: 172–173) disagrees.

[51] Among many North American Indians, the old men were the most influential in the affairs of the village: they spoke most frequently in council and their advice was usually followed.

what they say is believed. Hence, I shall make a better report of your doctrine, when I return to my country, than will the children that you seek.
[JR 16: 169–171.]

Certain of these men were chiefs. These were of two types: those
concerned with affairs of state, with the affairs of both Huron and
foreigners, as, for example, feasts, dances, games, lacrosse matches,
and funeral ceremonies, and those concerned with affairs of war (JR
10: 229–231; 16: 229). The councils of war were held in the house of
the war chief, a house called *otinontsiskiaj ondaon*, "the house of cut-
off heads." Councils held to govern the country and relating to the
maintenance of order were held in the *endionrra ondaon*, "house of
the council" (JR 13: 59). The latter councils, councils of peace, were
called *endionraondaoné* (JR 10: 261–263).[52]

There were as many kinds of chiefs as there were "affairs." In the
large villages, there were sometimes several administrative and war
chiefs who divided among them the families of the village as into so
many chieftainships.[53] Most of these chieftainships belonged to certain families, but there were certain chiefs whose influence was derived from their intellectual superiority, popularity, wealth, or other
such quality (JR 10: 231), or bravery (C 157).[54] No chief by virtue

---

[52] In the 19th century, the Wyandot still were reported as having tribal and war councils (Powell 1881: 61, 68). Apparently, the same distinction held among the Iroquois,
although Morgan (1901 (1): 67–68) states that "The Iroquois had no distinct class of
war-chiefs, raised up and set apart to command in time of war." The Iroquois did, however, have two hereditary chieftainships, held by the Seneca, whose function, the general
management of military affairs (Morgan 1901 (1): 69–71), was probably similar to that
of the Huron. Parker (1916: 34, 41) says that war chieftainships were held by those
families who also held League chieftainship titles and Hewitt (1918: 531; 1932: 486)
says that the clan or the lineage in the clan had a war chieftain. But as these men
worked some years after war had ceased to be important among the Iroquois, it seems
likely that there once was more organization concerning war activities. The League
organization, concerned with the affairs of state, has had a greater chance of survival than
the organization for war and has survived, although in somewhat modified form, on the
various reservations.

[53] This description probably indicates that the inheritance of the Huron chieftainships
was in the clans, as is the inheritance of tribal and war chieftainships among the Wyandot, although sometimes the rule of matrilineal inheritance was not followed (Powell
1881: 61–62, 68; Connelley 1899 b: 30; 1899 c: 107, 120–121). Similarly, among the
Iroquois, the inheritance of the tribal chieftainships and the two war chieftainships is
within the clan (Morgan 1901 (1): 57–71; cf. Beauchamp 1907: 346–347; Shimony 1961 a:
passim). Although it is commonly said that the chieftainships belong to a clan, it is more
accurate to say, of course, that they belong to a lineage within the clan. The Iroquois
word for lineage, as well as matrilocal extended family, is *ohwachira*, or in the r-less
Iroquois languages *ohwachia* (Hewitt 1918: 530–532; 1932: 476–478; 1944: 82; Shimony
1961 a: 20, 26–27). The chieftainship title in the Iroquois League is also associated with
a tribe, for each title belongs to a particular clan in a particular tribe.

[54] Among the Wyandot, the tribal council might confer a special name on a man for
distinguished services to the tribe (Connelley 1899 c: 109). And, among the Iroquois,
such chiefs whose position is not contingent on membership in a particular clan, called
"Chiefs" by Morgan and "Pine Tree Chiefs" by others, have some influence in Iroquois
councils. They are selected on the basis of personal ability and renown alone, and some
such chiefs attained this recognition on the basis of their ability to lead in war (Morgan
1901 (1): 66–68, 94; Beauchamp 1907: 347; Parker 1916: 11, 41; see also Jackson
1830 b: 30–31).

of election was of higher rank than other chiefs, but a chief held first
rank by virtue of his preeminence, eloquence, free expenditure,
courage, and wise conduct. Affairs of the village were referred principally to that chief in the village who had these qualifications, and
affairs of the country to those leading chiefs with the greatest ability.
Their relatives acted as lieutenants and councilors (JR 10: 231–233).[55]
The chiefs had charge of making the announcements and of managing
the ceremonials (JR 17: 129).

At Quieunonascaran [at least at the time of Sagard's visit] lived
the great chief of the Bear Nation, whom the Huron denoted
garihoüa andionxra to distinguish him from the ordinary warrior
called *garihoüa doutagueta*. In all the other villages within his juris-
diction, he had under him other chiefs, both for war and police, who
gave him messages and information on vital matters. In his own
village there were also three other chiefs, who always participated in
the councils with the village elders, and an assessor and lieutenant
who in his absence, or when otherwise so instructed, had the necessary
proclamations and notices issued throughout the village (S 149).

Each of the groups that comprised the Huron League, the "little
nations," [56] retained its name, a knowledge of its history, some minor
special interests, and its war chief and council chief (JR 16: 229).
The name of the country and the chief were the same; for example, if one spoke of *Anenkhiondic* [*Auoindaon* (S 91)], the
principal chief of the whole country (JR 10: 289), the Bear Nation
was being referred to, and peace treaties were made in his name (JR
10: 231). He lived at Ossosané (JR 13: 165–169). *Endahiaconc*
[*Entauaque* (S 91)] was first chief of the village of Teanaostahé and
of the nation of *Atignenongach* (JR 13: 125) and *Atironta*, chief of
the Arendahronons (S 91). In the past, only worthy men were chiefs
(*enondecha*), the term also used for country, nation, or district, as
though a good chief and the country were synonymous. At the time
of the Jesuits, they were no longer so named, but rather *atiwarontas*,
atiwanens, *ondakhienhai*, "big stones, the elders, the stay-at-homes"
(JR 10: 231–233).

Each individual had his own name. When a man died, his name
was given to someone else so that, if possible, no name was ever lost.
After the death, the relatives of the deceased met to decide which

---

[55] Among the Iroquois each federal chief (sachem) has an assistant, subchief, from his
clan. The subchief has no voice in council unless the chief is unable to attend and deputizes
him to act in his place (Morgan 1881: 31; Hewitt 1918: 532). The influence of the
members of the chief's clan is also apparent in that the clan could depose a chief if he
acted contrary to their wishes (Hewitt 1918: 531; 1932: 479–480; 1944: 85; see note
62, p. 46 for the role of the clan members in the selection of a chief).

[56] This is probably a reference to clans. Although the Jesuit Relations contain only a
few statements that may be interpreted as referring to clans, it is likely that the Huron
had such an organization: both the Wyandot and the Iroquois have matrilineal clans.

individual should take the name. Gifts were presented to the chiefs who gave them to the person assuming the name of the deceased. The person so chosen gave his name to another relative. When a new name was taken, the duties associated with that name also were assumed (cf. JR 20: 35). Thus, if the deceased had been a chief, the new possessor of that name became a chief (JR 23: 165–167). If while alive the man had been esteemed in the country, the one who took his name, "resuscitated him," gave a magnificent feast for the entire country so that he might be known thereafter under his name. He then recruited young men to go on a war expedition with him in order to perform some daring exploit that would make it evident that he had inherited not only the name but also the virtues and courage of the deceased (JR 10: 275–277).[57]

After the name had been transferred, they "dried their tears and ceased to weep"; they had placed the dead one among the living, had resuscitated him, and had made him immortal. The raising of the chief involved much ceremony.[58] All the principal men of the country were called together and a council was held.[59] After the new chief had been elected, he was resuscitated (JR 23: 167; S 209–210) : all rose except the one upon whom the name of the dead man was to be bestowed and put their hands down to pretend to lift him from the ground, indicating that they drew out of the

---

[57] The transference of the name of the deceased to his successor survives in the ceremony to "raise up" a new chief, i.e., to transfer his name (title) to his successor (Morgan 1901(1) : 64–67; see note 58, p. 45). Certain of the Faithkeepers, deacons of the present Longhouse, also hold their position by virtue of belonging to a certain family and these deacons ought to be given the name that accompanies the office (Shimony 1961 a: 77). The personal names given to the young child also belong to the clan among both the Iroquois (Goldenweiser 1912: 386; 1914: 366–368; Hewitt 1918: 534; 1932: 486; Morgan 1901(1) : 85; 1901(2) : 238; Shimony 1961 a: 210–214) and Wyandot (Barbeau 1912: 383; 1917: 402; Connelley 1899 b: 32–37; 1899 c: 107–108; Powell 1881: 59). These names are occasionally changed by formal announcement of such changes during certain ceremonials.

[58] To maintain as Hale (1883: 48) did that the custom of raising up chiefs among the Huron was merely a tribal custom, but became among the Iroquois an important institution essential to the maintenance of the state, is probably to misinterpret the data. Among the Iroquois, as among the Huron, the important chiefs were the tribal chiefs: the Iroquois federal chiefs were and are tribal chiefs. As the Huron also had a confederacy, it would seem likely that these tribal chiefs were also the chiefs of the Huron confederacy. The statement that the raising up of a Huron chief involved much ceremony probably indicates that the Huron had a ceremony comparable to the Iroquois Condolence Ceremony for the raising up of a chief. The Iroquois ceremonial is well known (see Beauchamp 1891 b: 39–41; 1907: 350–404; Deserontyon 1928; Fenton 1946; Hale 1883; Hewitt 1944; Hewitt and Fenton 1945; Morgan 1901 (1) : 109–119; Shimony 1961 a: 256–260). As was the Huron ceremonial, the Iroquois one is concerned with resuscitation. For example, one of the five sections of the Condolence Ceremony, the Requickening, restores the chief through the 14 articles, burdens, or matters. The first of these "wipe away the tears"; the second removes obstructions from the ears; the third removes obstructions from the throat; the fourth restores the internal organs; the fifth wipes clean the bloody husk mat bed; the sixth lets daylight into the darkness of grief; the seventh restores the light of the sky; the eighth restores the loss of the sun; and so on (Fenton 1946: 114–120).

[59] Similarly, the Iroquois Condolence involves the important men of the country; the investiture is in a council of all the federal chiefs.

tomb that great man who was dead and restored him to life in the person of the other, who then rose to his feet. After great applause, he received the presents offered him (S 209–210). Each nation gave its distinct kind of presents. Some, as they presented their gifts, said, "May these grasp the arm of the deceased, to draw him from the grave." Others said, "May these support his head, lest he fall back again." Another gave him weapons to repel the enemies. Still another said, "And I make the earth solid under his feet, so that it may remain immovable during his reign" (JR 23: 167–169). [60] There followed feasts (S 210). [61] If at the feast two women did not come to pitch the tone, "they expected to see only broken heads under the new chief" (JR 17: 161). [62] During the feast, the men told stories of their ancestors so that the young could learn them. [63] When these men were requested to tell a story, they were given a little bundle of foot-long straws. These straws served as counters to aid the memory of those present: the storytellers distributed them in various lots according to the number of tales they told (JR 30: 61). [64] The ceremony to resurrect a chief took place in the spring if events did not hasten or delay the affair (JR 10: 235). [65]

Chieftainships, then, were partly elected and partly inherited: a chief was elected from among the relatives of the deceased chief. [66]

---

[60] This Huron practice seems comparable to the Iroquois one of sending a string of wampum to the mourning moiety with the recitation of each burden in the Requickening portion of the Condolence Ceremony. The first three strings are, however, customarily omitted (Hewitt 1944: 69).

[61] A feast also follows the Iroquois ceremony.

[62] This may refer to the importance of the women of the clan in the selection of a chief. In Iroquois procedure, the clan mother of the clan which holds the federal chieftainship title "appoints" the successor, and the women of the clan have much to say regarding the choice of the successor. The election is also confirmed by the men of the clan and the League council (Beauchamp 1907: 346; Hewitt 1918: 531; 1932: 478–479; Parker 1916: 11, 41, 107). Wyandot procedure is similar (Powell 1881: 61–62).

[63] Similarly, among the Iroquois, after the new chief's name had been proclaimed, the wampum belts, the historical records of the League, were explained, one by one (Hale 1883: 61) and before opening the meeting of the League council for business, the Iroquois recounted the founding of the League and rehearsed the laws of the Condolence (Fenton 1949 a: 237). Apparently, if necessary, a Condolence Ceremony preceded the discussion of business at a meeting of the federal chiefs and if no such ceremony was necessary (no federal chief had died since the last meeting), it was given in abbreviated form.

[64] Sticks often served the Iroquois as mnemonic devices (see, for example, Beauchamp 1905: 169–171; Hewitt 1918: 539; Hewitt and Fenton 1945: 304). In the Condolence Ceremony, a cane with pegs is used as a mnemonic device in the roll call of the chiefs (Hewitt and Fenton 1945: 304). In the Condolence Ceremony and at other times, wampum strings and belts also serve as mnemonic devices.

[65] This reference to the performance of the Condolence Ceremony in the spring and a similar reference to a Wyandot ceremonial held in the spring in which the customs of the people were recited (Finley 1840: 57) would be consistent with Iroquois practice if these rites were held before the last killing frost in the spring. The Iroquois Condolence is held in the autumn or winter as the rites are thought to be destructive to growing things (Hewitt 1917: 323; 1918: 542; 1944: 66).

[66] This Jesuit statement parallels that of Morgan (1901(1): 83): "it appears, so far as positive enactments were concerned, that the office of sachem was hereditary in the particular tribe [i.e., clan] in which it ran; while it was elective, as between the male members of the tribe itself."

Further, a chief's children did not usually succeed him, but properly his nephew or grandson.[67] The person chosen had to have suitable qualifications, had to be willing to accept the position, and had to be acceptable to the whole country. Some refused the honor, sometimes because they did not have the aptitude for speaking, lacked sufficient discretion or patience, or preferred a quiet life. A chief was always, as it were, in the field: if a council was held 5 or 6 leagues away he had to go, summer or winter, regardless of the weather. If there was an assembly in the village, it was held in the chief's house and if there was anything to be made public, he had to do it. The chief's power was the power of the position and persuasion; he did not govern by means of command and absolute power as he had no force to compel men to do what he wished (cf. C 157–158). The chief's authority was solely civil; he could only present what was to be done for the good of the village or the country. Individuals acted as they wished. Some chiefs knew well how to secure obedience, especially when they had the affection of their subjects. Others were hampered in securing their positions by the memory of their ancestors who had badly served the country and could secure them only through giving presents, to the old men, which were accepted in their assembly and put into the public coffers (JR 10: 233–235).

A chief had symbols of his authority and was entrusted with public presents. These were "not the regalia nor the immense riches of European princes," but were what the Indians considered "the most honored and the most precious treasures of the country" (JR 28: 87). The chief had a package of council sticks, *atsatonewai*, which were "all the books and papers of the country" (JR 10: 293).[68]

The office had its compensations. Members of the council were invited to all feasts and received the best portions at them.[69] When anyone made a present, the chiefs got the best part of it. And, when a Huron or a stranger wanted to obtain something from

---

[67] This reference to a chief's nephew as succeeding him is probably a reference to inheritance of the chieftainship in the matrilineal line. In practice, the inheritance of the Iroquois chieftainships is similar to that recorded for the Huron. The best evidence comes from Goldenweiser's (1914: 369) study. In a total of 68 cases, he found that the deceased chief was followed by his brother in 21 cases, by his maternal nephew in 32 cases, by his grandson in 5 cases, by his great-grandson in 3 cases, and by irregular succession in 7 cases.

It may be of some interest to note that patrilateral cross-cousin marriage (marriage of a man to his father's sister's daughter) on the part of a chief's son would result in the possibility that the chieftainship would go to the chief's grandson. However, this does not seem to have been Huron (see below, "Marriage") or Iroquois (see note 35, p. 126) practice.

[68] The council sticks were probably some of the mnemonic devices mentioned above (note 64, p. 46). With the increased availability of wampum after European contact (see note 26, p. 21), wampum strings and belts were probably more often used than sticks. This substitution has meant that the chiefs are now keepers of wampum rather than sticks.

[69] The chiefs and the important participants in an Iroquois ceremonial today are given the first, and probably the largest, portions of the most desired food, although an attempt is made to distribute it equally among all present.

the country, he would "grease the palms of the principal chiefs, at whose beck and call all the rest moved." This led to some accusations of corruption; "the mere suspicion of these secret presents stirs up sometimes great debates and divisions" (JR 10: 253).[70]

COUNCILS

The council of the village,[71] composed of the old men and the head-men (C 157; S 148), was held in the chief's house (JR 10: 233; S 149) unless it was considered expedient to hold it elsewhere (S 149). These meetings were held almost every day (JR 10: 213). After the council meeting had been announced, a great fire, around which all the counsellors sat on mats, was made in the house or appointed place. The great chief held first rank and was seated so that he could see in front of him all his counsellors and assistants. Women and girls took no part in this meeting [72] nor did young men from 25 to 30 years old unless it was a general council, in which case they learned of it from a special announcement. If it was a secret council or one to plan a surprise attack, it was held at night and included only the principal counsellors who, if possible, said nothing until the proposed action had been carried out. When all had gathered and the house closed, they sat in their places for a long time before speaking, keeping their pipes in their mouths. Then the chief spoke for a considerable time in a loud and clear voice about the matter to be dealt with in the council. When he finished speaking, those who had something to say gave in a few words their reasons and opinions (S 149–150). The advice of those who were considered to have good judgment was requested by those present. Such advice might be followed exactly (C 157). Although anyone could express an opinion, the old men controlled the council (JR 10: 213). The council decided and promulgated everything by means of entreaties and suggestions and by majority vote, which was col-

---

[70] This description is somewhat overdrawn. Some of the presents given to the chiefs were undoubtedly those customarily given to indicate good faith, as the giving of wampum indicates good faith. The people did not move at the beck and call of their chiefs; chiefs ruled by persuasion as is indicated in these 17th-century reports. Suspicion of corruption is as general among North American Indians as it is among Whites (for a recent example among the Iroquois, see Shimony 1961 a : 91).

[71] Although there is no such village council now (perhaps a consequence of the establishment of reservations coupled with the conversion of a goodly number of Iroquois to Christianity), it was important in the past. As Fenton (1951 b : 50) says, "A constantly recurring theme in Iroquois mythology and history is the village, its headman, and the council of elders."

[72] Despite the extensive characterization of Iroquois society as being a matriarchy, women had, usually, no voice in council meetings. They exercised their influence behind the scenes, not directly by speaking or attending council meetings. Even today women do not speak in the Longhouse (Shimony 1961 a : 89).

lected by means of little ends of reeds or straws (C 157; S 148–150).[73] The decisions of this group were announced by the chief throughout the village (cf. JR 10:233; 15:157), as was the announcement that an assembly was called (JR 17:93).

Whenever any member of the council offered to do something for the good of the village or to go elsewhere in the service of the village, he was requested to present himself. If he was judged capable of carrying out his proposal, council members encouraged him by speeches to do his duty for the welfare of the others. Then he could accept or refuse the responsibility. Few refused, however, since by acceptance they were held in good repute (C 158–159).

Usually, long trips were made only with the permission of the chiefs. Each year in a special council, the number of men who could leave the village was determined, so that the village would not be unprotected (C 166; S 99).

In addition to these councils, there were general assemblies which included people from distant regions. Every year a representative from each province came to the place appointed for the assembly. For three weeks or a month, there were great feasts and dances, mutual presents were given, friendships were renewed and plans made as to how the enemy could be destroyed (C 159-160; S 150).[74]

If the council involved the nation, it usually met in the village of the principal chief of the entire country and sometimes in the house of this chief. His house was adorned with mats, or strewn with fir branches, with several fires, according to the season of the year. In the past, each brought his fagot to put on the fire.[75] At the time of the Jesuits, however, the women assumed this responsibility and made the fires but did not stay for the meeting. If it were summer, the council was held in the middle of the village or, if there was need for secrecy, in the forest. The meetings usually were held at night and often the entire night was spent in these discussions (cf. JR 19: 177). Decisions were made by a plurality of votes; the usual way of arriving at these decisions was to say to the old men, "Do you give advice; you are the masters" (JR 10:251).

These meetings were called in the following fashion. The chief, after consulting in private with the other chiefs and old men of his village, and after having decided that the matter warranted a public

---

[73] It seems unlikely on the basis of what is known about Iroquoian behavior and Indian behavior, in general, that decisions were made by majority vote of the council. The procedure was probably unanimous decision, the subject being discussed and compromised until all agreed. The reeds or straws probably were used as a device for attaining unanimity (William N. Fenton: personal communication).

[74] This statement implies that the Huron had League councils as did the Iroquois.

[75] Morgan (1901 (2) : 231) said that the Iroquois chiefs brought fagots to League meetings.

meeting, sent invitations to the council, to as many persons of each village as he wished. These invitations were taken by messengers, usually young men who had volunteered. Sometimes an old man was the messenger in order that the summons be more efficacious; the Indians did not always trust the young people. The summons was a request, not a command. These messengers told the chief of the village or, in his absence, the next in authority, the day on which the council was to be held (JR 10: 253-255).

When each man arrived at the meeting, he took a seat near those of his village or nation, so that he could consult with them (JR 10: 255). For example, in one such council consisting of three nations and the Jesuits, the Bear Nation sat along one side of the house, the Jesuits in the middle of the same side, and the two other nations, each with four very populous villages, on the other side (JR 15: 39). If someone was absent, the matter was discussed to ascertain if the meeting should begin. If they decided to hold the council, it was opened, but not always by the leaders: difficulty in speaking, unwillingness, or even dignity might dispose these men against talking first. First, greetings were said, thanks for the trouble taken in coming, and thanksgivings for a safe arrival, that everyone arrived without accident, that no one had been surprised by enemies, had fallen into a stream or river, or had been injured (JR 10: 255). Also as a part of the introduction, a cake of tobacco in a dish might be distributed to the more prominent members present. The Indians never spoke of business nor came to any conclusion without having a pipe in their mouths; they said the smoke went to their brains and gave them enlightenment on their difficulties (JR 10: 219; 15: 27). Then, the matter to be discussed was brought up (JR 10: 255-257).

As all affairs of importance were conducted by means of presents, and because wampum was valuable and all-powerful, it might be given in a council meeting. In one instance, when giving a collar of 1,200 beads of wampum, the Jesuits said it was to smooth the difficulties of the road to Paradise, employing the customary phrase when presents were made in connection with some difficult enterprise (JR 10: 29).

After the subject of the meeting had been presented, each nation or village consulted among themselves to decide what they would reply. Then, they gave their answer. The manner of speaking in councils differed from ordinary speech and had a different name (*acwentonch*): in it, the voice was raised and quavered. A speaker spoke slowly, decidedly, and distinctly, and often repeated the same reason several times. Before he gave advice, he summarized the proposition and all the other considerations brought forward. Some words were used only in these speeches, and metaphors, various circumlocutions, and other rhetorical devices were frequently employed. For example, when speaking of the Bear Nation, they would say, "the Bear has said, has done so and so; the Bear is cunning, is bad; the hands of the Bear are dangerous." When they spoke of the man who conducted the Feast of the Dead, they said, "he who eats souls." When speaking of a nation, they often spoke only of the principal chief; thus, in speaking of the Montagnet, they might say "Atsirond (one of their chiefs) says" [compare above]. Each speaker ended with the words *condayauendi ierhayde cha nonhwicwahachen*, 'that is my thought on the subject under discussion.' The assembly then responded with a "very strong respiration drawn from the pit of the stomach," *haau*. When a person spoke to their liking, the *haau* was "given forth with much more effort" (JR 10:257-259).[76]

In one council between the Jesuits and the Indians, some fell asleep and others left, but the principal men remained until after midnight (JR 15:47).

Various matters were discussed in council. For example, after a house in which only four or five children lived had been burned, the old men met in council to decide what should be done to assist the orphans. As all the stores of corn had been destroyed with the house, at the council each house said that it would furnish three sacks of corn. Everyone helped, giving whatever he could. One gave a plate, another a chest, and some even gave beaver robes. The children found themselves richer, at least in robes and clothing, than they had been before (JR 14:43-45).

All the villages had a kind of stock of wampum necklaces, glass beads, axes, knives, and other things obtained for the community in war, peace treaties, exchanges of prisoners, tolls from tribes which crossed their country, and by other means.[77] These items were deposited with one of the chiefs, appointed as treasurer of the country. When a present might be made for the common benefit and safety of all, as to be released from making war and to secure peace, the council met. After having expounded on the necessity of making the gift and having determined its amount and quality, they notified the treasurer to search his coffers and produce the gift. If he found that the finances were exhausted, every man taxed himself, giving what he could pay according to his convenience and good will and without compulsion (S 266-267).

---

[76] The manner of speaking in councils, the use of metaphor, and the response of the audience are also Iroquois practices.

[77] Hewitt (1932: 480) mentions treasuries of the clan which contained strings and belts of wampum; quill and feather work; furs; corn; meal; fresh, dried, and smoked meats; and other things. They were guarded by women of the clan appointed for this purpose.

CRIME

Murderers, thieves, traitors, and witches were punished (JR 10: 215; for punishment of witches see section on witchcraft).

For the crime of murder, payment had to be made to the deceased's family by the village of the murderer (JR 15: 157).[78] The relatives addressed themselves to the village of the murderer and that village had to give as many as 60 presents, the least of which had to be of the value of a new beaver robe (JR 10: 215–217; cf. JR 28: 49). If the murdered was a member of another tribe, then war was declared between the two tribes, unless that of the murderer gave large presents (S 163–164). Thus, if a Huron killed an Algonquin, the whole country assembled and agreed on the number of presents to be given to the tribe (JR 28: 49; cf. JR 33: 231–249 for the council concerned with the murder of a Frenchman by a Huron). And, if the Algonquin killed a Huron, they gave presents to the Huron. In one case, a Huron man, who had gone to kill a prisoner the Huron had given the Algonquin, was killed by the Algonquins. As a result, they had to give the Huron fifty wampum belts, a hundred fathoms of wampum, a large number of kettles and hatchets, and two female prisoners (C 102–103). If a Huron murdered a foreigner, a bundle of small sticks, a little larger and thicker than matches, tied together, was given by the tribe of the murdered to that of the murderer to indicate the number of presents they desired. The chiefs then divided the sticks among themselves to decide what each nation would give. Then the chiefs returned to their villages to exhort the people to provide the required number of presents (JR 33:239–241).

If the village or the relatives of the murdered were not given gifts by that of the murderer, the village or relatives would take up arms against them: it was an insult (JR 10: 219; S 163). But this rarely happened (S 163).

The usual number of gifts for the murder of a Huron man by another Huron was 30 presents and for the murder of a woman, 40. The price was higher for the death of a woman, the Huron said, because,

---

[78] It seems likely that the Jesuits were in error and the payment had to be made to the clan rather than the village. Among the Wyandot, if a man murdered a member of his clan, the matter was brought up in the clan council; if a man murdered a member of a different clan, the matter was settled in a meeting of the two clans (Powell 1881: 66–67; cf. Finley 1840: 59). Similarly, among the Iroquois, the clans of the murderer and the murdered meet in separate councils, or if they were of different phratries, the phratries might meet in separate councils (Morgan 1881: 12; 1901(1): 322–324); the members of the lineage or clan were obligated to purchase the life of one of its members who had forfeited it by homicide and to pay for the life of the victim (Hewitt 1918: 533–534). Apparently, with the establishment of the League, if the murderer and murdered were of different tribes, the matter was considered in a League council (Hale 1883: 68).

as they peopled the country, they were more valuable (JR 33: 243).[79] Each of these gifts was presented by the chief with a long speech; a ceremony sometimes lasting entire days (JR 10: 217). Those who received the gifts carefully examined them and rejected those that did not please them. Those not acceptable had to be replaced with gifts that were (JR 33: 245).

There were two kinds of presents given: some, as the first nine (*andaonhaan*), were given to the relatives to make peace and to take away all bitterness from their hearts and the desire for revenge; others (*andaerraehaan*, 'what is hung upon a pole') were put on a pole which was raised above the head of the murderer. Each of these presents had its particular name. Those of the first nine, the most important, follow. Sometimes each of these presents was a thousand wampum beads. The chief held the first present in his hand and said, *condayee onsahachoutawas*, 'There is something by which he withdraws the hatchet from the wound, and makes it fall from the hands of him who would wish to avenge this injury.' For the second present he said, *condayee oscotaweanon*, 'There is something with which he wipes away the blood from the wound in the head.' These first two presents represented the regret of the murderer for having killed the man and expressed his wish to restore his life. On giving the third present, the chief said *condayee onsahondechari*, 'This is to restore the country.' For the fourth, he said *condayee onsahondwaronti, etotonhwentsiai*, 'This is to put a stone upon the opening and the division of the ground that was made by this murder.' The fifth was made to smooth the roads and to clear away the brushwood; the chief said *condayee onsa hannonkiai*, in order that one might go henceforth in perfect security over the paths and from village to village. The last four presents were addressed to the relatives, to console them and to wipe away their tears. For the sixth, the chief said *condayee onsa hoheronti*, 'Behold, here is something for him (his father, mother, or the one who would avenge his death) to smoke.' The next was to restore completely the mind of the offended person, *condayee onsa hondionroenkhra*. The eighth was to give a drink to the mother of the deceased and to heal her as having been seriously sick because of the death of her son, *condayee onsa aweannoncwa d'ocweton*. The ninth was to place a mat for her on which she might rest herself and sleep during the time of her mourning, *condayee onsa hohiendaen*. After the giving of these principal presents, others were given as

---

[79] At the time the Iroquois League was established, the price for murder was fixed. The settlement for the murder of one man by another was 20 strings of wampum; 10 for the life he had taken and 10 for his life that he had forfeited by committing the murder. The price was double for a woman. The settlement for the murder of a woman by a man was 30 strings of wampum; 20 for the life of the woman and 10 for the forfeited life of the murderer. The settlement for the murder of a woman by a woman was 40 strings of wampum; 20 for the life of the woman who had been murdered and 20 for the life of the murderer (Hewitt 1917: 323; 1918: 541; 1932: 484–485; 1933).

further consolations and these represented all the things the deceased
would use during life.   One was called his robe; others, his canoe, his
paddle, his net, his bows, his arrows, and so on.   After this, the relatives of the deceased considered themselves perfectly satisfied (JR 10:
217–221).[80]

In the past, the murderer had also to endure a punishment.   The
dead body was stretched upon a scaffold and the murderer had to lie
under it and receive upon himself all the putrid matter which exuded
from the corpse.   A dish of food was placed beside him and this was
soon filled with filth and corrupt blood which fell into it.   To get the
dish pushed back a little the murderer had to give a present of seven
hundred wampum beads (*hassaendista*).   The murderer remained in
this position as long as the relatives wished.   Finally, he made
another rich present (*akhiataendista*).   If, after all this, the relatives
of the dead man revenged the death, all punishment fell on them
and they had to give presents even to the relatives of the first murderer (JR 10: 221–223).[81]

Inflicted wounds also were healed only by giving presents, as belts
and hatchets.   The value of these presents varied according to the
seriousness of the wound (JR 10: 223).

The presents given to the French for the murder of one of their
number were as follows.   The first present of the chiefs was to open
the door of the Jesuits' house to them and the second, to allow them
to enter.   After they had entered, the first present was "the wiping
away of tears":   "We wipe away your tears by this gift so that your
sight may no longer dim when you cast your eyes on this country
which has committed the murder."   Next came the present called "a
beverage":   "This is to restore your voice which you have lost, so that
it may speak kindly."   The third was to calm the agitated mind.   The

---

[80] The names of these presents resemble the names of the 14 burdens or matters in the
Iroquois Condolence Ceremony (see note 58, p. 45). Its resemblance is perhaps not acci-
dental; the 10th burden is called the "20 matters," the 20 strings of wampum that are the
penalty for murder (Fenton 1946 : 120; Hewitt 1944 : 75).

A procedure similar to that described for the Huron and that of the Iroquois Condolence
Ceremony is recorded by Sir William Johnson for a council meeting between Iroquois and
Whites concerning a murder (Beauchamp 1886 : 90).

[81] Finley describes a similar Wyandot procedure. He states that after the defeat of the
Wyandot by the Iroquois, murder was frequent, and to stop it, the council of the tribe
decreed to put to death every murderer (Finley 1840 : 62). He goes on to say:

When the sentence of guilt was passed, the body of the murdered person was
taken and placed on a smooth piece of bark, supported by a scaffold of forks and
poles, 2 or 3 feet from the ground, and so fixed that all the matter from the putrefying carcass should drop from a certain place. The murderer was then tied, and so
firmly pinioned to the ground by tugs and stakes, as not to be able to move in the
least. A gag was then put into his mouth, so as to keep it open, which was so placed
as to receive the drops from the putrefying body. In this position he lay, without a
moment's respite, until death came to his relief; and this, the chief said, would be
from 10 to 15 days. A few were put to death in this way, which so effectively broke
up the practice of killing and robbing, that it is hardly ever known for an Indian to
touch the property of another, even in the woods, unless hunger compels him to take
some meat to subsist upon. [Finley 1840 : 63.]

fourth was to soothe the feelings of an irritated heart.   Most of these
gifts were wampum beads, shells, and other valuable gifts.   Next
were the 9 gifts to build a tomb for the deceased: 4 for the 4 posts that
support it, 4 for the crosspieces of the deceased's bed and 1 to serve the
deceased as a bolster.   Then the 8 chiefs of the 8 nations [82] each gave
a present for the 8 principal bones of the body: those of the feet, thighs,
and arms.   Then the Jesuits gave a gift of about 3,000 wampum beads
saying it was to make the "land level, so that it would receive them
more gently when they should be overthrown by the violence of the
reproaches that I was to address to them for having committed the
murder."   The next day the 50 presents were hung on a type of stage
(JR 33: 241–243).   In addition to these presents, others were given
to the French.   Three were required to dress the body.   The next
was a present to draw the hatchet out of the wound.   Then 3 presents
were given: the first, to close the earth; the second, to trample it down
(at this point the men began to dance to indicate their joy that the
earth no longer wished to swallow them); the third, to put a stone on
it that it might stay closed.   Next came 7 presents: the first, to restore
the voice of the missionaries; the second, to ask the French servants
not to turn their arms against the murderer, but against the Iroquois;
the third, to appease the Governor [of New France] when he heard of
the murder; the fourth, to rekindle the fire; the fifth, to reopen the
door; the sixth, to put the boat in the water; the seventh, to put the
paddle in the hands of the young boy who had charge of that boat.
The Jesuits could have asked for 2 other presents to rebuild their
house and church and to set up again 4 large crosses, but they did
not.   The final presents were 3 given by the 3 principal chiefs, to calm
the Jesuits' minds and to beg them to love the Huron always.   All
told, about 100 presents were given.   The Jesuits also gave some presents (JR 33: 245–247).

The Jesuits maintained that the Indians killed each other quite frequently, but that they imputed these murders to their enemies, who in
the summer and autumn were to be found in ambushes along the roads
(JR 20: 75).   And, apparently, some murders were planned so that
the blame fell on other Hurons.   In one case, a young Huron robbed
his father-in-law and carried his booty to his mother's house in another village.   In accordance with the custom of the country, the
father-in-law then went to this house and took all he found, "hardly
leaving the inmates enough with which to cover themselves."   The
boy then plotted to kill his brother so that the father-in-law, or at

---

[82] These "eight nations" may be a reference to clans and indicate that the Huron had
eight clans: Lloyd (in Morgan 1901(2): 225) citing Bressani's description of the same
event (JR 38: 273–287) says that the Huron had eight clans at this time.   Various later
lists of Wyandot and Huron clans give various total numbers (Barbeau 1912; 1917; Connelley 1899 b: 26–28; 1899 c: 106; Hewitt 1907 c: 590; Morgan 1901(2): 225; 1959:
59; Powell 1881: 59 ff.; Wilson 1885: 75).

least his village, would be blamed for the murder and would have to give presents both to him and the other relatives of the dead man. After the planned crime had been committed, the youth appeared and asserted that his father-in-law was the murderer, that the ill-will he had for his in-laws was well known, and that he had not been satisfied with robbing them, but had done greater harm by taking the life of one of them. As a result of this argument, the village of the accused had to give satisfaction, a moderate fine, in this case, as the dead man and his relatives were obscure people and had little status. Later a girl of the village appeared and said that she had witnessed the murder. The final outcome was that the father-in-law was not accused of the crime (JR 13:11–17).

Gambling was almost the sole cause for assaults and murders (JR 10:81).

Some crimes in addition to murder were probably avenged by individuals. For example, one man killed his sister who stole (JR 8:123).

Thieves were [usually] punished in the following manner: If an Indian found an object that belonged to him in the possession of another, he could take it back and all the thief's possessions. If the thief was fishing, for example, he could take his canoe, nets, fish, robe, and everything else he had (JR 10:223).[83]

Traitors who plotted to ruin the country were killed as quickly as possible (JR 8:123).[84]

SUICIDE

Occasionally, an individual committed suicide either by eating a poisonous root [*andachienrra* (JR 14:37), *ondachienroa* (JR 13:27), *ondachiera* (S 195) (in JR 19:173 called an aconite)] [85] that acted very quickly or by hanging himself. Apparently an antidote for the root was known: one Frenchman who ate it was cured by emetics which the Indians made him swallow (S 195). There were at least two reasons for taking one's own life: excessive grief or vengeance on parents (and relatives) for some wrong (JR 13:27; 14:37; 18:27–29; 19:171–175). One of the principal reasons the Huron indulged

---

[83] Finley (1840: 62) says that among the Wyandot, if one Indian stole from another, the person robbed could take as much property of the thief as would remunerate him for his loss and trouble. Powell (1881: 66) says that if the matter was not settled in a council of the clans of the two men involved, any property of the clan that was found could be seized.

Among the Iroquois the punishment for theft was public indignation (Morgan 1901(1): 324–325). Jackson (1830 b: 31) says that a person suspected of theft was called by the chiefs to appear in council. If he was guilty, he confessed and restored the property. Then every chief or warrior in the council could say what he thought and the thief had to listen. No other punishment was inflicted.

[84] Wyandot traitors were killed (Powell 1881: 67).

[85] Fenton (1941 b: 111–113) identifies this root as water hemlock (*Cicuta maculata* L.). It was not aconite (Fenton 1941 b: 109).

their children so much was that the children would commit suicide if they were treated with some severity by their parents (JR 14: 37). In one case a man poisoned himself "from the grief he felt because his wife had been taken away from him" (JR 8: 121). In another case, after he had lost a beaver robe and a collar of four hundred wampum beads at a game of straws, a man hanged himself from a tree rather than face his relatives. He had attempted suicide before, but a little girl had caught him in the act. When asked why he did it, he replied, "I do not know, but someone within me seems always to be saying, 'Hang yourself, hang yourself' " (JR 10: 81).[86]

ETIQUETTE

Certain behavior was expected of individuals, for otherwise they would be criticized on the spot. If an individual made too many blunders, he would be talked about in the village and lose all his influence. When two Hurons met, the only greeting they gave was to call each other by name or to say "my friend, my comrade" or, if it was an old man, "my uncle." If a Huron came into a house when the occupants were eating, they gave him something to eat. If he was given one of their dishes, he would taste it and give it back. But, if he was given a dish for himself, he would not eat it until he had shared it with his companions who usually took only a spoonful (JR 10: 213–215). It was a serious breach of etiquette to set one's foot in a house while a feast for a sick person was going on (JR 13: 193), but it was proper to feed and lodge travelers (S 88). When they visited one another, they made mutual presents. To show politeness, they did not bargain and were satisfied to take what was honestly and reasonably offered. They despised the proceeding of the French merchants who bargained for an hour to lessen the cost of a beaver skin (S 140). When the Indians wished to entertain someone and demonstrate their friendship for him, they presented him with a lighted pipe after having smoked it themselves (S 88).

The Huron paid each other no compliments [probably in the sense that they did not indulge in the polite formalities of "civilized" society]. If their hands were dirty, they wiped them on their hair or on the coats of their dogs. They never washed them unless they were extremely dirty (S 140). They belched before everybody during meals (S 141). When one Huron sneezed, the others responded with imprecations, abuse, and even invoked death upon the Iroquois and all their enemies (S 85).

[86] The motives and methods of Iroquois suicide are discussed in detail in Fenton's (1941 b) study (see also below "Birth and Childhood" and note 27, p. 124, for further material on Iroquoian child-training practices).

SUBSISTENCE

DIVISION OF LABOR

The subsistence base of the Huron was a mixed one including agriculture, hunting, gathering, and fishing (S 103). Women did all the agricultural work; the men hunted, fished, and traded (JR 15: 155; C 137). The women tilled the ground; planted and harvested the corn; stored it; prepared it for eating, pounding it and roasting it in the ashes (JR 14: 235; C 136, 156; S 101). They pounded the meal their husbands carried on summer trading expeditions (C 166; S 101–102). They attended to other household matters. They were expected to attend their husbands, carrying the baggage (C 136).[87]

The women also collected the necessary wood (C 136, 156; S 101). All the women helped each other collect this wood during 2 days in the month of March or April. In this way, each household was supplied with what it needed in a few days (C 156; S 94).[88] If a girl married at the time of year when it was difficult to gather wood, each woman and girl brought a load of wood from her own supply to the newly wed girl (C 156–157; S 123). They used only a very good wood and preferred to go a distance to obtain it, rather than use green wood and wood that made smoke. For these reasons, their fires were clear and were made with a small amount of wood. If they could not find trees that were quite dry, they felled those with dry branches and broke these into splinters and cut them to equal length. They did not make up fagots of twigs, nor use the trunks of the largest trees. Tree trunks were left on the ground to rot because, as they had no saw to cut them in pieces, they could only break them up if they were dry and rotten (S 94). [The Huron had stone hatchets (JR 17: 49) and traded for metal ones (see above, "Trade and War")]. Wood was carried tied up on their backs and attached to

---

[87] Iroquois women also did the agricultural work, although the men cleared the land, removing the trees by felling or girdling them, burning what material they could, and uprooting the partly burned and rotted tree trunks (Parker 1910 b: 21–22; Waugh 1916: 7). Women cleared rubbish off the fields, planted the corn, beans, and squashes, and harvested them, often helping each other in these tasks. They also, of course, prepared the meals and did other household tasks (Beauchamp 1900: 81; Hale 1883: 65; Jackson 1830 a: 12, 29, 32; 1830 b: 17; Seaver 1824: 184–185; Shimony 1961 a: 154 n.).

In the years following the American Revolution, the subsistence base of the Iroquois shifted to more intensive agricultural efforts and to plow agriculture, a shift brought about by the fact that hunting and trading were no longer as profitable as they had been and war was no longer feasible. This shift necessitated a change in the division of labor, the men taking up agricultural work (the various changes in the division of labor and in the settlement pattern during this period are well documented in Jackson 1830 a). In more recent times, wage work has become important to the Iroquois.

[88] The Iroquois had a similar custom. As Mary Jemison said, "Each squaw cuts her own wood; but it is all brought to the house under the direction of the overseer [an old woman appointed for the task]—each bringing one back load" (Seaver 1824: 185; see also Beauchamp 1900: 81; Jackson 1830 b: 18). Waugh (1916: 54) remarks that wood is gathered very often by women and the older men, who sometimes use a pack basket or sled to transport it. Jackson (1830 b: 18) says that Iroquois women gathered wood in the summer or early fall.

"a collar resting and supported on their forehead" [a tumpline] (S 92–93).

The Huron had wooden and earthen vessels (JR 17: 49). The women made the pottery, particularly the round pots without handles or feet, in which the food was cooked (S 102). To make the pots, suitable earth was sifted and pulverized very thoroughly and mixed with a little sandstone. A lump of this was shaped into a ball and a hole put in it with a fist. The hole was enlarged and scraped inside with a little wooden paddle. Then the earthenware pots [a pot or kettle was called *anoo* (S 106, 260)] were fired in an oven. Although the pots, without water in them, could withstand being set directly on the fire, they could not stand moisture and cold water for any length of time without becoming soft and easily broken. The pots did not have feet or handles and were quite round except for the mouth, which projected a little (S 109).[89]

The women also prepared the hemp and bark (S 101). In the proper season, the women gathered the plant named *ononhasquara* from which hemp was made (S 240). Apparently these hemp-gathering parties were large: on one occasion about 40 people gathered hemp for nets (JR 26: 203–205). During the winter, the hemp, beaten and twisted by the women and girls who rolled it on their thighs into twine, was made into snares and fishing nets by the men (S 98, 101, 240; C 136, 166–167).

During the winter, the women made the mats of reeds (and of maize leaves) that were used both to hang in the doors and to sit on. They dressed and softened the skins of beaver, moose, and other animals and made cloaks and coverings of them, which they painted with various colors. They also made the leather game bag or tobacco pouch and decorated it with red, black, white, and blue porcupine quills. They made the sashes, collars, and bracelets worn by both men and women. They also made the baskets, both of reeds and of birchbark, to hold beans, corn, peas, meat, fish, and other foods, and the bark bowls used for drinking and eating (S 102).[90]

In their leisure time they played games, went to dances and feasts, and gossiped. They were not admitted to many of the men's feasts, however, nor to any of their councils (S 101).

In addition to hunting, fishing, warring, and trading, the men made the houses and canoes (C 137; S 101).[91]

---

[89] Iroquois pottery making quickly lapsed after the introduction of metal kettles. Huron pottery is known, of course, from the archeological remains.

[90] Barbeau (1912: 385) also says that women dressed and tanned the hides, made clothes, baskets, bark containers, and other articles for household use. See Parker (1910 b: 82) for mention of a cornhusk lounging mat and Morgan (1850: 74; 1901(2): 23–24) and Waugh (1916: 64) for descriptions of bark bowls.

[91] In later times, Iroquoian men also hunted, fished, went to war and to trade, and built houses and canoes (Barbeau 1912: 385; Hale 1883: 65; Jackson 1830 b: 21; Parker 1910 b: 22–23). They also, as Fenton remarks, "made fishnets, and all the gear that they used except burden straps and clothing" (see Quain 1961: 536).

Two other items concerning material culture should be mentioned. To stick together broken pieces of their pipes or earthenware tobacco-burning tubes, the Huron used blood drawn from their arms after making a cut with a small sharp stone (S 197).

From the *atti* tree [probably the basswood], the Indians tore off long strips of bark (*oühara*). These were boiled to extract hemp from which ropes and bags were made. If the bark was not boiled, it was used in place of moose sinews for sewing robes and other articles, for fastening together birchbark dishes and bowls, for tying and holding the planks and poles of the houses, and for bandaging sores and wounds (S 240).

AGRICULTURE

Corn, beans, and squash (pumpkins) were grown by the Huron (JR 11: 7; 15: 153; C 50) and also sunflowers (C 50). Corn was the basic food in the diet and, fortunately, the yield of corn was great; sometimes, 100 grains for 1 (JR 15: 157). Tobacco was also grown (JR 11: 7).[92] As the soil of Huronia and nearby regions was sandy (JR 10: 35; C 51), frequent rain was needed to grow crops. If 3 days passed without rain, the crop began "to fade and hang its head" (JR 10:35; cf. JR 10:41).

All uncleared land was common property. An individual could clear and plant as much as he wished. This land then remained his for as long as he cultivated it. If, however, he did not use it, anyone else could plant it (S 103).[93]

---

[92] These crops, corn, beans, and squash (aptly termed "the Three Sisters" by the Iroquois because they are found together in the fields), and sunflowers and tobacco were, of course, the cultivated plants of the Iroquois and other agricultural North American Indians (Morgan 1850: 78–79; 1901(1): 152–153; 1901(2): 32–34; Waugh 1916: 3–4). Tobacco, at least now, is seldom really cultivated. It is commonly sown by scattering tobacco seeds from the doorway of the house; it then seeds itself in subsequent years (Fenton 1953: 132). The seeds of the sunflower provided an oil which is now used principally for ceremonial purposes, as on False Face masks (Parker 1910 b: 102; Speck 1949: 78–79; Waugh 1916: 78). Lard is a more modern substitute (Shimony 1961 a: 149–150). Iroquois women used to oil their hair with sunflower seed oil (Shimony 1961 a: 154, 168; see also above under "Dress" for a similar Huron custom).

[93] Use ownership of land, ownership of land by the user for as long as he cultivates it, is a common form of ownership of agricultural land among North American Indians. The effect of the practice is to distribute agricultural land in an equitable manner—each individual family having sufficient land for its needs.

Among the Iroquois, the land used by the women was also owned by the women (the matrilineage). This included agricultural land and land on which berries, nuts, roots bark, and medicines were collected. They also owned the house and the burial grounds (Goldenweiser 1913: 467–469; Hewitt 1918: 533–534; 1932: 479–480; Parker 1916: 42; Quain 1961: 248 n.). Among the Wyandot also, the women owned the agricultural land and the houses (Powell 1881: 65).

These principles of land ownership are illustrated in the manner of indicating the ownership of melons planted in patches in the woods which had been cleared by burning. The ownership of the patch was indicated by a pole painted with the clan totem and name sign of the owner. The clan totem indicated that the patch belonged to the clan and that, if necessary, any clansmen might take the fruit; the name sign indicated that the patch had been cleared, planted, and cultivated by that individual and he had, in practice, a prior right to the fruit (Parker 1910 b: 92; 1913; 39 n.).

Clearing of the land was done by cutting down the trees at a height of 2 or 3 feet above the ground. Then all the branches were stripped off and burned at the stump to kill the tree. In the course of time, the roots were removed. Then the women thoroughly cleared the ground between the trees. To plant the corn, round holes or pits were dug a pace apart by the women and into each of them was put 9 or 10 kernels (S 103; C 156). This seed first had been picked out, sorted, and soaked in water for a few days (S 103). They planted enough corn to last 2, 3, or 4 years in order to have enough for a bad year (S 103; C 156) or to trade it with other tribes for furs and other things. Each year, the corn was planted in the same places, which were hoed with a small wooden spade shaped like an ear with a handle at the end. The rest of the land was cleared of weeds.[94] As the fields appeared to be all paths, Sagard got lost in the cornfields more often than in the meadows and forests (S 103–104).

Each cornstalk bore 2 or 3 ears, each ear containing one or two hundred grains and sometimes four hundred or more. The stalk grew as high as a man or higher and was very thick. The corn ripened in 4 months, and in some places in 3. After the corn was picked, the leaves were turned up, tied around the ears, and arranged in bundles. These bundles were hung in rows along the whole length of the house from top to bottom on poles which formed a kind of rack, coming down as low as the edge of the roof in front of the bench. When the grain was dry and fit for storing the women and girls shelled it, cleaned it, and put it into the large vats or casks made for the purpose. These were then placed in the porch or in some corner of the house (S 104). [95]

If the crops failed, the Huron were faced with famine. During one such famine, they lived on acorns, pumpkins, and roots (JR 27: 65); during another, they relied on hunting (JR 26: 311–313). In the course of some famines, they bought corn from other groups (JR 8: 97; cf. JR 15: 157—a report of a famine in which Neutrals sold their children to get corn). Sometimes, it was necessary to sow the crops more than once. One spring, for example, white frosts and worms forced the Indians to sow three times (JR 8: 99).

---

[94] In recent times, the digging stick was not used (Waugh 1916: 15; cf. Parker 1910 b: 24–25), but the foot was used to make a hole for the seeds and to cover them, or the seeds were planted in the hole left after the cornstalk had been pulled up (Waugh 1916: 17). Before planting, the corn is soaked in water which has some herbs added. This slightly germinates the corn (see Waugh 1916: 18–19; Parker 1910 b: 26–27; Shimony 1961 a: 153–154 for full descriptions). Formerly, all the cultivation given was to pull up or trample the weeds in the fields (Waugh 1916: 20). Various devices were used to protect the corn from animals and birds (see Waugh 1916: 36–37 for descriptions).

[95] The Huron methods of harvesting and husking the corn were probably like those more recently described for the Iroquois, with the exception that corn is no longer stored in pits (see Waugh 1916: 39–44 and Parker 1910 b: 31–36 for detailed descriptions). Iroquois bark barrels for storage are described by Morgan (1850: 74; 1852: 107; 1901(2): 22–23).

GATHERING

Although agriculture was important in the economy of the Huron, it was not the only source of subsistence. Berries, particularly straw-berries, raspberries, and blackberries, were plentiful (JR 10: 103; C 50; S 72, 74, 238). Fruits were dried for winter use, to be used as preserves for the sick, to give taste to *sagamité*, and to put into the small cakes that were baked in the ashes (S 237).

Cranberries (*toca*) were put into little cakes or eaten raw (S 238). Mulberries were also picked (JR 13: 13). Plums (*tonestes*) were rough and sharp to the taste until touched by frost. So, after being gathered by the women, they were buried in the ground to sweeten before being eaten (S 238).[96]

Grapes were also plentiful (JR 10: 103; S 83, 239). [But the Jesuits found the native grapes not as good as they were beautiful (JR 13:85).]

Acorns were eaten after having been boiled several times to take away the bitter taste. Sometimes, a kind of tree bark, like willow bark, was eaten raw. But the Indians did not eat herbs, except some roots they called *sondhratatte* [perhaps ground nuts or cow parsnip] (S 108). *Orasqueinta* [Jerusalem-artichoke] was rare in Huronia; it was eaten raw or cooked as *sondhratates*. When ripe and full grown, onions [chives] (*anonque*) were baked in the ashes (S 239). Other wild foods are mentioned, including small cherries and black cherries (C 51), small wild apples, mayapples, walnuts (C 50), wild beans (S 70), wild pumpkins (S 72), and wild peas (S 90).[97]

FISHING

Fishing was also a significant part of the Huron economy.[98] The Indians knew in what season, as autumn or summer, particular kinds of fish were plentiful in what places. For example, some weeks after

---

[96] Various berries, including strawberries, raspberries, blackberries, cranberries, and mulberries, were also eaten by the Iroquois (Parker 1910 b: 95–96; Waugh 1916: 127–128). The importance of this type of food to the Iroquois is indicated by their important "first-fruits" ceremony, the Strawberry Ceremony and, in some longhouses, a Raspberry Ceremony. The strawberry is among the earliest berries to ripen and is followed shortly after by the raspberry and others (Waugh 1916: 125; see also note 37, p. 79; see also Shimony 1961 a: 158 ff. for descriptions of these Iroquois ceremonials and the use of berry juice in them). The earliest of the wild strawberries are thought to have great medicinal value (Parker 1913: 25 and 25 n.; see below under "Curing Ceremonies" for an example of dried strawberries being used as part of a cure).

[97] The Iroquoians gathered more varieties of wild foods than the 17th-century observers noted (an indication of the number of different plants utilized is to be found in Waugh 1916: 117–129; Parker 1910 b: 93–109). The reasons for this neglect are obvious: gathering was probably not as important as hunting and fishing and, as it was done by the women, the French writers, being men, probably overlooked much of this activity.

[98] Fishing was also a significant part of the Iroquois economy and many kinds of fish were eaten (Waugh 1916: 136). Spears, nets, and weirs were used to take them (Beauchamp 1905: 130–131, 147–148). Among the Iroquois, spring was the fishing season (Morgan 1901 (1): 337), but great fish drives were also held in the summer before the new crop was ripe (Fenton 1942 a: 48).

the catch of big fish (*assihendo*), they went to catch another kind of fish (*einchataon*). It was used to flavor *sagamité* during the winter and much was made of it. The viscera of this fish were not removed; the fish were stored by hanging them in bunches on the poles of their houses (S 230). During another season of the year, a fish similar to a herring but smaller (*auhaitsiq*) was caught with a seine net. People cooperated in catching this fish, and divided the catch by large bowlfuls. It was eaten fresh or smoked. Many other kinds of fish were caught (S 231). The fish that were caught might be dried or smoked (JR 10: 101; 34: 215) to preserve them (C 56).

The fall was the season for fishing; at this time of the year numbers of people were engaged in it (JR 13: 115; 15: 57–59, 113, 125; cf. JR 8: 87–89). But fishing was also important in the early spring (JR 14: 57; 17: 197) and in the summer (JR 17: 51; C 166–167). One method of fishing was to set the nets by canoe (JR 23: 95). Another was to place the nets at some small openings in a number of weirs that almost closed the straits (C 56–57). Some fishing was done while the ice was on the lake (JR 19: 173) by means of lines or a seine net put through holes cut in several places (C 167; S 98). If using the latter method, the Indians made several round holes in the ice; the one through which they drew the seine, some 5 feet long and 3 wide. They then set the net at this opening and, fastening to the net a wooden pole 6 to 7 feet long, passed the pole from one hole to another under the ice. The one or two men at each hole, putting their hands through it, took hold of the pole to which was attached one end of the net. This process was repeated until the pole came back to the large hole. Then the net was dropped to the bottom; it sank because of the small stones attached to the end. When it was drawn up at its two ends, the fish were captured in the net (C 167–168).

Sagard's account of a fishing expedition to catch a large fish called *assihendo* [probably the whitefish] describes a procedure probably often followed. Sagard with four others left in a small canoe during the month of October and went north on Lake Huron (S 185). This lake contained many islands on which the Indians camped when going to fish or when journeying to tribes bordering on the lake (S 189). After a long sail, they stopped at an island suitable for fishing and put up a house near several others that had already been built there for the same purpose. On the evening of their arrival, they had a feast of two large fish which had been given them by a friend of one of the Indians as they had passed an island where he was fishing: it was their custom to give presents of a few fish when visiting friends during the fishing season. After the house had been erected in the Algonquin fashion, they chose their places in it, the four chief men

in the four corners and the others side by side. There were two
fires in the house (S 185).

Every evening the Indians took the nets a half league or a league
onto the lake. At daybreak, they drew in the nets and always brought
back many fish, such as *assihendo*, trout, and sturgeon. These they
gutted, cutting them open as one did cod, and spread them out on
racks made of poles to dry in the sun (S 185–186). The squirrels
were chased away from the drying fish by the Indians' shouting,
clapping their hands, and shooting arrows at them (S 190). If it
rained so that the weather was unfavorable for the drying of meat
or fish, they smoked it on frames or poles and packed it into casks
to protect it from dogs and mice. This they used for feasts and as
a relish for their soup, especially in the winter. Sometimes they
boiled the biggest and fattest *assihendos* to extract the oil from them,
skimming it from the top of the boiling mass with a spoon, and then
put it into bottles (of the rind of a fruit that comes from a distant
country) (S 186). When there was a strong wind, the Indians did
not put their nets in the water, although they did if the winds were
moderate (S 190).

In the stomachs of many fish were found hooks made of a bit of
wood, with a bone attached for a barb and tied with hemp cord. As
the line was too weak, the fish had been lost (S 189).

When the fishing was good and there were a number of houses,
many feasts were given (S 186).

In each house, there was usually a fish-preacher who preached a
sermon to the fish. Such men were in great demand, for the Indians
believed that they had great power to attract the fish into the nets.
One such man preached every day after supper. After first ordering
silence and telling everyone to lie flat on their backs as he did, he
spoke, saying that the Huron did not burn fishbones and begged the
fish to allow themselves to be caught and so be of service to their
friends who respected them and did not burn their bones (S 188).

In order to have good fishing, the Indians sometimes burned
tobacco and offered an invocation. They also threw tobacco into the
water for certain spirits that controlled the water, or rather to the soul
of the water, to allow them to catch many fish (S 189).

After a month or more had passed, the big fish changed their
feeding grounds and the Indians returned to their villages (S 190).

Fishing was important enough to the Huron to warrant other ritual
attention: in one ceremony, two virgin girls were married to a net to
insure an abundant catch of fish for the season (JR 17: 197–201; 10:
167; "Ceremony of The Marriage of Two Virgins to The Seine," p. 79).

HUNTING

Hunting was important to the Huron. Although occasionally the priests write of the scarcity of game and fresh fish in Huronia (cf. JR 7: 223; 17: 17; S 82), they do so usually when stressing the hardships of life among the Indians. In other places, they mention an abundance of game and fish (JR 11: 7; 15: 153), perhaps in an attempt to advertise the country.

Hunting probably varied with area and season. Game was scarce except during the autumn (JR 13: 109, 113, 255; cf. JR 8: 149) when some hunted deer, bear, and beaver (C 81). There is mention of an Indian hunting beaver about the end of the autumn (JR 26: 249). In another report, the Jesuits speak of the difficulty the Huron had in observing Lent, for this was the time when the hunters returned and the only time they had a little meat (JR 17: 141–143; cf. JR 21: 197— the supply of meat was great among the Neutral for one year because of heavy snows that facilitated hunting). They also speak of game as being scarce during Lent, that the hunters had to travel 200 to 300 leagues in order to find bears, deer, and "cows" [JR 15: 183; perhaps "wild cows" were deer (cf. JR 29: 221)]. In another place the Jesuits speak of hunting as being no longer successful, for the mild weather had ceased early in February and it was not the season for game (JR 13: 263). These apparent contradictions indicate that hunting took place in the late fall and early winter.[99] They also indicate that game was scarce near the villages and that the Indians had to travel considerable distances to obtain it. This interpretation explains why the missionaries often went without meat; their servants could not travel on long hunting expeditions, although occasionally they could take game and birds nearby.

Bears and deer were hunted (JR 15: 99, 183; 23: 63; 30: 53) with bow and arrow (JR 26: 313) or traps (JR 30: 53; C 85).

Animal drives were probably important.[1] In one place where deer and bears were abundant, four or five hundred Indians formed a line in the woods extending between points which jutted into the river. With bow and arrow in hand, they marched, shouting and making much noise in order to frighten the animals, until they reached the end of the point. There the animals were forced either to pass through the line and be shot by the hunters or to go into the water. Indians in their canoes easily approached the animals swimming along the

---

[99] Fall was also the Iroquois hunting season, the Indians returning to the village before the Midwinter Ceremonial (Jackson 1830 a: 34; Morgan 1901(1): 337; De C. Smith 1889 b: 282).

[1] Iroquois deer drives also have been described (Jackson 1830 b: 26; Morgan 1901(1): 336). Jesse Cornplanter said that communal hunts were held only in preparation for ceremonials (Quain 1961: 252 n.).

shore and killed them with a sword blade attached to a stick like a half-pike. Similar drives took place on the islands where there were large quantities of game (C 60–61).

On another deer hunt, 25 Indians built 2 or 3 houses out of pieces of wood fitted together, chinked with moss, and covered with bark. Then they built a triangular enclosure, closed on 2 sides and open on 1, of large wooden stakes joined closely together. The enclosure was from 8 to 9 feet high and each of the sides was nearly 1,500 paces long. At the end of this triangle was a small enclosure that narrowed the farther it went and was covered in part with branches. It had only one opening 5 feet wide which the deer were to enter. This structure took less than 10 days to build. In the meanwhile, some Indians had gone to catch trout and pike of great size. After the enclosure was ready, the hunters went to the woods a half-hour before daybreak. From there, about a half-league from the enclosure and separated from each other by some 80 paces, the men marched slowly toward the enclosure, striking 2 sticks together, and driving the deer before them. When they reached the end of the triangle, they began to shout and imitate wolves. The deer, frightened by this noise, entered the small enclosure where they were easily captured. This procedure was repeated every 2 days. In 38 days, the Indians captured 120 deer. They kept the fat, which they used as the French did butter, for the winter and took home some meat for their feasts. The trip back was made after the frost when travel was easier over this very marshy country (C 82–85).

A bear, after having been captured, might be fattened for 2 or 3 years and then killed for a feast (C 130). The bear was shut up in the middle of the house in a little round enclosure made of stakes driven into the ground. He was given the remains of *sagamité* to eat (S 220). Perhaps other wild animals also were kept: one Indian raised in his house a bustard which the Jesuits bought for a deer skin (JR 13: 97).

Other animals were taken. Rabbits were snared (S 223). Cranes [great blue heron] and geese were hunted with a bow and arrow or caught in snares (S 220–221). Crows were not eaten (S 221) but eagles were (S 259). Wild turkeys were found in some regions, especially near the Tobacco League (S 220). Turtles were eaten after they were cooked alive in the hot ashes or boiled with their flippers sticking up (S 235, 251).[2]

Dogs were eaten as meat (JR 7: 223; C 129; S 226) and for this purpose were raised as sheep were in France (JR 7: 223; cf. S 226).

[2] For kinds of birds and animals taken, see Waugh 1916: 134–136.

Often the killing of a dog was part of a religious ceremony (JR 9:111; 17: 195; 21: 161–163; 23: 173, and passim below).[3] Dogs also were used in hunting, at least in hunting bear (JR 14: 33–35).

The special relationship between men, animals, and dogs is indicated in the Huron belief that while hunting, the bones of deer, moose, and other animals or, while fishing, fishbones, should not be thrown to the dogs or into the fire and that the fat of the animals should not drop into the fire. If this happened, the other animals [of the same species] would hear of it and would not let themselves be taken (JR 10: 167; S 186–187; C 91–92). Animals taken when the hunter was lost were not eaten (C 91–92).

The Canadian beaver was "the main inducement for many merchants of France to cross the great Ocean. . . . Such a quantity of them is brought every year that I cannot think but that the end is in sight" (S 232). Beavers were usually hunted in the winter as during that season they stayed in their houses and their fur was better. When the Indians wished to catch a beaver, they first blocked up all the passages by which it could escape. A hole was then broken through the ice of the lake and one Indian put his arm into it waiting for the beaver to come up, while another walked over the ice striking it with a stick to frighten the beaver back to its lair. When the animal came up, it was seized by the back of the neck, a skillful operation, as it could bite. The Indians also took beaver in the summer: nets with poles were sunk into the water and as the beaver came out of their houses they were caught and killed. Beaver was eaten fresh or smoked. The skin was carefully dressed and bartered to the French or used for clothing. The four large teeth were used to scrape the bowls made out of tree knots (S 233–234).

MEALS AND THEIR PREPARATION

Usually the Huron had two meals a day, one in the morning (at 9 o'clock) and the other in the evening (at 5 o'clock), although they would eat at other times (JR 8: 113; 15: 183; C 130).[4] Corn pounded in a wooden mortar (JR 8:111) or ground between two stones (JR 19: 235), figured prominently in the dishes eaten, as did beans

---

[3] The custom of eating dogs as food is well known among North American Indians. The killing of a dog as a religious sacrifice lasted well into the 19th century as part of the Midwinter Ceremonial, although in these latter years it was not eaten.

[4] The early writers on the Iroquoians say that they had two meals a day (Jackson 1830 b: 17) ; the later writers say that the Iroquois had only one regular meal (in the morning), although food was eaten at other times during the day (Morgan 1852: 115; 1901(1) : 318–319; Parker 1910 b: 61; Waugh 1916: 46–47). The preparations for this morning meal are still remembered—older informants in this century saying that women used to get up early in the morning to pound corn for this meal.

(C 125).[5] Pounded corn was called *ottet* (S 71). The number of different ways of preparing corn, over 20 (JR 10:103),[6] attests to its importance.

The ordinary meal frequently consisted of corn roasted in the embers or ground into meal and mixed with water (JR 15: 161–163; 23:187). Corn might be roasted whole before the fire or the kernels stripped off and roasted like peas in the ashes (S 72). Roasted young corn was highly esteemed (C 129).

Most commonly, the corn was not roasted, but mixed with water and boiled. The boiled corn was sometimes flavored by the addition of ashes, little waterflies, or some rotten, powdered, or boiled fish (JR 15: 163; 17: 17; S 71, 80) or some small things called *auhaitsi-que* (S 71). *Leindohy*, corn that had rotted in mud or stagnant and marshy water for 3 or 4 months, might also be added (S 71–72).

The ordinary *sagamité* (S 107) or *migan* (C 126) [an Algonquian word], called *ottet* (S 107), was made in the following manner: Two or three handfuls of raw pounded (ground) meal which had not had the hull removed was put into an earthen pot full of water. This was boiled very clear and stirred from time to time with the *estoqua* [paddle] to prevent the meal from sticking to the bottom of the pot or burning. If available, a small quantity of fish, fresh or dried, or meat was added (C 126–127; S 107). If pumpkin was in season, it was sometimes added after having been cut up into small pieces. But often nothing was added (S 107).[7] Two kinds of *migan* were made. If made of venison, it smelled badly [to Champlain], but if it were made of fish, it did not. If fish had been added, it was taken out and pounded very fine, without removing the bones, scales, or entrails, and put back into the pot (C 127). Meat or fish might be divided and eaten before the soup (S 107).

Another method of preparing *migan* was to cook whole, with fish or meat when they had it, young corn that had been roasted before it was ripe and preserved (C 127–128).[8]

---

[5] These are the well-known Indian methods of preparing corn, the more important method in eastern North America being that using the wooden mortar and pestle. It is that method which is still used among the Iroquois. The method of grinding corn between two stones was also used until quite recent times (Morgan 1850: 75–78; 1901(2): 28–30; Parker 1910 b: 46–48, 54; Waugh 1916: 58–60, 185). This change is probably a result of changing dietary habits; the Iroquois now usually prepare old Indian dishes only for ceremonials.

[6] A similar variety of methods of preparing corn is indicated in the various studies of food preparation (Harrington 1908; Parker 1910 b; Waugh 1916).

[7] According to more recent Iroquois recipes for making hominy (*sagamité*), the flour is made of flint corn, pounded with ashes to make the pounding easier, sifted and pounded again, and then winnowed by tossing in a bowl or basket. Meat, beans, sunflower oil, pounded and sifted dried pumpkin, or rotten salmon may be added to the soup (Harrington 1908: 586–587; Parker 1910 b: 73–74; Waugh 1916: 91–94; Shimony 1961 a: 147 n.).

[8] For recent descriptions of early hominy see Harrington 1908: 589; Parker 1910 b: 69; Waugh 1916: 93–94.

Neintahouy was made in the following manner: The women roasted a number of ears of green corn, either by propping them up before the fire, leaning them against a stick resting on two stones and turning them until they were roasted, or by putting them into a heap of well-heated sand. After the roasting, the grains were stripped off and spread out on a bark to dry further. When sufficiently dry, the corn was mixed with a third to a quarter as much beans (*ogaressa*) and stored in a cask. When they wished to eat it, it was boiled whole, with a little meat or fish, if they had any (S 106).[9]

To make *eschionque* (S 106) [cornmeal], a quantity of dried corn was roasted in the ashes and sand of a fire, as for peas, and pounded very fine. Then, with a little fan of tree bark, the fine flour was taken away and this was called *eschionque* (S 106; C 128) and stored for use on journeys (C 128).[10] The cornmeal might be eaten dry, cooked in a pot, or steeped in warm or cold water (S 106–107). If cooked, some fish or meat was first cut up and boiled in a large kettle with some pumpkin, if they liked (C 128; S 107). The fat from the meat and fish was skimmed from the surface with a spoon (C 128). Then enough meal was added to make the soup sufficiently thick and the soup stirred constantly with a spatula [*estoqua* (S 107)] to prevent it from sticking together in lumps. When served, it was put into bowls with a spoonful of the fat, or a little oil or melted fat, if they had any, on top (C 128; S 107). This was often done for feasts, but not ordinarily (C 129).[11]

The hull of this flour, called *acointa*, that is, "peas" (cf. S 102), was boiled separately in water with fish, if there was any, and eaten. Corn that had not been pounded was similarly prepared, but it was very hard to cook (S 107).

To make *leindohy*, or stinking corn (S 107), the women put a large number of ears of corn, not dry and ripe, into the mud of a pool of stagnant water for 2 or 3 months. Then it was taken out and cooked like *neintahouy*, boiled with meat or fish, for important feasts. It might also be roasted under hot ashes. Corn prepared in this fashion was considered good; the Indians sucked it and licked their fingers as

---

[9] For similar Iroquois recipes see Harrington 1908 : 589–590 ; Parker 1910 b : 77 ; Waugh 1916 : 96–97.

[10] The Iroquois similarly made a parched corn traveling food by shelling the corn, parching it, and pounding it to a fine meal with a little maple sugar (sugar was not added if intended for hunters or athletes). Sometimes dried fruit was pounded with it (Jackson 1830 b : 18 ; Harrington 1908 : 587 ; Morgan 1850 : 77 ; 1901(2) : 31 ; Parker 1910 b : 75–77 ; Waugh 1916 : 88–89, 149).

[11] The Iroquois also make a mush of parched and pounded corn which is served with melted fat ladled on top. While cooking, the mush is stirred constantly with a wooden spatula by the Iroquois as the French said the Huron did. This dish is now made in connection with the False Face rites (Harrington 1908 : 587 ; Parker 1910 b : 79 ; Shimony 1961 a : 145 n. ; Waugh 1916 : 103). The stirrer is described in Harrington 1908 : 580 ; Morgan 1852 : 78–79 ; 1901(2) : 44–45 ; Parker 1910 b : 52–53 ; Waugh 1916 : 70.

they handled these ears, as if it were sugarcane (S 107–108; C 129–130).[12]

The ordinary meal of soup was sometimes supplemented with un- leavened cornbread baked under the ashes (JR 17: 17; 21: 223; 23: 123). This bread occasionally had beans or wild fruits added to it (JR 17: 17). To make bread, corn was first pounded into flour in a wooden mortar and the hull removed by fans made of tree bark (C 125). The corn was boiled for a short time in water and wiped and dried a little (S 104), then crushed and kneaded with warm water, shaped like cakes or tarts (an inch long), and baked in the ashes (S 105–106; C 126). To the dough might be added beans that had been boiled separately. Sometimes dried or fresh fruits, such as raspberries, blueberries, strawberries, and blackberries, were added (S 105; C 125–126). Sometimes, although not often as it was scarce, pieces of deer fat were added (C 126). The cakes might be wrapped in corn leaves (S 105). If baked under the ashes without being wrapped in corn leaves, the bread was washed before it was eaten (S 105; C 126).[13] All bread was called *andataroni*, except that called *coinkia*, bread shaped like two balls joined together (S 105) and boiled (several times) in water after having been wrapped in corn leaves (S 105; C 126).[14]

Another kind of bread[15] was made from corn before it was thor- oughly dry and ripe. To make this, the women, girls, and children bit off the grains of corn and spit them into large pots placed near them. It was then pounded in a large mortar. The paste, as it was very soft, was wrapped in leaves before baking under the ashes in the usual manner. This "chewed bread" was the most highly prized (S 105).

The deer and fish they obtained were set aside for the feasts (C 129) at which time smoked fish or meat or both were added to the corn (JR 10: 179–181; 14: 95). An ordinary feast consisted of 2 or 3 smoked fish cooked with corn (JR 14: 95).

The food eaten while on a trip was also corn; corn coarsely ground between 2 stones and then boiled in water (JR 8: 77–79; 10: 89; 15: 153).

Corn [*honneha?*] stalks were also sucked (S 70, 72).[16]

---

[12] This method of preparing corn is not remembered by the Iroquois (Parker 1910 b: 79–80; Waugh 1916: 101).

[13] As in the descriptions of Iroquois methods of preparing bread (Harrington 1908: 585– 588; Parker 1910 b: 69–73; Waugh 1916: 80–87), boiled cornbread, early bread, and dumplings are mentioned in addition to baked corn bread, it seems likely the Huron had a similar variety of cornbreads.

[14] This is one recipe for Iroquois wedding cakes (Harrington 1908: 587–588; Parker 1910 b: 71–72; Waugh 1916: 86–87).

[15] For Iroquois green corn leaf bread or tamales, see Harrington 1908: 589; Parker 1910 b: 66; Waugh 1916: 99–100.

[16] The older people at the time of Waugh's (1916: 101, 146) study of Iroquois foods remembered chewing cornstalks.

Squashes (pumpkins) were prepared by cooking them under the ashes (JR 10: 103; 15: 163; S 72; C 131) or by boiling them (S 72; C 131).[17]

No salt was used (S 80, 112).[18]

SEASONAL CYCLE

The various economic activities of the Huron took them away from the village for much of the year. In the spring, the people left the village to engage in various summer occupations; trading, hunting, fishing, warfare, and agriculture (JR 8: 143; 10: 51-53; 14: 57; 16: 249; 17: 99, 103, 115). The men spent the spring and summer trading; the women spent these months in the fields (JR 13: 11) and at least some of them lived in houses near these fields (JR 8: 143; 14: 49; 20:39; cf. JR 20: 45—house occupied when snowing). Fishing, most important in the fall, was followed by a hunting season. The people returned to the village about December (JR 8: 143; cf. JR 15: 113— return from fishing in December; JR 19: 125—about All Saints' the people returned from trading expeditions to live in the houses until spring).[19] [There is an example in the Jesuit Relations of a man going to trade in the fall (JR 17: 79–81).] Perhaps it was this seasonal movement that led the Jesuits to say that the Huron regulated "the seasons of the year by the wild beasts, the fish, the birds, and the vegetation." Years, days, and months were counted by the moon (JR 15:157).[20]

The dispersal of the Huron from spring until summer hampered the work of the Jesuit missionaries. In the summer, they could not do their proselytizing, as the people were not in the villages (JR 8: 143; 10: 53; 13: 11) and so spent their time in spiritual exercises and in compiling a dictionary and grammar of the Huron language (JR 10: 55; cf. JR 14: 9—from the 20th of February to Passion week of 1638 the chief occupation of the Jesuits was the study of the Huron language). In the winter, the missionaries' difficulties were of a different type. There were many people in the villages, but with supplies for the winter gathered in and with much leisure, the Huron

---

[17] The Iroquois also prepared squashes by boiling or baking them (Jackson 1830 b: 18; Parker 1910 b: 92; Waugh 1916: 114).

[18] Beauchamp (1895: 214) says that it is well known that the Iroquois did not originally use salt. Even today, at least at Tonawanda, dishes made according to old Iroquois recipes do not contain salt, although the Indians liberally salt them before eating (see also Speck 1949: 41; Waugh 1916: 150; Shimony 1961 a: 188 says that food now is salted on the Six Nations Reserve). Waugh (1916: 152) suggests the ashes added to boiled corn by the Huron was a substitute for salt.

[19] The seasonal cycle of the Iroquois was probably similar. From harvest to Midwinter, the Iroquois participated in the fall hunt, returning to the village in time for Midwinter. They stayed in the village until early spring. Then they left to go to sugar-brush sites, for a longer period in March and April to hunt pigeon at pigeon roosts, and to fish at nearby fishing sites (Fenton 1951 b: 42; see notes 98, p. 62, and 99, p. 65).

[20] The Iroquois count months by the moon (Waugh 1916: 32–36).

spent their time feasting, dancing, and playing games (cf. C 129, 137, 164; S 98).[21] The Indians were so occupied that they had no time for the priests.

RELIGION [22]

FEASTS [23]

In general, Huron feasts for one's friends and the leading men of the village [sometimes the number of guests totaled as many as 200 to 400 (JR 23: 161) or 500 (C 164) people] were to announce a great joy or great sorrow (JR 23: 161). A feast giver was an honored man; one of the most respected men in the country was so, the Huron said, "because he was a peaceable man, who did no harm to anyone and who greatly delighted in merrymaking and in giving feasts" (JR 17: 153).

At these feasts, there was an abundance of good food (JR 17: 163). Strangers were given the best of what had been prepared (JR 8: 127). The whole head of the animal that provided the feast was always given as a present to the head chief or to some other brave

---

[21] Finley (1840: 49) says that there were many feasts among the Wyandot if the harvest was good and game plentiful. The winter is still the time of great Iroquois ritual activity. Not only is the longest and most complex ceremonial, Midwinter (New Year's) held in the winter, but also there are almost nightly winter meetings of the medicine societies in private houses (Fenton 1953: 76). These meetings are to effect new cures and to renew old ones, for the ritual that effected the initial cure ought to be repeated every year or so in order to maintain health (see Fenton 1953: passim; Shimony 1961 a: passim). Several factors probably contribute to this great ritual activity concerned with individual health and welfare in the winter: leisure time, with some attendant boredom and anxiety, and perhaps also an increase in the actual incidence of illness in the winter months.

[22] The 17th-century French descriptions of Huron religion emphasize the ceremonies given by an individual in order to cure his illness or, in general, to obtain good fortune in his endeavors or to prevent illness or other ill fortune and virtually ignore the communal calendric ceremonials. In the 19th- and 20th-century descriptions of Iroquois religion, the emphasis is exactly reversed: the rituals concerned with individual crises have been most often ignored and the calendric ceremonials described at length. Although this change probably reflects some actual change in Iroquoian religion, it should not be taken to mean that Iroquoian religion has been completely transformed. Rather, it seems likely that both types of ceremonials existed among the Iroquoians of the 17th century, as both types exist among the Iroquois today. The early observers of the Huron probably neglected the communal calendric rituals—they are not as striking, or as "colorful," as the individual crises rites. That the religious tradition concerned with individual crises is still a strong one is evidenced in such publications as those of Fenton (1953), Shimony (1961 a; 1961 b), and Speck (1949).

Part of this shift in religious emphasis is probably also the result of the teachings of Handsome Lake, the Seneca prophet who successfully introduced his "New Religion" to the Iroquois at the beginning of the 19th century. This religion is a compound of old Iroquois and Christian religions with some unique elements added. It quickly supplanted the older form of Iroquois religion. Although Handsome Lake condemned the medicine societies, one of the mainstays of the individual crises rites, his attempt was not successful and they still flourish. Handsome Lake did confirm the "Four Sacred Ceremonies" (Feather Dance, Thanksgiving Dance, Adónwe', and Bowl Game), rituals of the calendric ceremonials, and at least some of the ceremonials themselves. This explicit approval may have contributed to the emphasis of these rituals in present Iroquois religion.

[23] Although the French called these events "feasts," the word should not be construed to mean secular affairs. On the contrary, the feast probably marked the occasion as being one of religious import. Today, feasting is important in the medicinal complex (Shimony 1961 a: 276), as well as in the communal calendric ceremonials.

man by the master of the feast.[24]   If the animal was a large one, as a bear, moose, sturgeon, or one of their human enemies, everyone received a piece of meat and the remainder was cut into small pieces and put into the soup. Customarily, the man who gave the feast ate nothing, but smoked, sang, or entertained his guests with talk. Contrary to custom, some did eat, but not often (S 113; cf. S 259). A dog might be eaten at these feasts (JR 17: 165; 23: 159).

Sometimes the Indians held festivals at which nothing was consumed except the tobacco smoked in their pipes, which they called *anondahoin*. At other festivals, they ate nothing but bread or bran cakes. Usually these festivals were prompted by the dreams of the giver or by those of the medicine man (S 112).

When a Huron wished to give a feast for his friends, he sent the invitations early. [25] Those invited came, for it was an insult to refuse except for a really valid reason (and if it was a feast at which everything must be eaten). For this reason, a man would leave one feast and go on to another (in which case they bought themselves off if they could not eat). For the feast a kettle, large or small depending on the number of persons attending, was put on the fire. When the food was cooked, messengers went to tell the people to come, saying to them, *saconcheta, saconcheta,* 'Come to the feast, come to the feast.' The guests came immediately, each carrying with him his dish and spoon.[26] If the feast was given by the Algonquin, the Huron would take a little meal in their bowls as the Aquanaque [Abnaki] were poor and hunger-bitten. After entering the house, they seated themselves on the mats on either side of the house (or on little twigs or cedar

---

[24] The role of the animal head in past and present Iroquois ritual has been summarized by Fenton (1953 : 106–107) as follows :

> Feasts on an animal head echo an earlier ceremonial cannibalism. The Huron, Mohawk, and Oneida tribes held feasts where the head, frequently the head of an enemy captive after torture, went into the kettle and then as a choice morsel went first to the chiefs. In the war feast the head, often a dog's head cooked in the soup, was presented to the captain who carried it in his hands inciting others to enlist. By the middle of the eighteenth century, the accounts refer to whole hogs being boiled in the corn soup and warriors successively danced with the hog's head in their hands. Thus, pork replaced the dog as the war feast food, and later it supplanted the bear and venison in all feasts, until today the pig's head is the ceremonial head, the pièce de résistance. . . . On certain occasions, an individual may pick up the head and march toward the women's end of the longhouse, chanting a personal song, praising the exploits of his ancestors, or ridiculing his father's clansman's daughter. In all the medicine feasts, requiring the use of a head, except at Tonawanda and Onondaga where chicken is cooked for Eagle Dance, the head man or woman passes the head first to the ritual sponsor, who occupies the position of the ancient war leader, and after him among the singers, dancers, speakers, and other functionaries. [See also above, "Torture of Prisoners."]

[25] Similarly, if an Iroquois gives a ceremony, he invites, often by messenger, people to come and participate. When the people have assembled, the speaker gives the Thanksgiving Address, explains why the people have been assembled, mentions the participants, explains the ritual, and thanks the people. The ritual is then performed. After this the speaker thanks the participants again and briefly repeats the Thanksgiving Address. The feast food is then distributed (Shimony 1961 a: 274–275). The form of the calendric ceremonials is similar (see Shimony 1961 a: passim; Fenton 1936: passim).

[26] Fenton (1953: 153) suggests that this custom of bringing dishes and spoons to a feast survives in the present Iroquois practice of bringing to a feast pails in which to carry food home.

boughs), the men at the upper end and the women and children next
to them lower down. When all had gathered, words were spoken.
After this no one, whether invited or not, could enter, as by so doing
he would bring misfortune or prevent the effect of the feast, which
was always celebrated for some purpose. The words announcing the
feast were spoken loudly and distinctly by the master of the feast or
by a person chosen by him. He said *nequarré*, 'the kettle has boiled'
and all replied *ho* and struck the ground with their fists; he then
named the contents of the kettle: *gagnenon youry*, 'there is a dog
cooked,' *sconoton youry*, 'there is a deer cooked,' etc., naming all the
contents of the kettle, and all replied *ho* after each thing was named
and struck the ground with their fists. This done, the servers went
from row to row taking each person's bowl and filling it with broth
with their large spoons (S 110–111). Thus, each person present was
given a bowl filled with food from the kettle. When each had eaten
all in his bowl, it was refilled until the kettle was empty. Everyone
had to eat all that was given him (if it was a feast at which all must be
eaten). If he failed to eat it all, he tried to get someone else to finish
it for him in return for a gift. If he found such a person, he also
had to give a small present to the master of the feast (JR 10: 179;
S 111). If he failed to find someone, he was left in a little enclosure
for 24 hours to finish it himself (JR 10: 179). At the end of one
feast for a sick man, there remained two or three persons, to each of
whom the sick man had given enough food for four. They ate a very
long time, encouraging one another. Finally, they had to disgorge,
and did so at intervals, not ending their eating for this reason. Meanwhile, the sick man thanked them, assured them that they were doing
well, and said that he was under great obligation to them (JR 13:
195).[27]

---

[27] The "eat-all" feast may not have been as common as this section suggests; it probably
was only one type of feast. In any case, it has become much less frequently given. Shimony
(1961 a: 287) mentions such a feast being given to "feed" a hunting charm. In this
recent ritual, the food not eaten is thrown into the fire—probably an instance of culture
change. Old custom was, of course, to eat everything. Hewitt (Curtin and Hewitt 1918:
811 n. 413) says that if any food was not eaten, the purpose of the feast would be defeated
by hostile sorcerers. This mention of witchcraft is interesting, for Shimony (1961 a: 285–
288) also emphasizes the witchcraft associations of the hunting charms, at least in present
Iroquois thought. This tends to confirm the possibility that the eat-all feasts were associated with the hunting charms—although witchcraft may be practiced by other means and
although this emphasis on witchcraft simply may be the result of the fact that as the
hunting charms are no longer useful in hunting because hunting is no longer important to
the Iroquois, but still having power, this power has been perverted and is used for witchcraft. The association of the eat-all feasts with the hunting charms is also suggested by
the legend for which Hewitt appends the footnote on the eat-all feast; this feast was given
after a hunter returned with the game he had killed (Curtin and Hewitt 1918: 515). It
also would help explain the greater prevalence of such feasts in the 17th century (hunting
and therefore hunting charms were more important then than in the 19th and 20th centuries) and would help explain the present witchcraft associations (both hunting and
witchcraft are occupations that rely on individual skill and power, a power that can be
enhanced by the use of charms owned by the individual rather than by the collective group).
It may be that the war feasts were also eat-all feasts, for Finley (1840: 51–52) mentions
such a feast in connection with the Wyandot war feast. To get out of eating all, a man
could give a present of tobacco to the giver of the feast and if no one in the company would
eat for him, someone else was called in.

The Huron had four types of feasts: the *athataion* (JR 10: 61, 177) [*atsataion* (JR 15: 67), *astataion* (JR 13: 55)], or farewell feast; the *atouront aochien* (or *atouronta ochien*), or singing feast; the *enditeuhwa*, or thanksgiving feast, and the *awataerohi*, a type of curing ceremony (JR 10: 177–179).[28] [The farewell feast is discussed under the section dealing with death customs and the *awataerohi*, under "Curing Ceremonies."]

It is not clear from the Relations what the *enditeuhwa* feasts were. The word may refer to the custom of giving a feast to rejoice for good fortune—as in the case of a Christian Huron who gave a feast after he had been cured (JR 15: 85). The products obtained from the summer's activity, from fishing, hunting, and trading, were exchanged as gifts when the Huron returned to their villages, and if what they had obtained was unusually good, a feast for the whole village or for their friends was given (JR 8: 127; 10: 213; 15: 113; 33: 209; cf. JR 23: 63). The word may also refer to this type of feast.

The *atouronta ochien*, singing feast, was held on three occasions: when a man wished to become renowned; when taking a new name, particularly that of a deceased chief [see above under "Chiefs"]; and before going to war (JR 10: 181). At the feast, the invited warriors might incite each other by their songs to perform some deed of valor (JR 23: 63; cf. JR 23: 159).[29]

When the people arrived for the ceremony, they sometimes began the singing before eating and sometimes after. If the ceremony lasted an entire day, as it often did, food was served both in the morn-

---

[28] This classification of the Huron ceremonials is not entirely clear. The farewell feast was given when a man felt that he was about to die and was a farewell to the friends of this world (see note 46, p. 39, and also "Death" below). The singing feasts include what is now called the Condolence Ceremony (see note 58, p. 45) and the war ceremony. The *awataerohi* was one type of curing ceremony, but one wonders why the Jesuits did not include all curing ceremonies under this category and mention only that ceremony which perhaps most impressed them. The real problem concerns the *enditeuhwa*, Thanksgiving feast. On the basis of the Relations, it would seem that this feast was given to announce and rejoice in good fortune. As the calendric ceremonials among the Iroquois today have as their stated function the giving of thanks, it is tempting to interpret this reference as one to the communal calendric rituals that the Jesuits ignore. However, much Iroquois ritual centers on the giving of thanks. The Thanksgiving Speech, for example, "is the most ubiquitous of all Seneca rituals, for it opens and closes nearly every ceremony" (Chafe 1961 b: 2).

[29] The comparable Iroquois ceremony is perhaps the War Dance (*Wasáse'*), which Morgan (1901(1) : 257–258) says was performed before going to war and on the return of the war party, as well as at the ceremony for raising up chiefs and for the entertainment of a guest (see Morgan 1901(1) : 258–268 for a description of this dance). Although according to informants this dance is of Sioux origin (Morgan 1901(1) : 258), its general pattern is similar to that of other rituals associated with war, including the Adónwe' rite, the Thanksgiving Dance, and Eagle (medicine society) Dance (Fenton 1953: 102–109 and passim). The War Dance (*Wasáse'*) is now given in the late spring or summer to honor the Thunder and to bring rain (Converse 1908: 40 n.; Fenton 1936: 8–9; 1941 c: 160; Parker 1913: 104; Shimony 1961 a: 162–165; Speck 1949: 117–118; cf. Morgan 1901(1): 188–189).

ing and in the afternoon. The food was plentiful. Sometimes in the "singing feasts," the most magnificent of the feasts, as many as 30 or 40 kettles of food containing as many as 30 deer were eaten. At one such feast there were 25 kettles in which there were 50 very large fish and 120 smaller fish. At another, there were 30 kettles containing 20 deer and 4 bears (JR 10: 179–181).

A large number of people came to such feasts. For example, eight or nine villages might be invited or even the entire country. The man in charge of the feast sent to each village as many sticks as the number of people from that village who were invited (JR 10: 181).

At the feast, there was also singing and dancing, during which some knocked down their enemies, as if in sport. They usually cried, *hen, hen* or *hééééé* or *wiiiiiii* (JR 10: 181–183).[30] At these war feasts and those to honor a victory, the young men, following the example of the old men, one after the other held a tomahawk or other weapon in his hand and fenced and fought from one end of the place where the feast was being held to the other, as if they were actually fighting the enemy. And to show that they would not lack courage while fighting the enemy, they chanted abuses, curses, and threats against the enemy and promised themselves victory over them. If the feast was one to rejoice in a victory, after they had chanted praises for the chiefs who had killed the enemy, they sat down and others took their place until the feast ended (S 113–114).

The origin of this rite was ascribed to a certain giant. When they lived on the shore of the sea, one of the Huron wounded the giant in the forehead because he had not replied *kwai*, the usual response to a greeting [cf. *chay* in Appendix 3]. In punishment for this, the monster sowed the seeds of discord among them and, after recommending to them the war feasts, the *Ononharoia* [see below, "Curing Ceremonies"], and the response *wiiiiiii*, disappeared into the earth (JR 10: 183).[31]

DANCING

The Huron danced for one of four reasons: (1) to propitiate the spirits who they thought conferred benefits on them, (2) to welcome someone, (3) to rejoice for some victory, or (4) to prevent or cure disease. When they were to dance either naked or covered by a breechcloth, in accordance with the dream of a sick person or by order of the medicine man or the chiefs, a summons was given

[30] William N. Fenton has pointed out to me that these are the usual responses to the individual adônwe' chants (see note 46, p. 39).

[31] Iroquois ceremonials also have such myths to account for their origin, but it is not clear what the corresponding Iroquois myth is, if any. The myth is in the Iroquois pattern.

through all the streets of the village to notify and invite the young people. They were told the day and time of the feast, the reason for having the dance, and that they should come painted and wearing the finest things they had or else dressed as specifically directed.[32] The people in the surrounding villages received the same notice and were also invited to be present; they came, if they so wished. Meanwhile, one of the largest houses in the village was made ready (S 115).

When the spectators, the old men and old women and children, arrived, they sat down along the entire length of the house on the mats laid against the benches or sat on top of the benches. Then, two chiefs rose, each holding a tortoise shell in his hand (as was used in curing the sick). While standing in the midst of the dancers, they sang a song accompanied with the sound of the tortoise-shell rattle.[33] When they finished, all shouted loudly *he é é é*. Then they began another song or repeated the same one as many times as they had been ordered. Only the two chiefs sang; the others said only *hé, hé, hé*, like a man drawing in his breath violently, and at the end of each song giving a loud, long shout, *he é é é*. All the dances were round dances, or at least danced in an oval, according to the length and width of the house. The dancers did not hold hands, but kept their fists closed; the girls held their fists, one on the other, straight out from the body, and the men held their closed fists up in the air or in another way, like a man threatening a blow. While dancing they moved the body and legs, lifting one leg and then the other, stamping their feet on the ground in time with the song and raising them as if half leaping. The girls shook their whole body and their feet, turning around at the end of four or five short steps toward the man or woman next to them and making a bow by inclining the head. Those dancers, men or women, who danced most vigorously and made all the most appropriate facial gestures were considered to be the best dancers (S 115–116).[34]

The dances usually lasted for 1, 2, or 3 afternoons. They wore nothing more than breechcloths, if it was so authorized, as it usually was. But, for some special reason they might be ordered to take these off. The girls always wore their collars, earrings, and bracelets and sometimes painted themselves. The men wore their necklaces, feathers, painting, and such. Sometimes, they wore a bearskin covering the whole body, the ears erect on top of their head, and the

---

[32] See note 25, p. 73.

[33] The turtle rattle still is used by the Iroquois in certain dances (Fenton 1942 b: 9; Speck 1949 : 42–44).

[34] There is greater variety in mode of dancing than Sagard indicates (for recent descriptions, see especially Kurath 1951 ; Morgan 1901(1) : 249–279 ; Speck 1949 : 149–158 and passim). The dance described by Sagard may be the Feather Dance.

face covered except for the eyes; those so dressed acted only as door-keepers or jesters and took part in the dance only at intervals, being there for a different purpose [see below for other such masking].[35] On one occasion, while a dance was going on, one of these jesters entered the house carrying on his shoulders a big dog which had its legs tied and was muzzled. In the middle of the house, he took it by the 2 hind legs and dashed it on the ground several times until it was dead. Then he handed it to another person who took it to another house to prepare it for the feast at the end of the dance (S 117).

When the dance was ordered on behalf of a sick woman, she was brought to it on the third or last afternoon, if it was so ordered by the *oki*.[36] During the first verses or repetitions of the song, they carried her; during the second, they made her walk and dance a little, holding her up under the arms; during the third, if she was able, they made her dance a little by herself (S 117). Throughout this they cried loudly *etsagon outsahonne, achieteq anatetsence*, 'Take courage, woman, and you will be cured tomorrow.' After the dances were over, those who were asked to the feast went to it and the others returned home (S 118).

---

[35] It is difficult to know what the comparable custom is, if any, in present Iroquois culture. Certain of the False Faces act as "doorkeepers," preventing people from freely coming and going during certain of their rituals, but now, at least, the False Faces do not wear bearskins. (It is possible, of course, that they did in the past when bearskins were more easily obtainable). Some False Faces also are clowns, and the more serious Faces may on occasion engage in clowning, as when performing the serious rite of blowing ashes on the patient (see note 1, p. 108, for masks). For such reasons, Fenton (1937: 218; 1940 b: 413) thinks this passage refers to the False Faces and Husk Faces. Finley (1840: 57) mentions a doorkeeper in connection with the Wyandot spring ceremonial devoted to the recitations of the traditions of the people.

[36] On the basis of the material in the Jesuit Relations alone, the best translation of *oki* would seem to be spirit, with the secondary meaning of medicine man or a person or thing endowed with more than usual talents or power (see passim below). In Wyandot, this word, transcribed as *uki*, has been defined as essentially supernatural beings who are endowed with power that may be either harmful or useful to man. They are the super-natural guardians of individuals (they may appear during the puberty seclusion) and of clans and societies. Rivers, rocks, and other natural objects possess similar personal spirits (Barbeau 1915: 9–10). Hewitt, however, equates the Huron word *oki*, and its variants with the Iroquois word *otkon* and says that this "name is applied to any object or being which performs its functions and exercises its assumed magic power or *orenda* in such a manner as to be not only inimical to human welfare, but hostile to and destruc-tive of human life" (Hewitt 1910 b; see also Hewitt 1902: 37 n.). The Iroquois call witches, for example, *agotkon* or *hoññatkon*, 'They are *otkons*' (Hewitt 1910 c: 180). Hewitt contrasts *otkon* with *oyaron*, individual, clan, and tribal guardian spirits. A person's *oyaron* was revealed in a vision or dream, before or after birth. Sacrifices and offerings of dogs, other animals, food, clothing, etc. were made to *oyaron*. Warriors carried their personal *oyaron* wrapped in a sacred skin and invoked it to give victory, and a shaman's *oyaron* aided him in all things. But, if one failed to make a feast in its honor or give it an offering to keep it alive and to renew its strength, the *oyaron* would become angry and cause its owner trouble, illness, or even death (Hewitt 1910 c: 178–179). This description of *oyaron* sounds rather like that of the Huron *oki*. The apparent lack of linguistic distinction between good and bad power of the Huron-Wyandot *oki* (and the general lack of such a distinction among North American Indians) would seem to indicate that Hewitt's distinction between *otkon* (bad power) and *oyaron* (good power) is a recent one among the Iroquois and perhaps one influenced by Christian thought.

ECLIPSE

One medicine man made a feast in order to turn aside the unluckiness of a lunar eclipse. In another village, on the occasion of this eclipse, the people all cried as loudly as they could and shouted imprecations against their enemies saying, "May such and such a nation perish" and shot several arrows at the sky to deliver it from danger (JR 10: 59).[37] The Huron believed that the eclipse of the sun occurred when the great turtle who upheld the earth changed his position and brought his shell before the sun (JR 12: 73).[38] In Huron mythology, the earth was believed to have been pushed up out of the water by a tortoise of prodigious size. This tortoise still supports the earth, otherwise the earth would be submerged in the water (JR 30: 61–63).[39] The Huron thought that the earth had a hole in it and that the sun went into this hole when it set and remained hidden there until the next morning when it came out at the other end (S 183).

CEREMONY OF THE MARRIAGE OF TWO VIRGINS TO THE SEINE

Only one calendric ceremony, to insure successful fishing, is mentioned by the Jesuits. In the spring, two young, virgin girls (in at least one case these were about 6 or 7 years old in order to insure they were virgins) were married to the Seine. At this feast, the Seine was placed between the two girls and told to catch many fish (JR 10: 167; 17: 197–199). In consideration for their marriage with the Seine, the families of the girls were given part of the catch. This

---

[37] Similarly, the Iroquois shoot arrows, fire guns, urge their dogs to bark and howl, shout, and beat drums and kettles when there is an eclipse (Hewitt 1890: 389; 1891).

Shooting arrows at the sun is also part of the Sun Dance that used to be held among some Senecas, at least, in response to a dream (Converse 1908; 34 n.; Parker 1910 a: 473; 1913: 103), but now seems to be a calendric ceremony on the Six Nations Reserve (Shimony 1961 a: 157–158; Speck 1949: 36) and on the Cattaraugus Reservation (William C. Sturtevant: personal communication). It is no longer given at Tonawanda (Fenton 1941 c: 159). The ritual includes a tobacco invocation and concludes with the Feather Dance. The ceremonial seems to have had war associations—participants gave their war cries in it (Converse 1908: 34 n.; Parker 1910 a: 473; 1913: 103) and at Six Nations ends with the singing of individual adónwe' chants (Shimony 1961 a: 158; Speck 1949: 36). Its war connotations perhaps are substantiated by Fenton's (1942 b: 12) suggestion that the Feather Dance probably once was associated with war. (See "Torture of Prisoners" for the importance of the sun in that ritual.)

There is also a moon ceremony, the main ritual of which is a peach stone game (Converse 1908: 34 n.; Parker 1913: 103–104; Shimony 1961 a: 157).

Barbeau (1914: 305–306) reports that the Sun Dance is generally called the "War Dance" by Oklahoma Iroquois and the "Blackberry Feast" is given in honor of the moon. The latter is mainly a woman's dance.

[38] Iroquois explanations as to the cause of the eclipse are varied. At least some Iroquois believe that eclipses of the sun and moon are caused by a fire-dragon which attempts to swallow it (Hewitt 1890: 389; 1891). One eclipse of the sun in 1806 was thought to be caused by a recently deceased chief (Seaver 1824: 187–188).

The Wyandot thought that earthquakes were caused by the Turtle's shifting of his weight when he got tired (Connelley 1899 b: 70).

[39] The idea that the earth is supported by a turtle is a familiar Iroquoian one and is supported by the creation myth (see Appendix 2).

ceremony was introduced into Huronia by some neighboring Algonquin, the latter having gone to fish some years before and having caught nothing. Surprised and astonished at this unusual event, they did not know what to think. Then the *oki* [i.e., spirit] of the Seine appeared to them as a tall, well-formed man, who said, "I have lost my wife, and I cannot find one who has not known other men before me; that is the reason why you do not succeed, and you never will succeed until I have been given satisfaction in this respect." The Algonquins then held a council and decided that to appease the Seine they should present him with girls so young he would have no reason to complain and that they should give him two for one. This done, the fishing succeeded. The Huron, their neighbors, having heard about this, took up the custom and repeated it every year (JR 17: 199–201).[40]

SPIRITS

The Huron believed that animate spirits resided in the earth, the rivers, lakes, certain rocks, and the sky (JR 10: 159) and had control over journeying, trading, war feasts, disease, and other matters (S 171). To appease and obtain the favor of these spirits, tobacco was thrown into the fire and a prayer said. If, for example, the offering was to the Sky, the most important spirit, they would say, *aronhiaté onné aonstaniwas taitenr*, 'O Sky, here is what I offer thee in sacrifice; have pity on me, assist me.' Or, if the offering was to implore health, they would say, *taenguiaens*, 'Heal me' (JR 10: 159).[41]

The sky was important as it was an *oki*, a power which controlled the seasons, held in check the winds and the waves of the seas, and

---

[40] The Jesuit statement that the Ceremony of the Marriage of Two Virgins to the Seine was not an old Huron ceremony is supported by the evidence that the Iroquois have no such ceremony, for if the Iroquois also had had this ceremony, the possibility would exist that it was part of an earlier, general Iroquoian culture stratum.

[41] Similarly, to quote Morgan (1901(1) : 155) :

> The Iroquois believed that tobacco was given them as a means of communication with the spiritual world. By burning tobacco they could send up their petitions with its ascending incense, to the Great Spirit, and render their acknowledgments acceptably for his blessings. Without this instrumentality, the ear of *Hä-wen-né-yu* could not be gained. In like manner they returned their thanks at each recurring festival to the Invisible Aids, for their friendly offices, and protecting care.

The use of tobacco is ubiquitous in present Iroquois ritual. One of the important parts of the Midwinter Ceremonial, for example, is a tobacco invocation. A tobacco burning invocation is also part of the ritual pattern of medicine society meetings (Fenton 1953 : 144; Shimony 1961 a : 275–276), and also is given before the Society dance held during Midwinter. Tobacco is also burned as part of the dead feast (Shimony 1961 a : 280). Mistakes in the ritual may be rectified (forgiven) by tobacco (Shimony 1961 a : 276, 287). Tobacco is also offered to the first plant of the species found when collecting medicinal herbs (Fenton 1940 a : 794; 1949 b : 235; Parker 1913 : 55 n; Shimony 1961 a : 263–266). Tobacco is also used in sorcery : for example, a member of the False Face Society may cause False Face sickness by burning tobacco and reciting the proper incantation. Some are said to be able to cause lightning to strike at a particular time and place by use of a tobacco invocation to the Thunder. An, a man may impel his faithless wife to return by smoking tobacco (Skinner 1925 b : 129–130). These examples do not exhaust the rituals in which tobacco is offered.

assisted them in time of need. It was this *oki*, the Sky, who was evoked in an oath when some promise of importance or some bargain or peace treaty with the enemy was made. The oath was *hakhrihóté ekaronhiaté tout icwakhier ekentaté*, 'The Sky knows what we are doing today.' If they broke their word or their alliance, they believed that the Sky would punish them. The Indians also thought that it was not right to mock the Sky (JR 10: 161; cf. JR 33: 225).[42]

Tobacco frequently was used in ritual contexts and offered to the spirits with a prayer (S 171). In addition to those occasions mentioned above and below, it was thrown into the water of a great lake in order to calm it and to appease a spirit (*Iannaoa*) who, in despair, once cast himself into a lake and who caused these storms (JR 26: 309–311).[43] Before going to sleep, a man might throw some tobacco on the fire and pray to the spirits to take care of his house (JR 13: 263). It was offered to some rocks that the Huron passed when going to Quebec to trade. One of these was called *hihihouray*, 'a rock where the Owl makes its nest.' The most famous was named *tsanhohi arasta*, 'the home of *tsanhohi*,' a species of a bird of prey. This rock was a man who had been changed into stone; the Indians saw the shape of the head, arms, and body in this rock, one so high that arrows could not reach it. In it was a depression in which lived a spirit capable of making their journey successful. Therefore, they stopped and put tobacco into one of the clefts saying, *oki ca ichikhon condayee aenwaen ondayee d'aonstaancwas*, etc., 'spirit who dwellest

---

[42] Some would interpret the deity, the Sky, as being the elder of the Twin Brothers (see Appendix 2).

It is also possible that the Sky is a being quite distinct from the Elder Twin Brother. It is possible, for example, that Hawéniyu, "Great Spirit" or "Controller," which Handsome Lake called the Creator (Speck 1949: 29), has been substituted for the older "Sky" in Iroquoian religion by Handsome Lake: in present Iroquois cosmology, the Creator occupies the place of the Sky in the early accounts. If it did occur, the substitution probably would have been easy: the Iroquois think that the creatures of the world, both natural and supernatural, are arranged in a hierarchy that is also spatial, the most important being those who are highest (farther from the ground). This order is well known to the Iroquois, for it is the basis of the Thanksgiving Address, which is frequently given in present Iroquois ritual. (The most complete account of this speech is contained in Chafe 1961 b. A list of other versions is also contained in this volume, ibid.: 301–302, to which may be added the more recently published summary version in Shimony 1961 a: 133–140.) If this general arrangement of beings is pre-Handsome Lake (which is entirely possible) and if there was no conception of the Creator then, the highest being logically would be the Sky. A substitution of the Creator for the Sky would, of course, be consistent with Christian thought: the Christian Creator, God, lives in heaven, the Sky.

The winds in present Iroquois thought are controlled by the Four Beings ("Four Angels"), messengers to Handsome Lake (Chafe 1961 b: 9; Shimony 1961 a: 138; Speck 1949: 30), although wind may also figure as a spirit in his own right (see Chafe 1961 a: 8; Morgan 1901(1): 151–152). It is, however, a short step from control of winds by the Sky to control of winds by the Creator or his messengers.

[43] A similar Wyandot belief is that some of the great serpents were never killed and still live in the bottom of the Great Lakes. These beings sometimes cause such turbulence of the waters that they can be calmed only by throwing some offering into the lake (Connelley 1899 b: 86–87). The Iroquois have similar mythical serpents (Curtin and Hewitt 1918: 797 n. 135).

in this place, here is some tobacco which I present you; help us, guard us from shipwreck, defend us from our enemies, and cause that after having made good trades we may return safe and sound to our villages' (JR 10: 165–167). This [?] rock looked something like a head and two upraised arms. In the belly or middle was a deep cavern that was difficult to approach. The Indians believed that this rock had been a man who, while lifting up his arms and hands, had been transformed into rock. If they were in doubt about the success of their journey they would offer tobacco to the rock when passing in their canoes. They threw the tobacco into the water against the rock itself, saying "Here take courage, and let us have a good journey" and some other things (S 171).[44]

The Huron believed that thunder was a bird (JR 10: 45; 15: 181; S 183). *Onditachiaé* (*ondiaachiaé*), the thunder, in form, a man like a turkey cock, was renowned in the Tobacco Nation. He controlled the rains, winds, and thunder. The sky was his home.[45] When he was there, the weather was calm. When he came down to earth to get his supply of snakes and *oki*, the clouds rumbled.[46] Lightning was due to the flapping of his wings. If Thunder was loud, then it was his little ones who accompanied him and helped him make noise as best they could. In answer to the Jesuits' question, "Whence, then, came dryness?" their Indian informant replied that it came from the caterpillars, over whom *onditachiaé* had no control.[47] In answer to the question, "Why does lightning strike trees?" the Indian said, "It is there that it lays in its supply" (JR 10: 195–197).

A spirit called *aireskouy soutanditenr* was invoked at various times: while hunting in the forests and when in danger of shipwreck on the water (JR 33: 225).

TYPES OF ILLNESS

The Huron recognized three types of illness: (1) illnesses due to natural causes that were cured by natural remedies, (2) illnesses caused by the desires of the soul of the sick person that were cured by supplying these desires [called *ondinnonk* (JR 33: 191, 193), *ondinoc* (JR 17: 155), *ondinonc* (JR 17: 155, 163, 179, 191–195)],

---

[44] Beauchamp (1892: 227) thought that such "reverence to remarkable stones" became less common in more recent times.

[45] The Iroquois proper do not seem to have believed in a mythical "thunderbird," although the Huron and Petun did (Waugh 1916: 24). Shimony's (1961 a: 137 n.) reference to a "thunderbird" is probably a reference to the Dew Eagle (Fenton: personal communication; see Fenton 1953).

[46] The Iroquois believe that the Thunderers control certain mythical animals: magic snakes and the giant lizard; and certain real animals: worms in the earth, wood ticks, mosquitoes, and injurious bugs and rain, wind, and certain diseases (Shimony 1961 a: 137 n., 163).

[47] This statement apparently indicates that the power of the Thunderers was temporarily in abeyance and they were not fulfilling their hoped-for control over both rain and bugs.

and (3) illnesses caused by witchcraft that were cured by extracting the sorcerer's spell (JR 33 : 199).[48]

There were several methods for ascertaining the cause of the illness and its cure. The ill person himself might know a natural remedy [my inference], or he might have had a dream that indicated his soul had some desire that had to be satisfied before he would be well again [see below], or he might have had a dream that indicated a sorcerer had cast a spell which was causing the illness (JR 33: 219).[49] [In addition to the desires that were free, at least, voluntary in us, the Huron believed that souls had other desires which were inborn and concealed (JR 33 : 189)]. When a child was sick, the father or mother might dream the cure. For example, one mother dreamed that in order to make her son well he should have 100 cakes of tobacco and 4 beavers (JR 10 : 173).[50]

If the cause of the illness could not be ascertained by any of these methods, a medicine man[51] was summoned by the relatives to make the diagnosis. This man might say that the sickness was natural and prescribe a potion, an emetic, or he might suggest that a certain kind of water be applied to the diseased part, or he might prescribe the use of scarifications or poultices (JR 33 : 203).[52] To effect a cure, the medicine man called upon his spirit, blew on the place where the pain was, made incisions and sucked out the blood. He also ordered feasts and amusements as a preliminary to his cure. If he wished to get information about distant matters, he asked his spirit about it and

[48] The Iroquois still recognize illnesses of these types, and cures are still effected by use of herbal medicines and by ritual means. (These methods are discussed at greater length in the notes below.) Hewitt (1928 : 610 n. 64), in fact, gives this classification of causes as modern Iroquois. Although recent descriptions of curing do not emphasize the cause of illness as being the desires of the soul (see especially Shimony 1961 a : 261 ff.), such may still be the case. The methods of diagnosing and the actual curing procedures are similar for both 17th-century Huron and 20th-century Iroquois. And, oñn^{n} kwǎ't derived from a verb-stem meaning "to beg" or "to crave," is the general Iroquoian word rendered into English as "medicine" (Hewitt 1928 : 610 n. 64).

[49] Similar methods are still used for diagnosis. It should be emphasized, however, that ascertaining the cause of illness is usually not as straightforward a procedure as the ethnographies sometimes seem to indicate. Probably most often there is discussion of the symptoms and possible cures between the patient and members of his family and friends, and out of this discussion comes a decision as to what the course of action will be ("When members of the family are taken sick, they try various herbal medicines suggested by the elders" Fenton 1953 : 7, and see ibid. : 120–121 for examples of interpretation of the patient's dream by members of his family.) A simple remedy, as herbal medicine, usually is tried first, and if this is ineffectual, more drastic, more ritually powerful, and hence dangerous measures are taken (Shimony 1961 a : 262).

[50] Fenton (1953 : 129) makes a similar statement: "The child's parents decide that the ritual [in this case, of the Eagle Society] may help their sick child, or, the child is sick and they consult a clairvoyant. The patient may dream himself, or someone may dream that the ritual will help the person."

[51] The term "medicine man" is used here for those individuals who now usually are called "fortunetellers" by students of the Iroquois.

[52] Similarly, Iroquois fortunetellers may prescribe herbal medicines and may prescribe their own medicines (Shimony 1961 a : 272–273). Not all these seemingly natural cures are so conceived by the Iroquois. Emetics, for example, are often used in cures for witchcraft (see note 13, p. 117).

then told what his spirit had said (S 193).[53] He might say that the illness was caused by the desires of the sick person or by witches. [These causes and the methods used by the medicine men are discussed at length below.]

Gifts were given to medicine men to obtain a remedy from them (JR 13 : 145; 17 : 119; S 193).[54]

CURE OF NATURAL ILLNESSES

The medicine men always carried a bag of herbs and drugs with them when they went to doctor the sick. They also had an "apothecary" who went with them carrying the drugs and a tortoise shell which were used in the ritual (S 193).[55]

In the opinion of the Jesuits, Huron knowledge of medicinal plants was very slight and was limited to some powdered roots and some simples (JR 33: 203; cf. JR 13: 103).[56] One medicine they esteemed highly was *oscar* [perhaps wild sarsaparilla], used to heal

---

[53] This description is not complete. Medicine men cured by other means in addition to sucking, and not all sucking involved an actual cutting of the patient (see below, "Witchcraft"). Some Iroquoian medicine men probably could get information about distant places, perhaps through his spirit, but this does not seem to be elaborated in Iroquoian culture. It is Algonquian cultures, of course, which possess the "shaking tent" shaman, a man who does send spirits to find out what is happening at distant places. It is possible that Sagard is describing Algonquian rather than Iroquoian procedures in this passage.

[54] Fees are still given to fortunetellers (Fenton 1953: 129: Shimony 1961 a: 272) and to herbalists (see note 56, p. 84). The line between "fee" and "gift" is a thin one in Iroquois as well as in other Indian cultures.

[55] This description is probably somewhat oversimplified. The "bag of herbs and drugs" may have been a medicine bundle containing supernatural rather than natural aids, and the "apothecary" may have been an assistant who was learning the ritual, rather than a specialized office.

[56] The Jesuits probably underestimated the Huron use of medicinal plants. Jackson (1830 b: 32) remarked that the Indians were often skillful in the application of simples and had considerable knowledge of the medicinal qualities of different herbs and plants. More recent opinion is also that Iroquois knowledge and use of such plants is extensive (see Fenton 1939; 1940 a; 1941 a; 1949 b; Parker 1928). To the Iroquois, every plant has some purpose, and that purpose may be a curing one (Fenton 1940 a: 790). And, although the Jesuits thought Huron medicine quite inferior to theirs, from the vantage point of the 20th century, Indian and French medicine seems quite similar (Fenton 1941 a: 505–506). The effectiveness of Iroquois medicine is not easily judged because it is infused with certain "magical" practices. First, certain herbs themselves are used for "magical" purposes. For example, the root of the yellow leaf cup (*Polymnia uvedelia*) is used as a fumigant against ghosts, returning souls, and after having had a nightmare. Second, sympathetic magic is used in the preparation of the medicines. For example, barks are scraped upward if they are to be used for emetics and downward if they are to be used for a purgative. Third, certain medicines are used because there is some resemblance between the shape of the plant and the symptoms of the disease. For example, yellow-flowered or yellow-rooted plants are apt to be used to cure bile troubles or jaundice; the sycamore bark, for scabs; bloodroot, for wounds. Further, Iroquois medical knowledge includes witchcraft and a practitioner can use his knowledge to cure or to witch (Fenton 1940 a: 793, 795; 1949 b: 234–236; see also Shimony 1961 a: 263–267).

Knowledge of herbs is transmitted in certain families. As other curers, the practitioner may not ask for remuneration, but the sick are expected to give what they can (Fenton 1940 a: 793; Shimony 1961 a: 265).

wounds, ulcers, and other sores (S 195). A root, like a small carrot or peeled chestnut, known as *ooxrat* [Indian turnip] was used to purge the phlegm and moisture in the heads of old people and to clear the complexion. In order to get rid of the stinging pain, it was first cooked in hot ashes (S 195–196).[57] They also used emetics and hot rooms and sweats (S 192).[58]

In order to become more nimble in running and to purge out swellings, the Huron made incisions into the fat of their legs with sharp stones (S 196–197).[59] They also burned themselves on their arms with the pith of the elder tree for the pleasure of it, letting it burn and smoulder on them, so that a scar was made (S 197).

Injuries such as wounds caused by a thrust of the javelin or by the bite of a bear were treated by natural remedies. The Huron believed that these natural medicines should always cure if the disease were a purely natural one. Thus, if the sickness continued after it should have been cured, they concluded that there was a supernatural cause; that a sorcerer had cast a spell on the sick person, or that the soul of the sick person had some desire that troubled it; as they said, the desire was "killing the patient." Most disease was attributed to these latter two causes (JR 33 : 201).[60]

Perhaps some of the Huron's medicines had magical power as, for example, the powder that a medicine man ("physician") took out of his bag, put into his mouth, and then spit onto the broth the Jesuits had given a sick woman (JR 13 : 257).

---

[57] *Ooxrat* (burning root) probably was the fruit and root of Indian turnip or jack-in-the-pulpit (*Arisaema triphyllum* (L.) Schott) still used by the Iroquois as a snuff for catarrh (Fenton 1941 a : 515).

[58] The use of these emetics and sweats is discussed at greater length below. As do the herbal medicines, they also have magical aspects, and it is difficult to ascertain the actual effects of such procedures in terms of Western medicine.

[59] Goldenweiser (1913 : 470) mentions the scarification of a boy's shins with a stone every morning during his puberty seclusion. The boy also was supposed to run a great deal, bathe in cold water, and eat little. An Iroquois warrior might cut three slits in the back of his neck and rub the cuts with the oil extracted from enemy scalps to guard against sudden attack from behind. Should an enemy approach the scars would quiver and warn him of the danger (Parker 1913 : 30 n.; cf. above under "Torture of Prisoners" for a Huron man making a cut in his neck and letting the blood of a tortured prisoner run into it so that he would not be surprised by the enemy).

[60] This logic also appears now in Iroquois attitudes toward White medicine. As Shimony (1961 a : 269) says:

Longhouse members do talk in terms of "germs" and "high blood pressure," and on that level they understand natural cause-and-effect relationships. However, they continue suspiciously to wonder why they, as particular individuals, are subjected to the disease. This is especially true if the disease is lingering and hard to cure, or if the hospital is unable to diagnose why the patient "feels bad." Surely, there must then be something causing the disease which white man's medicine cannot understand and does not have the historical perspective to appreciate, and it is therefore necessary to find the true etiology of the disease (a typically "Indian" cause) and apply an "Indian" treatment. To determine the true etiology one has recourse to an Indian specialist, namely, the fortuneteller.

What might be considered natural remedies were not without a magical aspect. For example, the Wenrôhronon excelled in drawing the arrow from the body of a wounded man. But, in order to be effective, the extraction and the application of a certain root to the wound had to be performed in the presence of a pregnant woman (JR 15: 181; 17: 213).

The greater part of their remedies consisted, however, of dances, feasts, and ceremonies (JR 17: 121).

Men sweated to keep in health and prevent disease. When anyone wished to sweat, he asked several of his friends to sweat with him. A number of stones were heated red hot in a large fire and then taken out and placed in a pile in the middle of the house or wherever they wished to construct the sweat house if they were traveling. In a circle around the pile of stones, they put sticks in the ground, waist high or higher, and bent them over at the top. The naked men then sat on the ground in the space between the stones and the sticks. They were squeezed closely together around the pile of stones with their knees raised up to their stomachs. After they were in this position, the whole sweat house was covered with large pieces of bark and a number of skins so that no heat or air could get out. To heat themselves further, one sang and the rest shouted continually, as in their dances, *het, het, het*. When it got too hot, they let in a little air by taking off a skin from the top and sometimes drinking large potfuls of cold water; then the sweat house was covered again. Sometimes they burned tobacco. After taking the sweat, they bathed in a river, if there was one nearby, or washed themselves in cold water, if there was not. Bathing was followed by a feast that had been cooking while they were sweating (S 197–198).[61] [For other descriptions of the sweat house and sweatings, see below, passim.]

DREAMS AND THE DESIRES

One of the basic beliefs of the Huron was that the desires of the soul could cause illnesses and misfortune and were often revealed in dreams.[62]

The desire might be a dance or an object, as a canoe, a new robe, or a wampum collar (JR 15: 179), or a black or white dog or a large

---

[61] Sweat baths, although no longer taken by the Iroquois, are remembered. Purges, with some concomitant sweating, are still taken (Shimony 1961 a: 265–266; Parker 1913: 11 n.).

[62] The Iroquois concept of "health" is similarly a broad one; it "includes not only physical well-being, but also the maintenance of life, mental ease, and good luck" (Shimony 1961 a: 261; 1961 b: 207). Dreams also indicate to the Iroquois what should be done to maintain "health" (Fenton 1953: passim; Shimony 1961 a: passim). The Iroquoian emphasis on dreams and on the fulfillment of dreams, a view that is particularly apparent in the early descriptions of Iroquoian culture, is, as Wallace (1958) has pointed out, rather close to that of Freud.

fish for a feast (S 118).[63]   The health of the sick person was rapidly restored after these desires had been granted or obtained (JR 33 : 193, 205).   The announcement of the desire was made all through the village in order that a person having such an object could make a present of it to the sick person and thus restore his health.   In one case, a sick woman dreamed that she would be cured if a cat which a Recollet father had previously given to a great chief was given to her.   The chief was told of this and, although both he and his daughter were very fond of the cat, he gave it to the sick woman.   The chief's daughter fell sick and died of regret over the loss of the cat (S 118).   Sometimes, the desires could not be fulfilled and substitutions were made.   In one such instance, 10 cakes of tobacco were substituted for the 100 of the desire and 4 large fish for 4 beavers (JR 10 : 173; see above, under "Types of Illness").

As the sick man might dream that a feast would cure him, so also might he dream that certain details of the ceremony should be observed in order that he be cured.   For example, he might dream that the guests should enter by one of the doors and not by the other or that the guests should pass only on one side of the kettle (JR 10 : 185).   Sometimes the dream or the medicine man dictated that all those at the feast had to be several paces apart, not touching one another.   At other times, when the guests departed, they made an ugly grimace at the master of the feast or at the sick man as a farewell.   At others, they could not break wind for 24 hours, or else they would die, although they might have eaten *andataroni*, i.e., bran biscuits or pancakes, which were very windy substances.   Sometimes, after they had eaten and were quite full, they had to vomit up beside them all they had eaten, which they did with ease (S 112–113).[64]

If the desire had been for a dance and if the performance of this dance did not cure, it had not been performed properly; there had been defects and omissions in the forms and details of the ceremonies

---

[63] Dreams still may indicate to the Iroquois that any one of the standard songs, feasts, dances, games, medicine society rites, as well as herbal medicine, ought to be performed (Shimony 1961 a : 273; 1961 b : 210).   Dreaming that specific objects will cure apparently has lapsed.   Certain miniature objects, as miniature False Face masks, miniature canoes, miniature lacross sticks or snowsnakes, are given as tokens as part of the dream guessing and ceremonial friendship rituals, and are made for other reasons (Beauchamp 1905 : 188; 1922 : 37; Fenton 1937 : 233; 1940 b : 425; 1942 b : 16–17; 1953 : 123–124, 142; Harrington 1909 : 88–89; Hewitt : 1910 g : 942; Keppler 1941 : 29–30; De C. Smith 1889 a : 279; Shimony 1961 a : 183, 242; Skinner 1926; Speck 1949 : 83–84, 99, 122–123).   But these seem to be more in the nature of talismans and charms rather than comparable to the objects of the desires.   The earlier dream objects were apparently the objects themselves, not miniatures, and were given on occasions other than simply dream guessing and ritual friendship.

[64] Dreaming of specific ritual details that should be performed is not well documented in recent anthropological descriptions of Iroquois curing.   However, the ritual for establishing ceremonial friendship either seems to be dictated by the dream (see note 69, p. 89) and certain changes in the communal calendric ceremonials are made as a result of the dream (Fenton 1936 : 4–5).

(JR 17: 159, 161, 187). The ceremonies, including the songs, were for the most part dictated by the spirit, who cautioned and threatened that the ceremony would not be effective if they failed to carry out the least detail (JR 17: 155).[65]

The dreams or desires did not exclude the Christians. Sometimes, the dream indicated that the ill person should be baptized; the Jesuits won some converts this way (JR 15: 73; 17: 137; cf. JR 10: 13; 13: 191; 23: 171). In fact, the Huron sought baptism almost entirely as an aid to health (JR 10: 13).[66] But, some Huron believed that baptism killed people (JR 17: 97). In one case, a girl dreamed that she would die if she was baptized (JR 13: 225). In another, the Jesuits were accused of killing a woman who had been baptized and were asked if presents had been given to satisfy the relatives of the woman (JR 15: 105).[67] [It should be remembered that these French Catholics believed that baptism could cure the ill and that they most frequently baptized the dying.]

In one instance, after a sick man complained to the council that the Christians did not attend the ceremony to cure him, the chiefs criticized the Christians for their conduct (JR 23: 45). In another instance, a man dreamed that a particular Christian should say three words in favor of his spirit else misfortune befall him. To fulfill his dream, he invited the Christian to the sweat house to torture these words out of him (JR 26: 245–249).

In general, if the desires were not granted (were not satisfied), the soul became angry and not only did it not permit the person happiness but might revolt against the body, causing illness (JR 33: 189). Failure to satisfy the desire might incur the risk of some great misfortune (JR 17: 163; cf. JR 10: 169). As a result, most Hurons were very careful to note their dreams so that they could provide the soul with what it desired. If, for example, a man had seen a spear in his dream, he tried to get it. Or, if he had dreamed that he gave a feast, he would give one if he could (JR 33: 191).

Sometimes dreams foretold propitious events. For example, a man might dream that he captured an enemy and killed him with a war hatchet. He would then give a feast at which he related his dream and asked for a war hatchet, which one of the guests gave him. This feast compelled the soul to keep its word and to do it sooner. If it were not given, the soul might not keep its word. Similarly, songs to

---

[65] Mistakes in the performance of the ritual are still of concern to the Iroquois and can be dangerous if they are not explained to the spirit force (Shimony 1961 a: 141; see note 41, p. 80).

[66] It is possible that at this time the Huron thought that Roman Catholicism was just another medicine society with its curing rituals, especially baptism, and that if the ritual of the society was performed when called for in a dream, it would cure.

[67] The implication here is that the Jesuits were being accused of murdering the woman by witchcraft, and as murder necessitated the giving of gifts to the family of the murdered person (see above, "Crime"), the Jesuits were asked for them.

hasten the foretold event might be given in these dreams (JR 33: 195–197).

A sort of war god, a little dwarf, appeared to many before going to war. If he caressed them, it was a sign that they would return victorious; if he struck them on the forehead, they could go to war without losing their lives (JR 10: 183). The god of war, *ondoutaehte* [*ondoutaeté* (JR 33: 225)], a frightful-looking man, might appear to an individual as either a man or woman. In one instance, this spirit was seen by a young man about 30 years old as a woman armed with firebrands and flames. After she had told him that she would burn him, he became furious and threw himself into the fires but did not feel any pain. After several days of singing continually without losing his voice, the spirit that possessed him was questioned. She demanded a set of armor (in the Indian style which covered a man from head to foot), an ensign of a wolf's muzzle, and other war equipment. As these things could not be given her, she appeared a second time to the man holding by its hair a head which she said was that of a certain Iroquois chief. Then, he saw a man's brains and was told that they were the brains of another of their enemies. She said that they could have carried off the spoils of the Iroquois the following summer, but now she would go to the Mohawk where she would be honored. She departed leaving terror in the hearts of the Huron (JR 23: 153–155).[68]

Dreams apparently also could dictate friendships. One woman had a dream in which her spirit commanded her to become friends with a Christian Indian woman. In order to accomplish this, she gave gifts to the woman: a dog, as she knew that the woman's cherished dog had died, a blanket, and a load of wood, and, finally, she publicly invited both the woman and her husband to a feast (JR 23: 125).[69]

In some dreams, the manner of preventing an unfortunate outcome was indicated. One man, for example, dreamed that he would die in a particular manner unless he offered a feast of two dogs. As he was a Christian, he did not give this feast and 14 months later died in the manner indicated by the dream (JR 21: 161–163).

Some dreams that foretold misfortune were enacted to prevent the misfortune. For example, one man dreamed that the Iroquois captured and burned him. A council was called to decide how to avert the misfortune predicted by the dream. The result was that the chiefs had 12 or 13 fires lighted at the place where they burned their

---

[68] See also below, "Medicine Men" for medicine men dreaming of success in war and note 87, p. 96, for mention of the comparable Iroquois custom.

[69] This is probably an instance of ritual friendship, a formal and lifelong relationship between two individuals that entails certain rights and obligations. Such ritual friendships may be established on the prescription of a fortuneteller or a dream. In the latter case, the ritual duplicates the dream as much as possible (Fenton 1953: 119, 123–126; Shimony 1961 a: 218–224). The Wyandot apparently also had ritual friendship (Powell 1881: 68).

captives. Then, each took a firebrand or flaming torch and burned the man who had the dream. Shrieking, he avoided one fire only to fall into another and in this fashion went three times around the house. As he left the house, he seized a dog that was held there for him and, placing it on his shoulders, carried it around the other houses. The dog, a consecrated victim which he offered to the spirit of war instead of himself, was then killed with a club, roasted in the flames, and eaten at a public feast similar to that at which captives were eaten (JR 23: 171–173).[70]

Dreams also might indicate what *not* to do. One man, when he was young, dreamed that he should not have a dog feast or have anyone make such a feast for him or else misfortune would befall him. He obeyed this dream until a friend at a village he was visiting wished to make a dog feast for him. Because he was now a Christian, he thought that his dream was no longer true and allowed the friend to give the feast. When he returned home, he found two of his children sick (JR 21: 161).

Dreams also had their general influence on the lives of the people. The dream often was taken into account at council meetings;[71] trade, fishing, and hunting usually were undertaken in response to a dream, almost as if only to satisfy it (JR 10:171). If a man had been successful in hunting or fishing, it was because of his dream (JR 10: 171; 15: 99). The dream was the oracle of these Indians. It predicted future events; it warned them of misfortunes that threatened them; it was the usual physician when they became ill. It was "the most absolute master" they had. If, for example, a chief said one thing and the dream another, the dream was obeyed (JR 10: 169). Not all dreams, of course, were true and most were not true: only a person who had dreamed true several times was considered to have true dreams (JR 10: 171).

The dream was consulted on various occasions. Sometimes in order to decide what action should be taken, a man would fast to get a dream [or vision].[72] These and other dreams dictated their feasts,

---

[70] Although during the 17th century, dogs were sacrificed on many different occasions, the offering of a dog may have been especially associated with the war feasts (see quotation from Fenton 1953 in note 24, p. 73, and Morgan 1901(2): 265. The acting out of the dream is not unknown to the Iroquois (see previous note) and, as Shimony (1961 a: 273) points out, the prescription of certain rituals as the result of a dream are reenactments of those dreams. In a sense, much of Huron and Iroquois ritual for the maintenance of health and good luck rests on this principle of reenactment of dreams. The therapeutic value of such a procedure has, of course, been suggested by Freud. This has led Wallace (1958: 244 ff.) to call these dreams "symptomatic dreams" in contrast to "visitation dreams," the power-giving dreams in which a guardian spirit appeared.

[71] Compare Jackson's (1830 b: 28) statement almost two centuries later: "They are superstitious in the extreme, with respect to dreams, and witchcraft, and councils are often called, on the most trifling occurrances of this nature."

[72] The word "vision" has been inserted here, as it seems likely that fasting would induce a vision rather than a dream. The French made no distinction between visions and dreams, and it is apparent that, although the dream was far more important in Iroquoian cultures than the vision, both were valued.

hunting, fishing, war, trade, remedies, dances, games, and songs (JR 8: 121; 10: 169–171, 175; 15: 177–179). The dream was the "God of the Hurons" [73] (JR 10: 171; 15: 177; cf. JR 17: 15; 23: 171) and the authors of these dreams, the spirits, were "the real masters of the country." The latter regulated and decreed everything, in dreams and otherwise (JR 17: 161).

When dreaming of something that was far away, the Huron thought that the soul issued forth from the body and proceeded to the place where those objects were that were pictured in the dream. They said it was not the sensitive soul that issued forth but only the rational one, which was not dependent upon the body for its workings (JR 33: 191). [74]

Women especially, and men rarely, dreamed at night of such things as representations of the death of relatives and other imaginary terrors [S 75; Sagard and Champlain (passim) both emphasize the curing of women rather than men, perhaps a reflection of this tendency for woment to be more prone to dreams, if the statement is true]. [75]

MEDICINE MEN

If the sick person did not know the cause of his illness, he consulted a medicine man [called *arendiouane* (JR 8: 123), *arendiowane* (JR 10: 35), *arendiwane* (JR 10: 197), *arendioané* (JR 13: 187), *arendioouané* (JR 14: 29, 59), *arendiwané* (JR 15: 137), *arendioouanne* (JR 33: 221) [76] or the diagnosticians who were called *ocata* (JR 17: 211) or *saokata* (JR 33: 193) [77] and the "apothecaries" and those who cured

[73] Connelley (1899 a: 118; 1899 b: 43) reports an actual God of Dreams among the Wyandot. Dreams, of course, were of great importance to the Wyandot at this time.

[74] Also compare Connelley's (1899 a: 118; 1899 b: 43) statement that the Wyandot medicine man could detach his soul from his body and send it to the God of Dreams for information. While his soul was away, the medicine man was in a trancelike condition. Similarly, Parker (1913: 61 n.) notes the Iroquois belief that "the soul may pass from a living body and enter any object or go to any place to acquire wisdom and returning reveal it to the person in dreams and visions."

[75] Although both Sagard and Champlain indicate that many more women than men had dreams and consequently curing ceremonies performed for them, later writers, the Jesuits and anthropologists, mention no such sex distinction. It is possible that Champlain's and Sagard's statements are based on inadequate information. It is also possible that Sagard, at least, was thinking of something similar to the 'Ohgíwe Society ("The Singers for the Dead"), an Iroquois medicine society composed of women that deals with dreaming of the dead (Beauchamp 1922: 162–163; Fenton and Kurath 1951; Morgan 1901(1): 275–276; Parker 1909: 178; Shimony 1961 a: 231–233; Speck 1949: 120–122). Certain other medicine societies are dominated by women (Fenton 1936: 17; Parker 1909: passim).

[76] This word is a compound of *arendi-* or *orenda-*, roughly meaning 'supernatural power,' and *-wane* or *-wanen*, 'large,' 'great,' 'powerful,' and thus means 'his orenda is powerful' or 'one whose orenda is powerful' (Hewitt 1902: 38; 1910 c: 178). The Seneca cognate has apparently lost its meaning of 'supernatural power' and is now used only in the meaning 'song' (Chafe 1961 a: 156; cf. Hewitt 1902: 43, "the Iroquois *orenda,* a subsumed mystic potence, is regarded as related directly to *singing* and with anything used as a charm, amulet, or mascot, as well as with the ideas of *hoping, praying,* or *submitting*" and ibid.: 40, "Let it be noted, too, that this is the only word signifying to sing, to chant, in the earlier speech of the Iroquoian peoples").

[77] Hewitt (1910 c: 178) translates this word, *saïotkatta,* in Huron, as "one who examines another by seeing," literally, "one customarily looks at another." The cognate *aksãktõ* is still used by the Iroquois to designate a fortuneteller (Shimony 1961 a: 270).

by extracting the spell, *ontetsans* (JR 17: 211) or *aretsan* (JR 17: 213) [78]]. Such a man usually said that the illness was caused by the desires. Sometimes without much ceremony, he mentioned four or five things the patient desired. If he thought the patient was not likely to recover, he mentioned a thing that he thought the man could not procure [79] and, if the man died, his death was attributed to a desire which could not be gratified (JR 33: 203–205).

Medicine men also were called *oki* (C 144; S 170, 193) [*oki* (JR 10: 49, 161; S 170, passim), *oky* (JR 33: 193), *ondaki* (JR 8: 109), *oqui* (C 143, passim)], as were admired and esteemed people (JR 10: 49). When a man did the extraordinary or was more capable than most or a valiant warrior, he was called *oki* (C 143). "Mad" persons were called *oki* (S 170; C 144). Some spirits (S 170) and charms (see below, "Charms") were called *oki*.[80]

The *arendiwane* had an *oki*, a powerful spirit who entered his body, who appeared to him in his dreams, or who immediately after awakening showed him the cause of the illness. The spirit might appear in one of a number of forms, as an eagle, a raven (JR 33: 193), crow or other bird, or as a flame or ghost (JR 15: 177) and reveal the secret for the recovery of health or for success (JR 17: 153–155). This secret was called *ondinoc*, 'a desire inspired by the spirit.' If a Huron was asked the cause of this desire, he answered *ondays ihatonc oki haendaerandic*, 'the thing under the form of which my familiar spirit appeared to me gave me this advice' (JR 17: 155). Other less important secrets and desires came from certain dreams for which the spirit was believed to be the author. These dreams the Indians dared not disobey, as otherwise they exposed themselves to great misfortune (JR 17: 163).[81]

These medicine men (*saokata*) had the sight to penetrate, as it were, into the depths of the soul and to see the desires that the sick man had

---

[78] The word *ontetsans* resembles the Seneca *hadé:jen⁸s*, 'conductor' or master of ceremonies (Fenton: personal communication: see also 1953: 134). Compare also *shadédjẽ⁸t* "dispenser of herbal medicines" (Shimony 1961 a: 263). On the basis of the material in the Jesuit Relations, it is possible that the word *arendiwane* was used as a general term for medicine man and that special words were used for certain types of medicine men, as the diagnosticians (the present fortunetellers) and the sucking shamans.

[79] In general, the present Iroquois fortuneteller prescribes simple and inexpensive remedies for minor ailments and more drastic measures if the illness is more serious, is lingering, or the patient is concerned (Shimony 1961 a: 272). Only in extreme cases, as repeated witchcraft, does the fortuneteller prescribe cures that are economically impossible for the patient to obtain (Shimony 1961 b: 209).

[80] The basic meaning of *oki* seems to have been "spirit" (see note 36, p. 78). To call medicine men and extraordinary and "mad" people *oki* was probably to refer to their spirits, or familiars.

[81] The idea of the familiar spirit seems to be lacking in current Iroquois culture. Fortunetellers now, for example, possess their ability by virtue of initial talent, gift, not apparently as the result of having a familiar (Fenton 1953: 70; Shimony 1961 a: 270; 1961 b: 207). The present absence of the idea in Iroquois thinking is probably the result of culture change, for it is mentioned in the 17th-century accounts and occasionally in the earlier anthropological ones.

dreamed about and had forgotten.[82] They could discern the desires of a child in the cradle as well as those of adults (JR 33: 191–193).

In order to see these hidden desires, they might employ one of a number of methods. Some looked into a basin full of water and saw on its surface a fine wampum collar, a robe of black squirrel skins, a richly painted skin of a wild ass (JR 33: 193–195), a canoe (JR 15: 179), or other objects that were the desires of the soul. Some saw these desires while looking into a fire (JR 8: 123) or by looking into water or a fire while singing and shaking a turtle rattle (JR 15: 179; 17: 213). Some fell into a "frenzy" by singing and saw the desires as if they were in front of their eyes (JR 33: 195). Some fasted in a little house for a number of days (JR 13: 237). Others secluded themselves in a sweat house (JR 10: 197; 13: 105) and in the darkness saw the sick person's desires (JR 33: 195). Feasts, dances, and songs were also employed in diagnosing (JR 8: 123).[83]

On one occasion, when a medicine man wished to find the cause of an epidemic, the sweat house was made of four or five poles set in a ring and crossed, making a sort of little arbor, covered with the bark of a tree. Into it, 12 or 13 men crowded, almost one upon another. In the middle of the sweat house were five or six large red-hot stones. Once inside they covered themselves with robes and skins in order to retain the heat better. The medicine man then began to sing and the others sang with him. A man was stationed outside to give the medicine man what he requested. After much singing he asked for some tobacco which he threw on the fire, saying *io sechongnac*. The whole affair lasted a good half-hour, after which they ate (JR 13: 203). Apparently, sometimes a number of men sweated in order to effect a cure. In one such incident, 20 men, including the sick man, sweated (JR 14: 65; see JR 26: 245 for another mention of a sweat house). At another time, after the priests had given some medicine to a sick chief, one of his relatives took a sweat bath during which he addressed himself to his spirit to make it effective (JR 13: 213). While taking a sweat bath the men might sing of dreams and war songs (JR 19: 259).

A dog feast, sometimes on the recommendation of an *arendiwane* (JR 10: 197), might be given to cure a sick person (JR 17: 211) or a number of those ill from an epidemic (JR 13: 235).

---

[82] This description is, in part, a translation of the term *saokata* (see note 77, p. 91).

[83] Not all these methods of diagnosing are currently used and some new ones have been introduced among the Iroquois. The common methods now employed are reading tea leaves and cards, dreaming at night after having put herbs (Speck 1949: 124 says a piece of the sick person's clothing) under the pillow, and scrying (Fenton 1953: 57, 70, 129; Shimony 1961 a: 271; 1961 b: 208). Scrying is usually reserved for the diagnosis of witchcraft suspicions (Shimony 1961 a: 271).

The medicine men could also prescribe general precautions against epidemics.[84] For example, one said that whoever stole the Algonquins' lines or the baits from their hooks would be stricken by the disease. As a result of this admonition several attributed the death of one man to the Algonquin. This man had committed a theft among them and they happened to catch him; he was attacked later by the disease (JR 14: 13). Another medicine man said that to put a quick end to an epidemic: first, the dead should be put in the ground and in the spring the bodies should be taken out and placed in dark tombs raised on four posts, as was usual; second, the dead should be given no more new mats; third, he should be given five cakes of tobacco. Toward evening, a council assembled outside the village. The children were warned by one of the chiefs not to make any noise. A large fire was lighted and the medicine man, after he had told those present of the importance of the affair, threw the five cakes of tobacco into the fire while addressing the sun, the spirits, and the disease, asking them to leave the country of the Huron and to go to that of the Iroquois (JR 13: 259–261).

One medicine man said that he could cure all the sick of a village by sprinkling them with a water about which his spirit had taught him. A council was held for 3 days to discuss the matter and 13 notable presents were given to him. Immediately after this, he sprinkled all the sick of the village (JR 19: 243).

One medicine man predicted how many would die during an epidemic and when it would end. His predictions did not come true and the people lost faith in him (JR 13: 213–215).

As the dreams of the individual could indicate more than the causes of illness, so there were other *arendiwane* in addition to those who cured (cf. JR 10: 195).[85] Some such men controlled the weather and predicted the course of future events (JR 8: 123; 10: 37, 193–195; 33: 221; C 144).[86] One boasted that he could bring and stop rain and prevent the frosts which injured the corn crop (JR 30: 63). Another saw in a dream, before three villages burned, three flames falling on them from the sky. In this instance, a feast of a white dog was then given in order to gain further information, but the *arendiwane* did not succeed in obtaining this knowledge (JR 8: 125; the villages referred to are probably those mentioned in JR 8: 105).

---

[84] Material on Iroquois control of epidemics is scanty, although it is known that the False Faces may be used to drive away epidemics (Morgan 1852: 99; 1901(1): 159; Taft 1914: 102; and see note 1, p. 108). Hewitt (1889) mentions that fires were extinguished if there was an epidemic.

[85] Iroquois fortunetellers can find lost objects, solve love affair problems, predict success or failure of agricultural endeavors and other undertakings (Waugh 1916: 29; and see following notes).

[86] The Iroquois have ceremonies to control the rain (Jackson 1830 b: 34; Waugh 1916: 25–29; see note 29, p. 75).

Similarly, the French priests who were thought able to cure illnesses were also thought to be able to control the weather and to see where the enemies were and how many they numbered (JR 8: 97; 10: 95, 109; 17: 119; S 173).

One summer, a famous medicine man was consulted about the expectation of a good harvest of corn. He said that to insure a good crop, each person should go each day to his field and, throwing some tobacco on the fire, say "Listen, O Sky! Taste my tobacco; have pity on us" and that no one should gather the hemp from which nets were made (JR 23: 55).

During a drought, one medicine man promised rain, and he was given a number of feasts and a present worth 10 hatchets. But this dreaming, feasting, and dancing did not bring rain. The *arendiwane* then said that the crops would not ripen, that he was prevented from making rain by a cross which was beside the Jesuits' door. The Jesuits were told to take down their cross, or they would be killed as sorcerers. Some said they would pull down the cross and some young people made a cross which they placed on top of a house and shot arrows at it. Then the Jesuits assembled the people of the village and explained to them their method of praying for rain. Fortunately for the Jesuits, it did rain (JR 10: 37–43).

A similar incident occurred during a drought in 1628. The *arendiwane* mentioned above said he could not make rain because the Thunder was afraid of the red cross in front of the Frenchman's house. Prayers were said and it did rain (JR 10: 43–49). In another instance, at the request of an Indian, Sagard prayed for the rain to stop so he could build a house. The rain did stop only to begin again after the house had been finished (S 78). The Indians also once asked the priests to pray for the cessation of rain that threatened their crops. They did and the rain ceased (S 178–182).

A medicine man in 1636 said that the corn would grow and the green ears would be roasted, but then there would be a white frost which would kill the crop and cause famine. He said, "The people are crying every day to the Sky, *aronhiaté onne aonstaancwas* [cf. above—*aronhiaté onné aonstaniwas taitenr*, 'O Sky, here is what I offer thee in sacrifice; have pity on me; assist one' (JR 10: 159)]; and yet nothing is given to it. This irritates the Sky and it will not fail to take revenge; when the corn shall begin to mature, it will without doubt vent upon it the effects of its wrath" (JR 10: 161–163). The prophecy, that a white frost would ruin the harvest, turned out to be false (JR 13: 85).

One man announced throughout the country that in order to insure a large catch of fish, the villages should give him certain little presents and, at the beginning of the fishing season and from time to time while it lasted, they should meet together and throw some cakes of tobacco into the fire in honor of his spirit. If they did not do this, they would not have a good catch. Some villages sent the gifts he had requested and they caught many fish. Only one village did not follow his advice. Several months later, returning from their fishery, two of the principal chiefs of this village and two of their relatives were drowned during a thunderstorm on the lake (JR 19: 87).

Some *arendiwane* were able to predict whether or not there would be success in war and were able to see what was at a distance, as whether the enemy was approaching the village, how many were coming and the places where they were hidden (JR 10: 197; 19: 83; 33: 221).[87] One old woman saw those who had gone to war and who were bringing back prisoners. Her method was to outline in her hut the Lake of the Iroquois [Lake Ontario] and on one side to make as many fires as those who went on the expedition and on the other side as many fires as they had enemies to fight. If the fires on the Huron side "ran over," it indicated that the warriors had crossed the lake; one fire extinguishing another meant that an enemy had been defeated; a fire only attracting another to itself without extinguishing it meant that a prisoner had been taken (JR 8: 125).

After having been asked about the enemy and after having performed many ceremonies, one individual said that he saw so many enemies in a particular guise and that they would arrive in the country in a certain number of days. But the people did not believe him. Then, one evening he followed his wife to the woods and killed her. He ran back to the village, uttering the cry of one who had discovered the enemy. The young men prepared for battle. The people went through the houses and ascertained that the woman was missing, but fright and the darkness of the night prevented them from pursuing the enemy and seeking the woman. The next morning they found her corpse, but finding no trail of an enemy, they soon suspected what had happened. The villagers did not say anything, however, for if it were known to be murder, then the relatives of the deceased, who was from another village, would have to be given satisfaction. Twenty days later, while the murderer was going through the village to raise the cry of another attack, committed in fact by the enemies, a man accused him of being a witch and killed him (JR 19: 83–87).

On another occasion, before setting out for war, a medicine man was consulted. A bark sweat house 3 or 4 feet high and wide was built for him and inside were placed hot stones. The medicine man shut himself inside the sweat house and sang while the warriors danced outside. Finally, his spirit gave him the answer and he yelled out,

---

[87] At least among the Iroquois, a war chief might go into seclusion and fast. If he had a dream or vision, he returned to the village and struck the war post. Then the warriors were summoned to a feast of dog flesh, a ceremony including dancing and striking the war post. Each warrior who struck the post pledged himself to join the war party which was to set out the next morning (Fenton 1953 : 104–106).

"Victory! I see the enemies coming toward us from the south. I see them take to flight. I see all of you making prisoners of them." On the basis of this advice, the warriors departed toward the south (JR 26: 175–177).

Some other medicine men could find lost objects (JR 10: 195) and could locate the thief (JR 33: 221).[88] A man who had been robbed might ask a medicine man to come to the house. The latter gave orders for a feast and then performed magic to discover the thief. This he could do, they said, if the thief was present at the time in the house, but not if he was absent (S 141).

Some medicine men could work wonders, as change a rod into a serpent or bring a dead animal back to life (JR 33: 221).[89]

ACQUISITION OF POWER

These medicine men probably obtained their power through visions [my inference]. In olden times, a man who wished to become a *arendiwane* fasted for an entire month in a separate house and saw no one except a man who carried wood to him and who also had fasted (JR 10: 199).[90]

Those who wished to become medicine men had to be deprived of all their possessions, had to abstain from women, and had to obey all that the spirit suggested (JR 15: 181).[91]

One Indian dreamed one night that he could become an *arendiwane* if he could fast 30 days. When he awoke, he resolved to keep this fast. However, he was invited to a feast of *awataerohi* [for a description of this ceremony, see below under "Curing Ceremonies"]; he was one of a few who could sing in this ritual. At this feast, he ate and sang so much he became mad and ran naked in the snow with a turtle rattle, "or more correctly, with the fool's cap in his hand," and sang night and day. The next day he went to the village of Wenrio where they made three or four feasts for his health, but he

---

[88] Some Iroquois fortunetellers specialized in finding lost or stolen objects, as clothing, cattle, horses, and spouses (Shimony 1961 a : 270 ; see also Parker 1913 : 49 n.; Waugh 1916 : 29).

[89] Wonder working is, of course, a common ability of North American Indian medicine men. Although one suspects that it was more frequently practiced in the past, it still is a part of Iroquois culture. For example, at Newtown, a medicine man of the Idos Society (Society of Mystic Animals) juggles hot stones, sees through a mask that has no eyeholes, and causes a doll to appear as a living person (Parker 1909 : 172). At Coldspring, men wearing masks also used by the False Faces appear in one ritual of the Idos Society and juggle hot stones or ashes (Fenton 1937 : 226 ; 1940 b : 421).

[90] Vision seeking was apparently not greatly elaborated in Huron culture, although it seems to have been present (see note 93, p. 100). The Jesuit statement that *in olden times* the medicine man fasted for a month may indicate that the vision quest was more prevalent before the 17th century.

[91] In the light of other American Indian cultures, this statement seems a little extreme. What may have been meant is that the spirit might order a man to give up certain of his possessions, not *all* of them, and that before performing certain rituals he had to abstain from sexual intercourse. The statement that the medicine man had to obey his spirit is probably correct as it stands.

returned as mad as when he left. A few days later he dreamed that he should receive a canoe, 8 beavers, 2 rays, 120 gulls' eggs, and a turtle, and that he should be adopted by a man as a son. As soon as he had told of his dream, the old people of the village met and talked it over. They then set about finding what he requested. The chief's father adopted him as his son the same day. For the gulls' eggs, small loaves were substituted, a substitution which kept all the women of the village busy. The feast took place in the evening, but without effect. The next day another feast was given at which masked and costumed people appeared. Some of the dancers wore sacks over their heads with only holes pierced for their eyes; others had straw stuffed around their waists to imitate pregnant women; [91a] still others were naked with their bodies painted white and their faces black, and on their heads were feathers or horns; others were painted red, black, and white. Although there was the threat of war and although all the youth had been invited to go to the village of Angwiens to work on a half-made palisade, they continued the ceremony. The chief cried in vain *enonou eienti ecwarhakhion*, 'Young men, come.' The ceremony accomplished no more than the preceding. After he had fasted 18 days without tasting anything except tobacco, he came to see the Jesuits. They gave him seven or eight raisins. He thanked them and said he would eat one every day in order not to break his fast. Later, making his usual round of the houses, he found the people preparing for a feast and said, "I shall prepare a feast; I wish this to be my feast." Immediately he put on his snowshoes and went himself to the neighboring villages to invite people. He returned almost 48 hours later and made 7 or 8 feasts. It was said that on his trip three remarkable things happened: he was not buried in the snow although it was 3 feet deep; he threw himself from the top of a large rock and was not hurt; he was not wet and his shoes were dry when he returned. He had done all this, as a spirit had guided him. At the end, he asked that the Jesuits see him. He told them of the progress and cause of his malady which he attributed to the breaking of his fast, and said that he had resolved to go on to the end, that is, as prescribed in his dream. Later, he told the Jesuits that he had become *oki*, a higher title than that to which he aspired. But still he was not free from his madness until he dreamed that the performance of a certain kind of dance would make him well. This ceremony was called *akhrendoiaen* as those who took part in the dance gave poison to each other. It had not been practiced before among the Nation of the Bear. Messengers were sent out and a fortnight

---

[91a] Fenton (1937: 218–219) suggests that the dancers wearing sacks over their heads were wearing masks comparable to the Iroquois Longnose mask—a mask which unlike the False Face and Husk Face masks is made of buckskin. The Longnose is a bogeyman, a cannibal clown, who sometimes kidnaps children, i.e., is used to frighten them (Fenton 1937: 222; 1940 b: 418). Fenton also suggests that the dancers with straw stuffed around their waists were Husk Face impersonators.

was passed in assembling the company [medicine society?] of about
80 people including 6 women [from other villages]. Although
fasting was thought to give the eyes the ability to see things far removed, the new *oki* did not see the distant objects correctly: he said
the members of the company were 2 leagues from the village, but actually they had not yet set out. When they did arrive within musket-
range, they stopped and began to sing and the people of the village replied. In the evening, while he was in the middle of the house on a
mat, the company danced in order to find the cause of his illness. The
dance ended when he fell over backward and vomited and was then
declared a member of the brotherhood. (The brethren were called
atirenda.) They then danced for the cure, a dance called *otakrendoiae*. In it, they killed each other with charms, bears' claws,
wolves' teeth, eagles' talons, certain stones, and dogs' sinews. After
having fallen under the charm and having been wounded, blood poured
from their mouths and nostrils or was simulated by a red powder they
took by stealth. The members of this society often avenged their
injuries and gave poison to their patients instead of medicine. They
were skilled in healing ruptures. Their medicines could not be
recognized or their secret discovered if they were to be successful,
and took "pleasure, so to speak, in silence and darkness." The ceremony was given because he asked for *oatarra*, a little idol in
the form of a doll, from a dozen sorcerers who had come to see him in
order to be cured; after he put it into his tobacco pouch, it began to
stir inside, and ordered the feasts and other ceremonies of the dance
(JR 10: 199–209).[92]

Another medicine man, it was reported, said the following about
himself:

> I am a spirit. I formerly lived under the ground in the house of the spirits,
> when the fancy seized me to become a man; and this is how it happened.
> Having heard one day, from this subterranean abode, the voices and cries of

---

[92] The description of this ceremony suggests the Midewiwin ceremonies of the various
Upper Great Lakes Indians (Kinietz 1940 : 160). One of the distinguishing characteristics
of the Midé Society ritual is that the members of the society are magically killed and
revived. Initiation into the society for curing purposes is not a distinctive trait: initiation
into the various Iroquois medicine societies, and into similar societies in other Indian cultures is often part of the curing procedure of that society. Although dolls may figure in
various ceremonies (as, for example, in the Idos Society ritual, Parker 1909 : 172), a doll
does figure in the Midé ritual (see Dockstader 1961 : pl. 225 for a doll that formed part of a
Saulteux Midé Society headman's bundle). The Wyandot seem also to have this ceremony (Finley 1840 : 50–51), but its introduction may have been late. The Jesuit statement
that the ceremony had not been performed before among the Bear tribe of the Huron adds
to the suspicion that this ceremony is that of the Midé: the prevalence of this ritual in the
Upper Great Lakes area and its absence in other areas make it a ceremony that could be
introduced to adjacent peoples.

Certain parallels to this Huron ceremony are to be found among the rituals of the Iroquois
medicine societies, particularly in certain ceremonies of the Idos Society (and see Fenton
1942 b: 21 for a mention of the "throwing" or "shooting sharp objects" by members of
the Society of Medicine Men). Interestingly, Parker (1909 : 172) says that the Iroquois
Idos Society was introduced from the Huron (but in 1913 : 29 n. says it was introduced by
the Nanticoke). Certain of the Idos rituals may be older.

some children who were guarding the crops and chasing the animals and birds away, I resolved to go out. I was no sooner upon the earth than I encountered a woman. I craftily entered her womb and there assumed a little body. I had with me a she-spirit, who did the same thing. As soon as we were about the size of an ear of corn, this woman wished to be delivered of her fruit, knowing that she had not conceived by human means and fearing that this *ocki* [*oki*] might bring her some misfortune. So she found means of hastening her time. Now it seems to me that in the meantime, being ashamed to see myself followed by a girl and fearing that she might afterward be taken for my wife, I beat her so hard that I left her for dead; in fact, she came dead into the world. This woman, being delivered, took us both, wrapped us in a beaver skin, carried us into the woods, placed us in the hollow of a tree, and abandoned us. We remained there until, when a man passed by, I began to weep and cry out, that he might hear me. He did, indeed, perceive me and he carried the news to the village. My mother came, took me again, bore me to her house, and brought me up. [JR 13:105–107.]

This man also said that when he was young the children ridiculed him as he was very ill-shapen [he was an extremely misshapen little hunchback (JR 13: 101)] and he had caused several of them to die (JR 13: 107). He said that when he died they should bury him in the ground in order that he might return to the place from which he had come. During his sickness, he complained that his twin sister was the cause of his death and had broken his leg because he had tried to treat patients other than those of one house (JR 13:245).

The medicine men were not the only ones who fasted. There is some indication that young men at puberty went on a vision quest: [93] one man, when he was about 15 or 16 years old, went into the woods and fasted, drinking only water for 16 days. Then he heard a voice from the sky saying that he should end his fast, and he saw an old man of great beauty coming down from the sky. The man approached and, looking kindly at him, said, "Have courage, I will take care of your life. It is a fortunate thing for you, to have taken me for your master. None of the spirits who haunt these countries shall have any power to harm you. One day you will see your hair as white as mine. You will have four children; the first two and the last will be males, and the third will be a girl; after that, your wife will hold the relation of a sister to you." Then, he held out a piece of human flesh which the boy refused, and then a piece of bear's fat saying, "Eat this." After the boy had eaten of it, the old man ascended toward the sky. After that he often appeared to the boy and promised to assist him. Nearly

---

[93] A vision quest at puberty was apparently a part of Iroquoian culture, but its relatively minor place is attested by the scarcity of data on it in all periods. Barbeau (1915: 10) mentions a puberty seclusion and *uki* (*oki*) in the form of animals that appeared to individuals then (and see note 36, p. 78). For the Iroquois, Converse (1908: 107–110) says that during the puberty vision quest, a fast of not less than 7 days, the spirit of the bear would appear if the dreamer was a member of the Bear clan and would show him his future guardian. Hewitt (1910 c: 178), Waugh (1916: 153), Goldenweiser (1913: 470), and Shimony (1961 a: 215–216) also mention puberty rites for boys and girls that included a fast and seclusion. Jesse Cornplanter maintained that visions were associated with preparation for war rather than puberty (Quain 1961: 275 n.).

all the predictions came true. He had four children and the third was a girl. Then, an illness forced him to become sexually continent. He was in excellent health; although approaching old age and although exposed to contagious diseases, he did not contract them. He was always a successful hunter and when he heard a number of cries from the sky, he knew he would take that many bears. Sometimes when he was alone in the house he would see a number of deer entering the dwelling. He told others of these appearances and the next day they would find in their traps the same number of animals he had seen in his dream. He attributed his luck in hunting to the piece of bear's fat that he had eaten. He thought that if he had eaten the piece of human flesh, he would have been successful in war (JR 23: 155–159).

The Indians fasted on other occasions. Some Hurons told the Jesuits that, in order to have success in hunting, they sometimes fasted for a week, eating and drinking nothing, and cutting themselves so that the blood ran profusely (JR 12: 69–71). At least one man shook a tortoise shell rattle in order to invoke the aid of the spirit before he went hunting (JR 20: 23).

CURING CEREMONIES

If the sick person was an important member of the village, the chiefs of that village (the "old men") held a meeting, as the matter was of public importance, to decide whether they would do anything to help. If there were a number ill, there might be considerable intrigue by many people on behalf of their relatives and friends, as not all could be helped. If the chiefs decided in favor of the sick man, a deputation went to him to ask what his soul desired. These desires might number as many as 25 valuable presents. [In one instance, the sick man wished a number of dogs of a certain shape and color and a quantity of flour in order to make a 3-day feast and some dances performed, particularly the ceremony of the *andacwander* (JR 17: 147).] The desires were reported back to the council, and the chiefs either exhorted the people at a public meeting to contribute the necessary gifts or went through the streets and houses three or four times announcing the desires of the sick man. It was deemed important that all the desires be given for, if one was not, the omission would be considered the cause of the man's death. The dances to be given in the patient's house for his recovery were announced at a public meeting. These dances were performed on three or four consecutive days. The relatives of the patient gave a feast at the end of the ceremony, the choicest food going to the important people of the village and to those who participated in the dancing. Then the patient never failed to say that he had been cured (JR 10: 175; 15: 179; 17: 147–149, 155; 33: 205–209; cf. JR 15: 117). The desires had been taken to the sick person at the time of the first assembly [i.e., dance]. There the chiefs had given them to the patient saying, "Listen, such a man or woman and you, voice of the spirit [who had indicated the desires], behold what such a man or woman gives" and threw the presents upon the patient (JR 17:155).

The origin of the [curing] feasts was ascribed to a meeting of wolves and the owl. The owl predicted the coming of *ontarraoura*, an animal allied to the lion, by its tail [the meaning of this passage is obscure (JR 10: 325 n. 17)].[94] *Ontarraoura* resuscitated the Good Hunter, a firm friend of the wolves, in the course of a great feast. From this myth, the Indians concluded that feasts were capable of healing the sick, for they had restored life to the dead (JR 10: 177).[95]

A brief description of one such curing ritual will indicate the nature of these ceremonies. To fulfill her desires, one sick woman had performed for her, by 50 persons, a dance that lasted 3 hours. Three days were spent preparing for this dance. On the day it was held, the chiefs made a series of more than five public announcements: to tell them, first, that they should begin to wash their bodies; second, that they should grease [paint?] themselves; third, that they should put on one ornament; fourth, that they should put on another. The final announcement was to urge all to be there and to arrive before those who were to dance. The dancers entered the house of the patient led by a chief who carried the objects that were the desires of the patient. Following him were the two leaders of the dance, each singing and shaking a turtle shell rattle. Behind these leaders were the men and women who danced. In the middle of the house was the patient. One of the leaders placed himself at her head and the other at her feet and continued to sing and shake their rattles. The dancers danced around the patient. However, the ceremony did not cure her. She said that it was because they had not conducted the ceremony properly. Five or six days later, she was carried to another village, where the dances were performed again. She returned to her village still ill and more ceremonies were performed, including many *awataerohi* feasts. These were not effective and she finally died (JR 17: 155–159).

In another instance, the medicine man said that there should be feasts on 3 consecutive days to cure a number of sick people. Toward evening, the men assembled. Before the ceremony began, a chief climbed to the top of the house and cried—

Come now, see us here assembled. Listen, you spirits whom the medicine men [who did not attend this ceremony] invoke, behold us about to make a feast and have a dance in your honor. Come, let the contagion cease and leave this

---

94 Beauchamp (1901 a : 153) thought this animal was a panther.

95 Myths of this general type—involving the Good Hunter who encounters animals or other supernaturals, learns their ritual, and returns to teach it to his people—are common in Iroquois mythology. Various Iroquois medicine societies have such myths which tell of the source of their ritual knowledge (Fenton 1953 : 80 ff., 173 ; Goldenweiser 1913 : 474 ; Parker 1909 : 164 ; Shimony 1961 a : 284).

town. But, if you still have a desire to eat human flesh, repair to the country of our enemies. We now associate ourselves with you to carry the sickness to them and to ruin them.

This speech ended, the men began to sing. Meanwhile, the associate medicine man made the rounds of all the houses to visit the sick. The entire night was spent alternately singing, while beating on pieces of bark, and dancing. The associate medicine man's visits took him until after daybreak. He then returned to the house where the dancing and singing were taking place. A chief marched before him carrying in one hand the bow of the medicine man and in the other a kettle filled with water with which he sprinkled the sick.[96] The associate medicine man gave those ill something to drink and fanned them at a distance with a turkey wing. Then followed a feast for the men. After they left, the women came to sing and dance, but not to feast. A second feast was made, but, for lack of fish, the third was not. Before he left, the associate medicine man gave a turkey wing as a token to each of the three men he had taught and said that their dreams would now prove true. He also commissioned these men to send to him, after a few days, a report of the success of their remedies. Four or five days later, they visited all the houses to ascertain the number cured and the number still sick. They found 25 cured and 25 sick. Their report was given to the medicine man. He sent back his associate, who said that the sick people should come to a certain house to be cured; but his remedy did not have the desired effect (JR 13: 237–243).

There were many curing dances that were given in response to the desires. One that the Jesuits often mentioned, perhaps because it was impressive and important (cf. JR 21: 151), was the *awataerohi* [*aoutaerohi* (JR 10: 183; 13: 31, 171, 187–189; 14: 59), *aoutaërohi* (JR 13: 229), *aoutaenhrohi* (JR 21: 151), *outaerohi* (JR 17: 171)].[97] This ceremony cured the disease of the same name, one caused by a spirit the size of a fist that lodged itself in the body of the sick man. Both the names of the ceremony and the disease were from the name of this spirit (JR 10: 183; 13: 171). As other curing rites, this

---

[96] The Iroquois Otter Society similarly sprinkle those ill with sickness caused by the otter and other water animals and, during Midwinter, the public also (Parker 1909: 170–171; Speck 1949: 65–67). The implication that the feast food in this Huron ceremony was fish suggests, most tentatively, that the ceremony was related to the Iroquois one. The Iroquois Otter Society is, however, composed of or dominated by women, and sprinkling also occurs in the Thunder Ceremony (Shimony 1961 a: 164).

[97] It is tempting to equate this ritual with that of the Iroquois Idos Society (see notes 89, p. 97; 92, p. 99). Both had juggling hot objects as part of their ritual, and both had masks. (The Iroquois False Face Society also wear masks and handle hot coals and ashes in the course of blowing ashes on the patient, but this society does not emphasize handling hot stones, and its members are masked while performing the ashing ritual, whereas apparently the Huron fire jugglers were not.)

The Wyandot also had a feast which was distinguished from their other feasts by being held at night and by the exhibition of many fire tricks (Finley 1840: 52).

ceremony was given if the sick man had dreamed that it would cure him or if a diagnostician had said it would (JR 10: 183). For example, one woman saw at the beginning of her illness a black man who touched her body. She simultaneously felt all on fire. Before the man disappeared he had begun to dance with the rest of the troop. When she told of this experience, all those present concluded that the *awataerohi* had caused her illness. Many feasts were then made for her recovery; among them was a feast of a dog on one day when she was very sick. As she opened her eyes while the dog was half alive on the coals, they thought that the medicine was operating. Next, a medicine man was called in to try to cure her. After taking a sweat bath to diagnose her illness, he said that she had been bewitched [for an account of this part of the treatment see below, "Witchcraft"] (JR 13: 31). Part of the ceremony consisted of the women singing and dancing (JR 13: 189; C 151; S 201) under the direction of the medicine man (C 151) while the "men struck violently against pieces of bark"—the whole creating an awful din (JR 13: 189). Stones which were heated red hot in the fire during the singing were handled by the medicine man. He then chewed hot coals and, with his hands so warmed by the coals, rubbed the disease-affected parts of the patient and blew or spit out on those parts some of the coals he had chewed (S 200–201). Or certain men took live coals in their bare hands and rubbed these coals over the stomach and body of the patient (JR 13: 189; 14: 63), threw fire from one side of the house to the other, swallowed red-hot coals, held them in their hands for a time, and threw red-hot ashes into the eyes of the spectators (C 151). During one such ceremony, a man put a large live coal in his mouth and growled like a bear into the ears of his patients. When the coal broke in his mouth, the ceremony was not deemed effective and consequently was repeated the next day. This time, the men carried red-hot stones the size of a goose egg instead of live coals in their mouths while holding their hands behind their backs and blew on the patients and growled in their ears (JR 14: 59–63). While coals were being thrown about, the occupants of the house feared that the contents of their house would be burned up. For this reason they removed everything in sight (C 152). When the medicine man arrived, his eyes were flashing and frightful and he stood or sat as he wished. Suddenly, he would lay hold of everything he found in his way and throw it from one side to the other. Then he would lie down and sleep for a time. Waking with a jump, he would seize fire and stones and throw them on all sides. Then he would sleep again and, on waking, would call several of his friends to sweat with him (C 152–153; S 201). While they were sweating, the kettle boiled in preparation for giving them something to eat. They sweated, covered with their robes, for 2 or 3 hours in a bark-covered sweat house containing a great many stones that had been heated red hot. All sang, occasionally stopping to get their breath. Then they drank many jugfuls of water (C 153).

During the curing ceremony, the place was kept as dark as possible; all openings that admitted light from above were covered. Only those who were invited might be present (S 200).

In one case, a blind man named Tsondacouané, having dreamed it was necessary for him to fast 6 days, resolved to fast for 7. An apartment was partitioned off for him at the end of the house and there he fasted, drinking only a little tepid water to warm his stomach. After a few days, he began to see the spirits dancing around the fireplace. On the sixth day, they spoke to him and said, "Tsondacouané, we come here to associate you with us. We are the spirits, and it is we who have ruined the country through contagion." Then one of them named all the others by name, "That one is called *Atechiategnon* ('he who changes and disguises himself') and is the spirit of *Tandehouaronnon* (a mountain near the village of Onnentisati)." After he had named five or six of the spirits, he said, "But you must know that the most evil is he of *Ondichaouan* (a large island nearby); this spirit is like a fire. It is he who feeds upon the corpses of those who are drowned in the great lake and who causes the storms and tempests and swamps the canoes. But now we wish to take pity upon the country, and to associate you with us, in order to stop the epidemic which prevails." Tsondacouané agreed and they taught him some remedies to cure the sick. Among other things, they recommended to him the feasts of *awataerohi*, saying that they feared nothing so much as those. They pretended to try to carry him away, but he resisted so well that they left him to make a dog feast, threatening to come and get him the next day if he failed to make the feasts. After the spirits had disappeared, Tsondacouané told all this to the chief, who reported it in council. A dog was immediately found with which he made a feast the same day. When all the people had assembled, the man began to cry out that the spirits were coming to carry him away, but that he did not fear them, only that all should sing a certain song. While they were singing, he said, "There! Two of them are approaching and what I say is not imagination, but the truth." A little while later, he told those who were preparing the feast, "Withdraw; here they are, quite near." The spirits then reproached him for failure to do several things he had been ordered to do and said that they had come to carry him off. They said, "Tsondacouané, you are now safe. We can do nothing more to you. You are associated with us, you must live hereafter as we do; and we must reveal to you our food, which is nothing more than clear soup with strawberries." In order not to get sick, the people ate dried strawberries (this was in January) and hung large masks at the doorways and scarecrowlike figures above the houses. One man had four or six of these straw archers hung on the poles of his fireside (JR 13: 227–231). The blind man said that all would be recovered at the end of the January moon. He also said that if some others did not give him a present of a net, they would die (JR 13: 233).

As the performance of the ceremony was dictated by a dream or vision, so the performers who handled the live coals might dream the power to do so. One man when a youth about 20 years old handled the coals, but found that he could not, like the others, handle hot coals. Thus he was very careful not to touch those that were too hot and made only a pretense of doing it. After a time, he dreamed that he was at an *awataerohi* and handling fire like the others. In this dream he heard a song that he remembered perfectly when he awoke. He sang his song at the next ceremony and, taking the live coals and hot stones in his hands and between his teeth and plunging his bare arm in boiling kettles, was neither injured nor felt any pain. On the contrary, he felt a coolness of the hands and mouth. From time to time, he dreamed that at a feast something was given or lent to him; he then wore it during the ceremony. Such a dream meant that he should not dance at the next ceremony without this object. The next time he would ask for the item of which he had dreamed, and it would be given to him so that he would dance (JR 21: 151–155).

This ceremony, which so impressed the Jesuits, was only one of the dances that were used for curing purposes. There were as many as 12 different dances used to cure as many illnesses. As for the *awataerohi*, a diagnostician or the dream of the ill man dictated which dance was given (JR 10: 185). [98]

One ceremony for the cure of an ill person was that of the *andacwander* [*andacwandet* (JR 17: 179)], a mating of men with girls at the end of the feast. In one such ceremony there were 13 girls, one for the patient himself (JR 17: 147). In another such ceremony, all the girls in the village assembled at a sick woman's bed and were asked, one by one, which of the young men they would like to have sleep with them the next night. The men selected were then notified by the masters of the ceremony and all came the next night to sleep, in the presence of the sick woman, with the girls who had chosen them. They occupied the house from one end to the other and passed the whole night thus while the two chiefs at the two ends of the house sang and rattled their tortoise shells from evening until the following morning when the ceremony was concluded (S 120).

---

[98] As the Iroquois have almost 12 medicine societies, it is tempting to think that the dances referred to are medicine society dances. They may be given, of course, in response to the dream of an ill person.

Another dance was designated, by the Jesuits at least, as the dance of the naked ones (JR 17: 81; cf. JR 17: 193—"nude dances"). To cure one sick woman, all the young men, women, and girls danced stark naked in her presence and one of the young men was required to make water in her mouth, which she had to swallow; this was done in accordance with her dream which she wished carried out without any omission (S 118).

After the medicine man had visited the sick man or woman and ascertained the cause of the illness, he might send for a large number of men, women, and girls, including three or four old women. They entered the house of the patient dancing, each having on his head the skin of a bear or other wild animal, the bear being the most common. Three or four other old women near the sick person received the presents from the dancers [for the sick person], each woman singing and stopping in turn. The presents [probably the desires] were food, wampum, and other things. After all the presents had been made, they all sang together, keeping time with sticks on dry tree bark. Then all the women and girls went to the end of the house to dance. The old women walked in front with their bearskins on their heads, and all the others followed them, one after the other. They had only two kinds of dances with regular time, one of 4 steps and the other of 12, as in the *trioly* of Brittany. The young men often danced with them. After dancing an hour or two, the old women led out the sick person to dance. The latter got up sadly and began to dance and after a short time danced and enjoyed it as much as the others (C 148–150). [This is probably a description of a ceremony for the cure of a sick woman that Champlain saw; see above under section headed "Dancing" for perhaps that is Sagard's description of such a ceremony. The phrasing and the details of these two descriptions are different, but one suspects Sagard used Champlain's description to jog his memory.]

In another type of ceremony, women walked on all fours like animals.[99] When the medicine man saw this, he began to sing and then he blew upon the patient, in the particular instance described, a woman, told her to drink certain waters and to make a feast of fish or meat that had to be found even though it was very scarce at the time. After the feast was over, each woman returned to her own house. Later the medicine man came back to visit the ill woman, blew on her, and sang with several others who had been summoned for this purpose while they rattled a dry tortoise shell filled with little pebbles. They told the patient to make three or four feasts and hold a singing and dancing

---

[99] Members of certain Iroquois medicine societies, as Bear and Buffalo, imitate the animal to which the society is dedicated. Persons also may become possessed upon witnessing a dance of the medicine society and will then have to be cured by that society (Fenton: personal communication).

party at which all the girls should appear adorned and painted (C 154–155; S 202).

In some other ceremonies, masked dancers appeared in order to drive away the disease (e.g., JR 13: 175).[1] The medicine man might order this. Those taking part disguised themselves, went and sang near the bed of the sick person, and then paraded through the village while the feast was being prepared for them. They returned to empty the kettle of its *migan* (C 155; S 202). In one such dance held for the recovery of a patient, the dancers appeared disguised as hunchbacks, wearing wooden masks and carrying sticks. The patient had dreamed about it 2 days before, the intervening time having been spent in preparations. At the end of the dance the medicine man said that all the masks should be hung on the ends of poles and placed over every house and straw men placed at the doors to frighten away the disease and the spirits who brought it (JR 13: 263). Five days before this, on the 5th of February, the medicine man had had published through the village the necessary prescriptions for shortening the end of the epidemic [see above] (JR 13: 259–261). On the 8th, the chief went through the houses again to publish a new order and to say that the medicine man would not return until the next day. He was sweating and feasting in order to invoke the assistance of the spirits and to make his remedies more efficacious. His prescription, in this case, consisted in taking the bark of ash, spruce, hemlock, and wild cherry, boiling them well in a great kettle and washing the whole body with this concoction. In using this remedy, care had to be taken not to go out of the house barefoot in the evening. This prescription was not for menstruating women. On the 9th, before going to sleep, at least one man [the host] threw some tobacco on his fire and prayed that his house be taken care of. On the 10th, the medicine man returned and demanded eight cakes of tobacco and three fish of different species: an *atsihiendo*, a fish they decoy from the edge of the water, and an eel. Four of the cakes of tobacco he used to make a sacrifice to the spirits, as he had done 2 days before. On the 11th, the chief made a round of all the houses and in a loud voice exhorted the women to take courage and not to allow themselves to be cast down with sorrow over the deaths of their relatives. When the young men should come bringing some hemp to spin, he said, it was their intention to make weapons to wage war in the spring against the Iroquois, to make

---

[1] Beauchamp (1905: 184–185) and Fenton (1937: 218–220; 1940 b: 412–416) suggest that masks may have been introduced to the Iroquois late in the 17th century because they are not mentioned earlier, but not all (Parker 1909: 181) have agreed. The issue is whether the lack of mention in the early 17th-century accounts of the Iroquois means that they had no masks or whether it simply means that no one happened to mention them because the trait was already a familiar one to the European observers of Iroquoian cultures (see especially Fenton 1937; 1940 b; 1940 c; Keppler 1941; Skinner 1925 a; Speck 1949: 68–109 for descriptions of the False Faces; for a description of a Wyandot False Face curing ceremony, see Finley 1840: 58).

the women secure and able to work peaceably in their fields. On the 12th, early in the morning, the man [the host] again threw some tobacco into the fire with the prayer that his family be preserved. Toward evening, a third offering of four cakes of tobacco was publicly made. Then, in all the houses, the men beat upon pieces of bark for a quarter of an hour making a terrific din to frighten and drive away the disease. The man [the host] then asked the wooden masks and straw men that had been hung over the houses to keep a good watch, and threw a piece of tobacco into the fire for them (JR 13: 261–267).

Those villages which had mummers or maskers invited other villages to come see them and attempt to win their utensils, if they could (C 166).[2]

At least some of these dances belong to fraternities [medicine societies], all of which had chiefs (JR 17: 139) or masters (JR 17: 197).[3] After a person had had the dance or feast of a society performed for him, he became a member of that society and, after his death, was succeeded in membership by one of his children. Some members of the society had a secret or a charm and a song that had been given to them in a dream. These gave them power, for example, to handle fire (JR 17: 197; cf. JR 30: 23).

Each family had certain illnesses and thus certain cures (JR 15: 181). The heads of most families had ceremonies that cured disease or insured success in certain activities.[4] [The Jesuit Relations do not state whether or not the head of the fraternity must be from a particular family.] These ceremonies were given by a spirit who appeared in a dream in the form of an animal such as a raven, other bird, or a snake, or were given in a dream of which the spirit was the author (JR 17: 153).

In addition to controlling certain diseases, each family had a distinct armorial bearing: a deer, snake, crow, the thunder (a bird) (JR 15: 181). [This may refer to clan symbols.]

At least some of these dances should not be danced by children. If children danced in play the dances they had seen at the ceremonies, they were immediately reprimanded as though they had profaned some holy thing (JR 17: 163).

---

[2] Champlain's association of maskers with betting games is obscure: Iroquois False Face and Husk Face rituals do not involve games. The statement would be consistent with the Iroquois data if Champlain was thinking of Midwinter; its rituals now include the appearance of the False Faces and the playing of the Bowl Game.

[3] This is the only statement in the Relations that specifically states the Huron had medicine societies. They were probably more important than this single reference implies (see notes above, passim).

Although membership in an Iroquois medicine society is often the result of having had a dream, membership also may be based on inheritance (Shimony 1961 a : 178–179, 231–232; Fenton 1953 : 119). Sickness also may run in certain families and this amounts practically to inheritance of membership in the medicine society (Fenton 1953 : 121).

[4] There are statements in the literature that Iroquois (Hewitt 1918 : 532–534; 1932 : 486) and Wyandot (Powell 1881 : 65) clans also owned certain rituals.

If their usual cures had no effect and there were many sick in the village, or at least an important man was ill (S 202), or a sick person dreamed that he would be cured by the dream-guessing feast, it was given (JR 10: 175). [This ceremony was called *ononharoia*—'turning the brain upside down' (JR 10:175, 183); *ononhara* (JR 10: 175); *ononhwaroia*—'turning round the head' (JR 17:167, 171); *ononhouaroia*—'upsetting of brain' (JR 23: 53, 103); *onnonhouaroia* (JR 30: 101); *lonouoyroya* (S 202).][5]

In the evening, after someone had said that this ceremony should be given, a band of people went through the houses, upsetting everything (JR 10: 175), breaking, and turning topsy-turvy everything in the houses. They threw fire and burning brands about the streets, shouting, singing, and running through the streets and around the walls all night (S 203). The next day they returned, announcing in loud voices, "We have dreamed." Those in the house tried to guess what had been dreamed by offering what they thought the dream was (JR 10: 175–177; cf. JR 23: 53). In each house and at each fire, they stopped for a short time and sang softly, "So-and-so gave me this, so-and-so gave me that" (C 165; S 203). Nothing was refused: hatchets, kettles, wampum, axes, knives, pruning hooks, pipes, dogs, skins of beaver, bear, deer, lynx, and other animals, fish, corn, tobacco, canoes, and other objects were offered (JR 10: 177; C 165; S 203) and hung around their necks (JR 10: 177). If nothing was given to them, they went outside the door and got a stone which they put beside the man or woman who gave nothing, and then went away singing; this was a sign of insult, reproach, and ill-will (C 165; S 203). When they had been offered what they had dreamed, they thanked the giver (JR 10: 177), uttered a cry as a sign of joy and ran out of the house, while those in the house struck their hands on the ground with their usual exclamations, *hé, é, é, é, é* to congratulate him (S 203). Other presents, as some leather or an awl if the dream was a shoe, were given to them (JR 10: 177). The gift belonged to him (S 203).

---

[5] The name of this Huron ceremony is cognate with one of the names of the Iroquois Midwinter ceremonial and it would appear, therefore, that the descriptions of it are descriptions of a Huron Midwinter ceremonial (Beauchamp 1888: 198, 198 n.; 1891 b: 41–42; Fenton 1942 b: 15; Hewitt 1910 g: 940). (The major descriptions of the Iroquois Midwinter include Morgan 1901(1): 199–213; Hewitt 1910 g; Fenton 1936; 1941 c; Speck 1949; Shimony 1961 a: 173–191). The dream-guessing rite now appears most prominently in the Onondaga Midwinter ceremonial where 3 days are devoted to it (Hewitt 1910 g: 942). At Six Nations it is a rite that now may be performed during the Midwinter ceremonial if someone wishes his dream guessed for curative purposes (Speck 1949: 60, 63, 122–123), but it is not given frequently (ibid.; Shimony 1961 a: 173).

It should be noted that the French accounts usually state that the dream-guessing ceremony was performed to cure an individual and no mention is made of the ceremony being a part of Midwinter. The origin of the ceremony as given by the Jesuits also suggests that the dream-guessing rite was a curing ceremony quite independent of Midwinter. On the other hand, the French may have been describing the Midwinter ceremonial although they did not explicitly say so. The third possibility is that the Huron performed the dream-guessing rite at times other than Midwinter to cure an individual if the patient's dream indicated it should be performed, as many other rituals associated with particular calendric ceremonials may be performed separately to cure among the Iroquois.

According to one account, they then went in a band to the woods and cast out, they said, their madness. The sick man then began to get better (JR 10: 177). Those who did not get what they dreamed thought they would soon die and some of the sick were carried from house to house hoping to get what they had dreamed and thus be cured (S 204). The festival usually lasted 3 days (S 203), or 7 or 8 hours (C 165).

An example will indicate the details of such a ceremony. While a curing ceremony was being celebrated in the village, a woman went out one night from her house with one of her daughters in her arms. The moon appeared to her as a beautiful tall woman, also holding in her arms a little girl. The moon told her that the various peoples of the area should offer her presents that were the product of their own country: for example, some tobacco from the Tobacco Nation, some robes of *outay* [probably the black squirrel (JR 17:243 n. 8)] from the Neutral Nation, a belt and leggings with their porcupine ornaments from the Askicwaneronons or Sorcerers, and a deer skin from the Ehonkeronons or Islanders. The moon also told her that the feast being performed was acceptable to her and that she wished others held. Finally, she said that she wished the woman to be like her, and that, as she was of fire, the woman should be dressed in the color of fire—in a red cap, a red plume, and a belt, leggings, shoes, and the rest of her clothes decorated with red ornaments. (This was the dress in which she appeared at the ceremony later performed for her.) When she had returned to her house, she suffered from a giddiness in the head and a contraction of the muscles that made the people conclude that she was sick of a disease for which the remedy was the *ononharoia* ceremony. The sick woman confirmed this belief by seeing in her dreams only shouting people going and coming through her house. She resolved to ask in public that they celebrate this feast for her. The chiefs from the village in which she was living went to the village in which she was born to ask this of the chiefs. They immediately summoned the council. In this council, the affair was declared one of those most important to the welfare of the country, and it was said that they ought to avoid any failure and give what the sick woman desired. The next morning, this decision was announced throughout the village and the people were exhorted to go promptly and bring the sick woman to the village and to prepare themselves for the feast. They did not walk but ran to the village. At noon the sick woman arrived, carried upon their shoulders in a kind of basket, with an escort of 25 or 30 persons, who were singing. A little while before she arrived, the general council had assembled. The deputies announced her arrival to the council. They said two men and two girls arrayed in robes and collars of such and such a fashion and with certain fish and presents in their hands should be sent to her, in order to learn from her own lips her desires and what was necessary for her recovery. Shortly, two men and two girls went loaded with all that the sick woman had desired, and they immediately returned, naked except for their clouts; all they had carried had been left with the sick woman. They repeated the desires whose fulfillment would bring about her recovery. She desired 22 presents be given her: one was 6 dogs of a certain form and color; another was 50 cakes of tobacco; another, a large canoe; another, a blue blanket that belonged to a Frenchman. The report having been made by the deputies, the chiefs began to exhort every one to satisfy promptly the desires of the sick woman. All the presents having been furnished and carried to the patient, the public announcement was made that in all the houses all the families should keep their fires lighted, and the places on both sides ready for the first visit which the sick woman was to make in the evening. The chiefs made another announcement after the sun had set, and all stirred up their fires and maintained them with great care. (The patient had said that these fires should be made as large and bright as possible.) The time having come when she was to set out, her muscles relaxed and she could walk, even better than before. Two people walked beside her, each one holding up one of her hands; thus supported she went through all the houses of the village. She walked with bare legs and feet through the middle of the houses and consequently through the middle of the fires, a total of 200 or 300 fires, without doing herself any harm. She even complained constantly of how little heat she sensed and how it did not relieve the cold she felt in her feet and legs. Those who held up her hands passed on either side of the fires. Having led her through all the houses, they took her back to the house where she was staying. Then all except perhaps a few old men painted themselves and, vying with one another in the frightful contortions of their faces, ran through the houses where the sick woman had passed. On all the three nights that the ceremony lasted, they had liberty to do anything; no one dared say a word to them. They upset kettles found over the fire, broke earthen pots, knocked down dogs, and threw fire and ashes everywhere so thoroughly that often in such ceremonies the houses and entire villages burned down. The more noise and uproar they made, the greater the relief of the patient. The next day everyone prepared to revisit all the houses where the sick woman had passed and particularly the one in which she was staying. At each fire each person told of his own desire (*ondinonc*) in a riddle. For example, one said, "What I desire and what I am seeking is that which bears a lake within itself," meaning a pumpkin or calabash. Another said, "What I ask for is seen in my eyes and will be marked with various colors" and as the Huron word that meant 'eye' also meant 'glass bead' what he desired was some type of glass beads of different colors. Another intimated that he desired an *andacwander* feast. In guessing the riddle, they threw an object at the person and said "It is that." If this was really his desire, he said that it had been found. Immediately, all those in the house rejoiced by striking against the pieces of bark that formed their house walls. The patient felt relieved each time a riddle had been guessed. (It was found in the council held at the end of this ceremony that 100 riddles had been guessed during the ceremony.) If what was guessed was not the answer to the riddle, the asker replied that they were near it, but that was not what he desired. He took the present, however, so that he might show it in other houses and thus better indicate what it was not, so that by elimination they were better prepared to tell what it was. Later, he brought back what was given him, keeping only that which was really his desire. Both the running through the houses and the guessing of riddles was repeated each of the 3 nights and 3 days that the ceremony lasted. On the third day, the sick woman went for the second time through the houses and indicated her last and principal desire in the form of a riddle, as the others had done previously. She was accompanied by a number of people, "with the faces, appearance, and attitudes of persons afflicted and penitent," some following her and some going before, none of whom might say a word. While this part of the ceremony was going on, no one should be outside of the houses, so those who were escorting the sick person gestured to those outside that they should go indoors. In each house, the woman related her troubles and indicated that her recovery depended upon the satisfaction of her last desire. This she gave in the form of a riddle and each one threw to the sick woman what he thought it might be. Those who were attending the sick woman collected all these things and went out laden with kettles, pots, skins, robes, blankets, cloaks, necklaces, belts, leggings, shoes, corn, fish; in short everything that was used by the Indians. Finally the woman gave so many hints that her answer was found. At once there was a general rejoicing of all the people, indicated by striking against the bark walls. She returned a third time through all the houses to thank them for the health she had recovered. After this, the last general council was held, at which time a report was made of all that had taken place. Then the last present, the last desire of the sick woman over and above what that individual who had guessed it had been able to give, was presented to her and the ceremony ended (JR 17: 165-187).

Sometimes the desire in this ceremony was that, among other things, the patient's house be furnished anew. In this case, the ill person had to give away all that he possessed during the 3 days in which people went through the houses stating their desires. If, as sometimes happened, a single wooden plate was retained for sentimental reasons, the patient was not cured and he was told in a dream the place and spot where he would die (JR 17: 193).

During the ceremony described above, a young man, while running through the houses acting as the mad man, encountered a spirit with whom he talked. This so upset his brain that he fell down and became insane. As a remedy, two dogs, one of which he held especially dear, were killed and a feast made (JR 17: 197).

The dream-guessing ceremony originated in a village where the chief saw the spirits on a lake engaged in it and begged them to come to his village to teach the ceremony. After much urging and many sacrifices of dogs, they finally consented. Later, the chiefs and the other villagers died, their deaths followed still later by the whole nation with the exception of a few who joined the Huron as refugees. From these, the Huron learned the ceremony (JR 17: 195).

In general, each nation of the Huron brought its special dances, customs, and ceremonies (all of which originated in the same manner) to Huronia. They were performed according to the dream (desire) of the sick person or by order of the diagnostician (JR 17: 195). Such observances were called *onderha*, 'the ground,' the prop and maintenance of their country (JR 17: 195–197).

GAMES

One of the three kinds of games, lacrosse, dish [bowl], or straw (JR 15: 155), might be played on the advice of a dream or of an *arendiwane*.[6] Of the three, lacrosse and the bowl game were considered the most effective healing games. For example, a sick man might dream that he would die unless lacrosse was played for his benefit. In response to his request, villages would play against each other and bet such articles as beaver robes and wampum collars. Sometimes a medicine man would say that the whole country was sick and would request that a game of lacrosse be played to heal it; this would be done for otherwise some great misfortune would befall the entire country (JR 10: 185–187, 197; 13: 131; cf. S 97–98—mention of the invitation to other villages to gamble and feast, but not in connection with the curing ceremonies).

During one epidemic, the disease did not cease to spread, although the young played lacrosse (JR 13: 131). In another instance, a man recovered 7 or 8 days after the bowl game had been played for his cure in his house for 2 or 3 days (JR 14: 81). At least once,

---

[6] Similarly, games are played for curing purposes among the Iroquois. The total inventory of such games, including the bowl game, lacrosse, football, tug-of-war, and snowsnake (Beauchamp 1896: 271; Harrington 1909: 89; Shimony 1961 a: 180, 278–279; Speck 1949: 115–118, 124–126, 141), is larger for the present Iroquois than that indicated in the 17th century Huron accounts. For descriptions of Iroquois games see Beauchamp 1896; 1905: 180–183; Culin 1907: passim; Hewitt 1892; Morgan 1850: 80–83; 1901(1): 280–304; Speck 1949: 141–144.

lacrosse was played because the medicine man had said that it would influence the weather (JR 14:47).[7] Sometimes, also, it was played in memory of an excellent player (JR 15:179).

For the game of straws (*aescara*) 300 or 400 little white reeds of equal length (about 1 foot long) were cut (S 96–97).[8]

For the bowl game,[9] six wild plum stones (JR 10:187), five or six fruit stones, or little balls the size of the tip of a little finger, slightly flattened (S 97) were put into a large wooden bowl (wooden dish). These dice were painted black on one side and white or yellow on the other. The players, squatting on the ground in a circle, took the bowl in turn in both hands and, lifting it a little from the ground, struck it sharply so that the dice sometimes fell on one side and sometimes on the other. A side scored when the stones fell either all white or all black (S 97; JR 10:187). The one who held the bowl kept saying *tet, tet, tet, tet* in order to effect a favorable outcome (S 97).

The use of this bowl game to cure is illustrated in the following description. A sick man told the chiefs that the bowl game should be played for his health. The chiefs called the council to fix the time and choose the village that should be invited. (The game was usually played between two villages.) An envoy was then sent to the other village with the invitation; if it was accepted, preparations were made in both villages. The men, having fasted and abstained from sexual intercourse, assembled at night for a feast to prepare themselves and to seek good luck and success for their side. To predict the result of the game, the man chosen to play took the dish, put the stones in it, and covered it so that no one could put his hand into it. Then the men sang a song. After that, the dish was uncovered and all the plum stones were found to be either all white or all black. Next, they displayed their charms and exhorted them. Then they lay down to sleep in this house and hoped to have some favorable dream. In the morning, they related their dreams and collected all the things that they dreamed would bring them good luck. These they put into their pouches. They also collected other people's charms that would bring them luck and had them sit nearest to the player so that they might assist him (cf. JR 17:159). If there was an old man whose presence

[7] Iroquois may play lacrosse as well as dance the War Dance during the Thunder Ceremony, a ceremonial directed to the Thunderers which is thought to bring rain (see note 29, p. 75). Either the War Dance or the lacrosse game, or both, also are performed to cure a sick person (Shimony 1961 a: 162—165, 278; Speck 1949: 118–119).

[8] See Beauchamp (1905:182) and Culin (1907:241–243) for later French descriptions of this game.

[9] The following description of how the bowl game is played could easily serve for present Iroquois practice. Sagard's indecision as to the number of stones may be a trick of his memory: at the present time, six are used. They are now peach stones, but peaches were unknown in America before European contact. The French description of the scoring is incomplete: currently, at least, if all stones fall either black or white, the score is five; if all stones except one fall so that the same color is up, the score is one. Beans are used to tally the score.

was considered efficacious to the charms, they might be taken to him or he might be brought to the game on the shoulders of the young men. The man who was selected to play either previously had had a dream indicating that he would win or had a charm. One man who had such a charm rubbed the plum stones with an ointment and rarely failed to win.[10] When the game started, the two parties took their places on the opposite sides of the house, filling it from top to bottom. The sick man was brought in in a blanket. Behind him walked the man who was to play for the village, his head and face wrapped in his garment. The two players were in the middle of the house with their assistants, who held the charms. The bets between individuals on both sides having been placed, the game was begun. Everyone shouted and gestured with the hands, eyes, and face to attract good luck. Some made contrary gestures and said other words to drive bad luck back to the other side. When the opposite side took the dish, they cried at the top of their voices *achinc, achinc, achinc*, 'Three, three, three,' or perhaps *ioio, ioio, ioio*, wishing him to throw only three white or three black. Beads, tobacco pouches, robes, shoes, leggings, and the like were bet and the betting was heavy. Sometimes so much was lost by one side, a participant returned home naked.[11] A loss, however, was taken cheerfully. The participants did not leave until the patient had thanked them for the health he had recovered through their help (JR 10: 187–189; 17: 201–207).

Another dice game,[12] using five or six fruit stones like those of apricots blackened on one side, was usually played by the women and girls although men and boys also played. They held the dice in their hands and threw them a little upward onto a piece of leather or skin stretched on the ground for that purpose. The stakes were collars, earrings, and other such possessions (S 97).

The stakes in such a game of chance were varied. One Huron, having lost all his wealth, staked his hair, which he also lost, the winner cutting it close to his scalp. Others gambled their little finger and, losing the bet, had it cut off without showing any sign of pain (JR 16: 201). Monetary losses might run to 200 or 300 écus (JR 15: 155). One village lost 30 wampum collars, each having 1,000 beads, equal to 50,000 pearls or pistoles in France (JR 17: 205; cf. JR 17: 77—an account of a Mohawk losing by gambling the wampum he had brought to another Iroquois nation to trade for beaver.)

[10] It is still said that there are medicines that will influence the outcome of the bowl game (Shimony 1961 a : 172).
[11] Compare Morgan's (1901(1) : 282; cf. 1850: 83) statement, "It often happened that the Indian gambled away every valuable article which he possessed; his tomahawk, his metal, his ornaments, and even his blanket."
[12] This game should not be confused with the bowl game; although the rules are somewhat similar, the two games are quite distinct.

Gambling was frequent and took up much of the Indians' time. Both men and women might stake all that they had on such games, appearing as cheerful and patient when they lost as though they had lost nothing. Some returned to their villages naked and singing after having lost everything (S 96).

WITCHCRAFT

Not all illness was caused by the desires. The diagnostician might find that the illness was not caused by the desires of the sick person, but by witchcraft (JR 17: 213); or the sick person might have a dream that indicated the cause of his illness was witchcraft (JR 33: 219). To treat this kind of disease, there was a special class of doctors [called *ontetsans* (JR 17:211) or *aretsan* (JR 17:213)]; those who cured by extracting the spell. This spell might be a knot or tuft of hair, a piece of a man's nail or animal's claw, a piece of leather, bone, or iron, a piece of a tree leaf or wood, some sand or pebble, or other such object (JR 33:199, 219). The charm was extracted, sometimes by giving an emetic and sometimes by sucking the diseased part of the body (JR 33: 199, 219).[13] [The general references to giving "potions" and to "blowing" by the medicine men (JR 8: 123; 13: 103, 137, and passim above), may refer to the extraction of the charm.] The doctor might extract the charm with the point of a knife without making any incision, saying he had drawn it from the heart or inside the patient's bones (JR 33: 199), or he might extract the charm from the material vomited up (JR 17: 213). In one instance, a woman was given some doses of water and she threw up a charm; a coal as large as a thumb. Another time, the *arendiwane* shook a man sick with a high fever, as one would shake a sieve, and sand came forth from all parts of his body (JR 10: 197). In a third instance, a sick man was given an emetic and threw up a charm that consisted of some hairs, a tobacco seed, a green leaf, and a little cedar twig. As one of these charms was broken and the other part had remained in his body, he died. In still another instance, a sick person vomited up a charm that was a grasshopper's leg twined about with a few hairs (JR 13: 157; cf. JR 15: 21—when a member of the Tobacco Nation vomited up a leaden pellet in some blood, it was concluded that a Frenchman had bewitched him).

Sorcerers sometimes used as a charm the flesh of a kind of monstrous serpent (*angont*[14]) who lived underground, in caves, under

---

[13] The Iroquois also hold that witchcraft charms may be extracted from the patient by giving an emetic or by sucking. The charms are similar to those of the Huron described below (Beauchamp 1893: 183; 1922: 61–66; De C. Smith 1889 a: 277–278; E. A. Smith 1883: 71–72; Snyderman 1949: 218; Parker 1913: 27 n.; see also Finley 1840: 65 for a Wyandot example of extracting a witch charm by cutting and sucking). Witches may also use other techniques (Parker 1913: 27 n.; Shimony 1961 a: 288).

[14] Shimony (1961 a: 287; cf. Speck 1949: 113) mentions a charm described either as a small stone or as a small piece of dried meat, called *oʔnĕ′yŏnt* or *oʔnĕ′yĕt*, that is said to be used for witchcraft. The word means 'sharp point' (William N. Fenton: personal communication).

rocks, in the woods, or in the mountains, but generally in the lakes and rivers. In order to cast a spell, the sorcerer rubbed some object, as a blade of corn, tuft of hair, piece of leather or wood, or animal claw, with a piece of the serpent's flesh. This caused the object to penetrate into a man's entrails and his bones, inducing illness unless removed (JR 33: 217).

The spells in a sick person could be quite numerous. Ten or twenty spells might be taken from the individual's body and, if he still was not cured, the disease was thought to be caused by some other spell which was yet more concealed and could not be removed (JR 33: 201).

The following is an example of a ceremony to cure a woman ill from witchcraft. Many feasts had been made for the recovery of this sick woman. Then, a medicine man was invited to try to cure her. He took a sweat bath to get knowledge of her disease. After throwing some tobacco into the fire, he saw five men and deduced that she had been witched and that she had five charms in her body. The most dangerous of these charms, and the one that would cause her death, was in her navel. Another man was called in to get the charms out. Such a person usually made three demands. First, the dogs must not bark as his cures could be made only in silence. Second, he cured only in a place apart and so would often have the patient carried into the woods. Third, the sky must be clear. In this instance, however, the patient was not carried out of the house, perhaps because the sky was cloudy. The medicine man did give her something to drink and it should have gone directly to her navel in order to be effective. It went, however, to her ears, which then became swollen, and she died shortly after. The medicine man said she had not been cured because he did not get all he had demanded; particularly a pipe of red stone and a pouch for his tobacco (JR 13: 31–33).

Sorcerers, *oky ontatechiata*, 'those who kill by spells' (JR 33: 221), might be put to death for their activities.[15] The witch was ascertained, sometimes, from the dream of the sick man. Occasionally a person was seen in the woods or in some out-of-the-way part of the country, and the person seeing him there would think that he was preparing spells. People accused of being sorcerers were killed without trial, for no one would dare undertake their defense or avenge their deaths (JR 8: 121–123; 10: 37, 223; 13: 111; 15: 53; 19: 83, 179; 30: 21; 33: 219–221).

In one instance, a woman accused of being a witch was killed in the following manner. The man who thought she was witching him sent for her under the pretext of inviting her to a feast.

---

[15] The Wyandot (Finley 1840: 63, 66; Powell 1881: 67) and Iroquois (Morgan 1901(1): 321–322) also killed witches.

When she arrived, her sentence was pronounced without any other form of trial. The woman, seeing there was no appeal, named the man who was to execute her. At the same time, she was dragged outside the house and her face and part of her body were burned with pieces of burning bark. Finally, "the one she had taken for godfather split her head." The following day her body was burned in the middle of the village. Some said that she confessed to having practiced witchcraft and named some of her accomplices. Others said that she spoke only in general terms and that the accomplices had all agreed not to expose one another if one was caught. After she had been captured, one of the chiefs said that she should be promptly killed, that the old men were too lenient and that if she were allowed to live until morning, her life would probably be spared (JR 14: 37-39).

In another instance, the people for a time talked about nothing else except the possibility of killing an old man. For a long time, he had been suspected of being a sorcerer and poisoner. Then, one testified that he believed that this old man was making him die. Some said that they had seen him at night roaming around the houses and casting flames from his mouth. A girl who had seen seven or eight of her relatives die within a few days went to his house to accuse him of causing their death. He was not there, but she talked to his wife so freely that the son, who happened to come in, laid down his robe and taking a hatchet went off in a rage to the house where these evil suspicions had originated. He sat down in the middle of the room and addressed one of the men there, "If you think it is we who make you die, take this hatchet and split open my head; I will not stir." The man replied, "We will not kill you now at your word, but the first time we shall take you in the act" (JR 13: 155–157). In another instance, an Indian accused the Jesuits of bringing the epidemic and said that if anyone in his house died, he would kill the first Frenchman he found (JR 13: 215).

The Jesuits were frequently accused of being witches (sorcerers) who brought disease (JR 10: 37; 13: 213–217; 14: 51, 53, 97, 103–105; 15: 25 ff., 53 ff., 105, 181; 17: 115–125; 18: 25, 41; 19: 91, 167, 183, 195; 21: 219–221). This idea had some justification; as the Hurons said, the priests did introduce disease into the villages where they were, practically causing the extinction of the people (JR 19: 91–93). In at least one instance, the Jesuits were not accused of being witches because they also came down with the disease (JR 13: 111).

An interesting synthesis of Huron and Christian ideas appears in the following example. A spirit in the form of a tall, handsome young man appeared to a man while fishing and said:

Fear not, I am the master of the earth, whom you Hurons honor under the name of *Iouskeha* [see p. 145, "Creation Myths"]; I am the one whom the

French wrongly call Jesus, but they do not know me. I have pity on your country, which I have taken under my protection; I come to teach you both the reasons and the remedies for your misfortune. It is the strangers who alone are the cause of it; they now travel two by two throughout the country, with the design of spreading the disease everywhere. They will not stop with that; after this smallpox which now depopulates your houses, there will follow certain colics which in less than three days will carry off all those whom this disease may not have removed. You can prevent this misfortune; drive out from your village the two black gowns [Jesuits] who are there. As for those who are now attacked by the smallpox, I wish you to serve me in curing them; prepare a quantity of such a water, run as fast as possible to the village, and tell the elders to carry and distribute this potion during the whole night. Then all the youth and the war chiefs will go acting like madmen through all the houses; but I wish them to continue even till the dawn of day.

Then the spirit disappeared. This man immediately hastened to the village and gave the warning to all he knew. Then the elders met two and three times in council. These ceremonies were received with approbation. Toward evening, one heard in all the streets nothing but the shouts of the chiefs, exhorting the youth to act bravely as mad men. These masqueraders withdrew a little after midnight. Six of the elders then bore in silence a great kettle full of that water and made all the sick people drink it after the young men had ceased their activities.[16] The ceremony was repeated the next night (Christmas) (JR 20: 27–31).

The Huron said that the witches could ruin them. If a person's trading or hunting had been successful, then a witch made him or a member of his family ill so that he had to spend all his profit on doctors and medicines (JR 8: 123).

CHARMS

Not all charms were witchcraft charms; some charms, or familiars, [*ascwandies* (JR 17: 159); *ascwandics* (JR 17: 203, 207, 211; cf. JR 17: 159); *aaskwandiks* (JR 21: 135); *aaskouandy* (JR 33: 211); *oky*—"most things that seem at all unnatural or extraordinary to our Hurons are easily accepted in their minds as *Oky*—that is, things that have supernatural virtue" (JR 33: 211) and cf. above, "Medicine Men"] brought good fortune. All (JR 17: 211) or nearly all (JR 15: 181) possessed these charms (JR 33: 211). Such things as an owl's claw or a serpent's skin could be charms (JR 26: 267).

Charms could be found. If, for example, after a hunter had had difficulty in killing a bear or stag, he found in its head or entrails something unusual as a stone or snake, he said that this was what gave the animal such strength and prevented it from dying. He kept the stone or snake so that it might bring him good fortune. Or, if

---

[16] Beauchamp (1901 a : 158), apparently referring to this episode, says that drinking medicine water was not customary among the Huron, but that it was among the Iroquois. This statement would seem to be in error.

a man found a stone of a peculiar shape, as one resembling a dish, spoon or small earthen vessel, in a tree or in the ground, he kept the stone as a charm; he believed that it belonged to some spirit who dwelt in the woods and who had lost it there (JR 33: 211).[17] These charms might alter their shape and appearance; the stone or snake found in the entrails of a deer might change into a bean, a grain of corn, a raven's beak, or an eagle's talon (JR 33: 211–213).

Charms made the owner lucky in hunting, fishing, trading, and gambling (JR 15: 79; 17: 209; 20: 217; 23: 185; 26: 267; 33: 213–215; and see p. 114, "Games"). Some had power for all these things, some were limited to a particular thing (JR 33: 213), and some were more powerful than others (JR 17: 211). The owner had to be advised, in a dream, of a charm's proper use (JR 33: 213). Some people had many charms (JR 17: 211). One man had three: one each for success in hunting, fishing, and trading (JR 23: 91). Some charms could bring success in love (JR 26: 267). Some charms were inherited from relatives (JR 10: 193; 15: 79; 17: 211).[18]

One man attributed his fishing success to the ashes of a certain little bird (*ohguione*) which he said penetrated the trunks of trees without resistance. When he went fishing, he mixed these ashes with a little water and rubbed this on his nets to insure an abundant catch (JR 10: 193).

Another used a charm when he went to trade. He would open the pouch where the charm was, request of it a wampum collar of so many beads or a robe of so many beaver skins and put some beads and a piece of beaver in the pouch. Then he would make a feast in honor of the charm. Having done all this, he would get what he wished in his trading. Such charms were powerful: this man's wife trembled whenever he brought it out in order to speak to it (JR 17: 209).

The owner of a charm commonly would give it a feast from time to time in order to make it more propitious to him. At other times, he would invoke it in his songs and would ask his friends to join him and help him in his prayers (JR 15: 181; 33: 213). If the charm had lost its power, it might be restored by giving a feast (JR 17: 209).[19]

---

[17] Witthoft and Hadlock (1946: 420) mention a Cayuga medicine bundle from Six Nations that contained a tiny sling and several sling stones which had belonged to the Little People (Pygmies), a species of tiny beings who live in the woods and rocky places and who hunt with slings. The skill of these people was probably thought to be transferred to the owner of the charm. Some Iroquois charms are found after a tree has been struck by lightning (Jackson 1830 b: 33; Converse 1908: 40 n.).

[18] Finley (1840: 64) mentions that Wyandot girls could purchase love charms from an old woman. Shimony (1961 a: 285–288) suggests that the hunting charms, now that hunting is no longer practiced by the Iroquois, have become charms to aid in witchcraft. These charms are inherited.

[19] Wyandot hunters similarly feasted the contents of their medicine bundles (Finley 1840: 53). De Cost Smith (1889 b: 283) in describing an Iroquois hunting fetish (a bone from a large snake) mentions that the owner gave it a feast, and the erstwhile hunting fetishes are also given feasts now among the Iroquois (Shimony 1961 a: 285–288; Speck 1949: 113–114).

Some charms were obtained in trade from neighboring tribes, especially from the Algonquin, who had powerful ones: the most costly and precious merchandise of the country (JR 17: 211).

A particularly powerful Algonquin charm (*onniont*) was a kind of serpent, almost in the shape of the armored fish, which pierced everything it met on its way, trees, bears, and rocks, without deviating from its course or stopping. If a person could kill the *onniont* or obtain a piece of it, he would have good luck. The *onniont*, however, did not live in Huronia and Huron knowledge of this creature was obtained from the Algonquin, who sold them a small piece of it for a high price (JR 33: 213–215).[20]

LIFE CYCLE

BIRTH AND CHILDHOOD

Other Huron ritual was associated with the life cycle: birth, marriage, and death.

In many different situations, a pregnant woman could give good or bad luck (JR 17: 213). Her condition could prevent her husband from taking game; if she looked at an animal that was being pursued, it could not be taken. If she entered the house of a sick person, he became worse. If people ate with her, they became ill (JR 15: 181).[21] (See above under "Cure of Natural Illnesses"—the presence of a pregnant woman was necessary for the successful extraction of an arrow.)

Girls were preferred: the Huron rejoiced more in the birth of a daughter than a son, in order that the country's inhabitants increase (JR 15: 181–183). They desired many children both to help support them in old age and to defend them against their enemies (S 127).[22]

Women gave birth "by themselves, and for the most part do not lie up." Some came from the woods, laden with a big bundle of

---

[20] See note 14, p. 117. The behavior of this being resembles that of certain Iroquois mythological creatures (see, for example, Converse 1908: 76). The buying and selling of charms is, of course, to be expected when such a high value is placed on them. It still occurs: the Iroquois of the Six Nations Reserve buy their supply of Little Water Medicine from the Indians of the Cattaraugus Reservation in New York (Shimony 1961 a: 284).

[21] Based on the idea that her condition could cause others harm, a pregnant woman is still subject to taboos which are similar to those mentioned by the Jesuits. Paralleling the Jesuit statement that a pregnant woman should not look at an animal is the current idea that a pregnant woman should not "associate with hunters or with medicine men or watch the making of medicine, since the animals would be scared by the contaminated hunter and the medicine would be spoiled" (Shimony 1961 a: 208) and paralleling the Jesuit statement that a pregnant woman should not eat with others is the current prohibition against using the common drinking cup at the Longhouse (Shimony 1961 a: 159, 161, 208, 216–217).

[22] Apparently now boys and girls are equally desired by the Iroquois (Randle 1951: 177).

wood, gave birth to a child as soon as they arrived, and immediately
were on their feet again (S 130).[23]

After the child was born, the mother pierced its ears with an awl
or fish bone and put in it the quill of a feather or other object to keep
the hole open. Later, wampum beads or other things were suspended
from it and hung around the neck of the child, however small it might
be. Some made the child swallow grease or oil as soon as it was born
(S 127).

A name was chosen from the great supply of those available. Some
names had no meaning; others did, such as *yocoisse*, the wind; *ongyata*, the neck; *tochingo*, crane; *sondaqua*, eagle; *scouta*, the head;
tonra, the belly; and *taihy*, a tree (S 128).[24]

The child was breast-fed (S 128). During the 2 or 3 years the
child was being nursed, the father abstained from sexual intercourse
with his wife (JR 8: 127).[25] The child was also fed meat that the
mother chewed well. If the mother died before the child was weaned,
the father took water in which corn had been boiled and filled his
mouth with it. Then, putting the child's mouth against his own, he
made the child swallow the liquid. Women used the same method to
feed puppies (S 128).

During the day, the child was put on a cradleboard (2 feet in
length and 1 in breadth) wrapped in fur or skins (C 141; S 129).
The cradleboard sometimes had a rest or small piece of wood bent
into a semicircle under the feet. The cradleboard was stood up on
the floor of the lodge, except when the child was taken outside. Then
the child on the board was carried on a woman's back by means of a
belt across the forehead, or it was wrapped up and carried in her dress
above the girdle either in front or back so that it could look from side
to side over her shoulders (S 129).[26]

The cradleboard was usually decorated with little paintings and
strings of wampum beads. The child was swaddled on the board so
that there was an opening in front of its private parts through which

---

[23] Now a midwife helps in the delivery (Shimony 1961 a : 207) and also did so 150 years
ago (Jackson 1830 b : 20).

[24] Sagard's statement that the name of a child was chosen from a great supply of
names may refer to the Iroquois custom of choosing a name from those thought to be
owned by the clan, but not being currently used because the persons bearing them had
died (see note 57, p. 45).

[25] The present average duration of nursing, 1 year to a year and 9 months for boys and
2 years for girls, is approximately that reported by the Jesuits, although the figures
indicate that the period may have been shortened somewhat. The post-partum sex taboo
seems not to be currently practiced, but rather prolonged breast feeding is used as a
common method of contraception (Shimony 1961 a : 209).

[26] Although the cradleboard is not used now (Shimony 1961 a : 209), it was used in
the past by the Iroquois (Beauchamp 1905: 167–169; Jackson 1830 b: 20–21; Morgan
1852: 76–77; 1901(2): 57–59) and Wyandot (Finley 1840: 48).

it made water. If the child was a girl, a leaf of corn was arranged upside down which served to carry the water outside without soiling the child. A very soft down of a kind of reed which was cleaned with the same down (or with the powder of dry rotten wood) was used in place of diapers (C 141; S 129).

At night, the child slept quite naked between the father and mother (C 141–142; S 129).

Children were left naked in the lodge and, even when older, rolled, ran about, and played both in the snow and during the hottest days in summer (S 130).

They did not obey their parents and were not punished for any fault. Everyone lived in complete freedom and did what he thought fit. Parents failed to correct their children and often suffered wrongdoing at their hands, sometimes being beaten and flouted to their face (C 142; S 130–131).[27]

YOUTH

The usual and daily practice of the boys was to shoot their bows and arrows. They also played a game with curved sticks, making them slide over the snow, and with a ball of light wood, as is done in France. They learned to throw the prong with which fish are speared and practiced other sports and exercises. They returned to the house at meal times or when they felt hungry. If a mother asked her son to go for water or wood or do similar household work, he replied that this was girl's work and did none of it.[28] Some mischievous boys delighted in cutting the cord that held up the door of the Recollects' house so that it fell when one opened it, but they denied doing it and took flight (S 132).

As boys had their special training and taught one another to shoot with the bow as soon as they began to walk, so the little girls had a small stick put into their hands to train and teach them early to

---

[27] This comment reflects a difference in child-training methods between the Iroquoians (and North American Indians, in general) and Europeans (and White Americans), a difference which has also been noted by more recent observers (as Randle 1951: 170), although their statements are not as extreme, and punishment, especially by using cold water, is mentioned (Jackson 1830 b: 19; Parker 1913: 33 n.; Shimony 1961 a: 209–210). The difference in emphasis probably rests ultimately on different attitudes toward the child: Indians tending to view the child as an individual with its own rights, needs, etc., and those of Western civilization tending to view the child as an unformed creature that must be molded by admonition and force into a human being. This difference is apparent in many ways. One such is that among Indians, learning tends to be by example rather than by formal instruction, a difference that has struck many observers. For example, it is reflected in Fenton's (1957: 33) statement, "What always amazes me, however, is to return to an Iroquois community and see a comparative youngster rise in the speaker's place without prolonged training under the older men."

[28] Iroquois boys still play games and do some hunting and trapping (Shimony 1961 a: 214–215). Although they rarely now are assigned tasks by their mothers, their grandmothers are apt to give them tasks (Randle 1951: 178). They now chop wood and fetch water (Shimony 1961 a: 215), a change that is probably part of the general change in tasks of men and women. This change began at the end of the 18th century when men took up agricultural pursuits, traditionally the occupation of Iroquois women.

pound corn. When somewhat grown, they and their companions played various games in the course of which they were trained quietly to perform small household duties (S 133).[29]

The girls vied with one another as to which should have the most lovers. If the mother found none for herself she freely offered her daughter and the daughter offered herself. The husband sometimes offered his wife, if she were willing, for some small present. There were also procurers in the villages who had no other occupation except bringing some of these women to the men who desired them (S 133–134).[30]

Huron women did not leave the house or village during their menstrual periods as did women of the "wandering peoples," but they did cook their food separately in little pots during their periods and did not allow others to eat their meats and soups (S 67).[31]

MARRIAGE

The Huron were monogamous, but divorce was frequent (JR 8: 119–121, 151; 15: 79; 17: 143; 23: 187; 27: 69; 28: 51–53).[32] Often a young woman might have 12 or 15 husbands, not including other men, for after nightfall the young women and girls and the young men went about from one house to another, regardless of whether or not they were married (C 137–139; S 124). Marriage was "nothing more than a conditional promise to live together so long as each shall continue to render the services that they mutually expect from each other" (JR 28: 51; cf. JR 21: 135). If the couple wished to separate, they were free to do so. It was sufficient for the man to say to his wife and her relatives that she was no good and might provide elsewhere for herself. Wives left their husbands with equal ease (S 124). If the couple had children, they rarely separated and then only for some important reason. If they did divorce, they did not remain unmarried for long, notwithstanding their children.[33] In some instances, the children remained with the father; in one instance, a baby son remained with the mother. (The daughters should go to the

---

[29] Iroquois children still help with household chores at an early age and older children care for the younger ones (Randle 1951: 170, 178; Shimony 1961 a: 215).

[30] Sagard's statement is probably a little extreme, although the attitudes of the Indians are different from those of Europeans.

[31] Menstrual taboos still include similar prohibitions: taboos against cooking for a man, drinking from the same glass, or biting the same bread as a man, as well as others, although they are not always observed (Shimony 1961 a: 216–217).

[32] Many writers on the Iroquois have made similar statements: that they are monogamous but that divorce is common (Jackson 1830 a: 55; 1830 b: 29; Morgan 1901(1): 315–316; 1901(2): 271; Shimony 1961 a: 227–228; Morgan's (1901(1): 315–316) statement that divorce was infrequent in ancient times is probably an exaggeration). The Wyandot apparently permitted polygyny (Finley 1840: 69–70; Powell 1881: 63) and Mary Jemison said that polygyny was occasionally practiced by the Iroquois (Seaver 1824: 180).

[33] Children, legitimate or illegitimate, are still not an impediment to marriage (Shimony 1961 a: 228; Randle 1951: 178–179).

mother and the sons to the father, but they did not always follow the rule (S 125).) [34]

The French idea of the indissolubility of marriage did not appeal to the Huron and was a great obstacle to conversion (JR 10: 63). One convert expressed the difficulty this way: "If we take a wife, at the first whim that seizes her, she will at once leave us; and then we are reduced to a wretched life, seeing that it is the women in our country who sow, plant, and cultivate the land, and prepare food for their husbands" (JR 14: 235). One very sick woman refused baptism when she was told that she could not separate from her husband after she had been baptized (JR 13: 141).

The Huron did not marry any relative in either the direct or collateral line, however distant the relationship (JR 8: 119; 10: 213), or a relative within three degrees of consanguinity (S 123). [35]

When a boy was of marriageable age, apparently his parents and relatives suggested to him a suitable girl to marry (JR 27: 31; 30: 37; 33: 87). In any event, when the young man wished to marry a girl, he had to ask her parents for her. Without this consent, the girl was not his, although most frequently the girl did not accept this parental advice. [36] The boy then painted his face and wore the finest ornaments he could get to appear more handsome to the girl and gave her a wampum necklace, bracelet, chain, or earring (C 137–138; S 122) or a beaver robe and perhaps a wampum collar (JR 14: 19). If the girl liked the suitor, she accepted the present, and the lover came and slept with her for three or four nights. The girl might do this in deference to her father's wishes and, still not liking the suitor then could reject him. He had no further recourse (C 138; S 122). If the boy and girl agreed to the marriage and had the consent of their parents, the second marriage ceremony followed. A feast of dog, bear, moose, fish, or other meat was prepared, and all the friends and relatives of

---

[34] Mary Jemison also said that the Iroquois mother takes the girls, and the father, the boys (Seaver 1824 : 180), although others say that the mother generally takes the children, especially if they are small (Jackson 1830 a : 64 ; 1830 b : 29–30 ; Shimony 1961 a : 228). Morgan's (1901(1) : 316) statement on the subject is somewhat colored by his concern with matrilineal descent.

[35] At least some Iroquois today hold that marriage is prohibited with any known relative (Shimony 1961 a : 30–31). Morgan (1901(1) : 79) states that the clan, and anciently the moiety, were exogamous. In present practice, the rule of clan exogamy occasionally is broken (Fenton 1951 b : 46 ; Shimony 1961 a : 31–32). The Wyandot also practiced clan exogamy (Powell 1881 : 63).

[36] Probably "parent" in these sentences should be read "mother." The Wyandot boy seeking a wife asks her mother, sometimes through his own mother (Powell 1881 : 63). A similar custom is reported also for the Iroquois : the boy told his mother, or other female relative, of his intentions and she told the mother, or other female relative, of the girl (Jackson 1830 b : 28). At least some marriages were arranged by the mothers (Jackson 1830 b : 28 ; Morgan 1901(1) : 312–313 ; Randle 1951: 170). The arrangement of marriages by the mothers may have been advantageous to the couple : women saw more of the young girls and could judge their characteristics (Parker 1910 b : 31). At the present time, mothers do not choose spouses for their children (Shimony 1961 a : 225).

the couple were invited. When all were assembled and seated according to rank around the house, the father of the girl or the master of ceremonies deputed to the office announced that the couple was being married and that that was the reason for the gathering and that the feast was prepared for the enjoyment of all. All greeted this with approval, ate of the kettle, and left (S 122–123).[37]

The parents of the girl desired that the suitor have not only a good address and be well painted and adorned, but also that he be bold in hunting, war, and fishing and capable of supporting the girl (S 123). For example, in one instance, an Indian made love to a girl and because she could not get her father's consent to the marriage, the boy carried her off and took her for a wife. There ensued a great quarrel and the girl was taken from him and returned to her father. The father had objected that the boy could not do anything, "though he amused himself with cooking in the French way and did not make a practice of hunting." In order to prove himself, the boy went fishing and caught a number of fish. Then the girl was given to him and he took her to his house (S 124).

Many young men had not wives (*aténonha*), but companions (*asqua*), because the marriage ceremony had not been performed. They lived together for as long as they wished, their relationship not hindering their freely seeing other friends, male or female, without fear of reproach. Premarital sex relationships were not frowned upon (S 121–122). When the girl became pregnant, the various lovers would come to her, each saying that the child was his. From them, she chose the one she liked best (C 139–140).

Probably both matrilocal and patrilocal residence were practiced by the Huron. The cases in the Relations do not indicate matrilocal residence (JR 13. 11; 17: 165, 19: 85, 147; cf. JR 13: 199—the case of a woman living in Huronia with her husband; she was of a strange nation "and spoke a language that I did not understand so well").[38]

---

[37] Jackson (1830 b: 29) and Mary Jemison (Seaver 1824: 180) also report that a present was given by the boy to the girl or her father. Powell (1881: 64) reports that presents were given by the man to the girl's mother and that a feast was part of the customary procedure among the Wyandot. Iroquois custom was for a girl to cook 20 cakes of boiled cornbread with berries in them, or a different number of cakes made by other recipes. These were taken to the house of the man where they were distributed among friends and relatives, and a feast made of them and meat provided by the father or male relatives of the young man. His mother filled the basket which contained the cakes with meat, and the girl's relatives later feasted on this gift (Waugh 1916: 82, 85–87; see also Morgan 1901(1): 313). This wedding bread (see note 14, p. 70) is still remembered by the Iroquois (Shimony 1961 a: 227).

[38] One supposes that marriage was matrilocal when the old longhouse was still in use, the members of the matrilineally related families living in one longhouse, although there probably were exceptions. With the change in house type, there may have occurred a change in rule of residence. Powell (1881: 64) says that the Wyandot couple resided matrilocally for a short time. Fenton (1951 b: 43) reports that the Iroquois couple now moves in with the set of parents that has room for them and that they move out as soon as they are able to build a house. He also suggests that residence may have been patrilocal in those marriages that were arranged by the mothers.

DESCENT

The father's successors and heirs were the children of his sisters, not his own children (C 140; S 130). The Jesuit statement that the chieftainship usually went to the deceased chief's *nephew* or grandson (JR 10:233) seems to indicate that they were matrilineal, as does their statement, "There have been near relatives, such as *nephews*, who at the death of their *uncles* did all they could to make them say that it was we who made them die . . . to solace themselves for the death of persons whom they tenderly cherished" (JR 17:123: italics mine). Also indicating matrilineal descent is the statement that a niece was a surer support for a man than were his own children (JR 26:297).[39]

The presence of clans is difficult to ascertain from the Relations. The Jesuits' mention that each family had a distinct armorial bearing, as a deer, snake, crow, or the thunder (JR 15:181) may indicate clans. The eight chiefs, "from the eight nations that constitute the Huron country" (JR 33:243; cf. JR 33:247 for another reference to this "eight") mentioned in the giving of gifts for reparation of the murder of a Frenchman may be an indication that there were eight clans (see note 82, p. 55).

KINSHIP TERMS

The following are some Huron kinship terms (from S 71, 85) :[40]

aystan (*yaistan*)—my father; sometimes used to address old men. [cf. below, *aistan* (JR 10:267)]
sendoné—my mother
houatinoron (*honratinoron*)—my uncle
ataquen (*attaquen*) (*ataquon*)—my brother
earassé (*sarassé*)—my cousin
ayein—my son [cf. below, *aien* (JR 10:267)]
hiuoittan (*hinoittan*)—my nephew [cf. above *chouatan* (JR 13:69)]
yatoro—my friend, my companion, my comrade, i.e., those of no relationship
eadsé—my kind friend, my companion; used to address girls
garihouanne—great chief

DEATH

The Huron was expected to be courageous in the face of approaching death. If the man was dying slowly of natural causes, he was often shown the clothing, the robe, leggings, moccasins, and belt, in which he was to be buried, and frequently he was prepared for burial

---

[39] There is very little material in the 17th-century accounts that indicates the Huron had matrilineal descent. As the Wyandot (Powell 1881: 59 ff.) and the Iroquois are matrilineal, the Huron probably were also—the few statements in the early reports only tend to support this contention.

[40] The terms for "cousin" and "uncle" probably mean "cross cousin" and "mother's brother," respectively (see Morgan 1871: 291–382).

before he expired (JR 10: 267; 13: 251).[41] One man, having been to the land of the dead and wishing to be dressed as the people there, had his entire face painted red and had brought and placed over him the finest articles he had. He was also given his plate and spoon. Thus he died (JR 17: 153).

A dying man often made a farewell feast for his friends, at which he partook of the best, and, sometimes at this feast, would sing [his war song] [42] without showing any dread of death (JR 10: 61, 267; 15: 67). To it were invited all the dying man's friends and important people, a total of about 100 participants (JR 34: 113).

Apparently a man might dream when he would die. One sick man, a chief, asked what the weather was and was told it was snowing. To this he replied, "I shall not die, then, today, for I am not to depart from this life except in fine weather" (JR 13: 213). In another case, a woman said that she would not die for 8 days and so it happened (JR 10: 13).[43]

As soon as the man had died, he was placed in a flexed position, "in a crouching posture, almost the same that a child has in its mother's womb" (JR 10: 267). The body was wrapped rather tightly in his finest robe and then placed on the mat on which he had died (S 205) or wrapped in furs and covered with tree bark (C 160). Someone remained with the body until it was taken to be buried (S 205).[44] The dead were painted (JR 38: 253).

The mourners wept, cried, groaned, and wailed to express their grief. The children cried *aistan* if the deceased was their father; the mother, *aien, aien,* 'my son, my son' (JR 10: 267). After the chief had been told of the death, he or his assistant went around the village saying, "All take courage, *etsagon, etsagon,* and all prepare the best feast you can, for such a one who has died."[45] Then each man prepared the finest feast he could with what material he could and sent a portion of it out to all the relatives and friends. This feast was called *agochin atiskein,* the feast of souls (S 205). After the chief had gone through the houses announcing the death, friends arrived and there was more weeping (JR 10: 267). Only the women and girls wept and lamented and they began and ended it on order of the chief or master of ceremonies. When the signal was given, all began to weep and lament and added to their sorrow by reciting the names

---

[41] Similarly, today the "dead clothes" of a dying person, the clothes in which he will be buried, are hung in his sight. In the past, he was dressed in them just before he died (Shimony 1961 a: 236; Morgan 1901(1): 168 also mentions dressing the body in its best clothes and painting the face).

[42] See note 46, p. 39.

[43] A similar, but by no means identical, belief of the Iroquois is that a sign, often a bird, indicates approaching death (Shimony 1961 a: 234).

[44] Similarly, today, the corpse should not be left alone (Shimony 1961 a: 237).

[45] Today, a messenger goes around to tell of the death and invite people to the wake, including a "midnight lunch" (Shimony 1961 a: 237).

of all their dead, saying, "And my father is dead, and my mother is dead, and my cousin is dead" and so with the rest of their dead. All burst into tears except the little girls. When there had been enough weeping, the chief said, "It's enough, stop weeping" and they all stopped. The men did not do this, but put on a mournful and melancholy look with their heads sunk on their knees (S 206). Often, at this time, someone of importance spoke in praise of the deceased, lauding his patience, his good nature, his liberality, his magnificence, and, if he had been a warrior, his courage (JR 10: 267).[46]

BURIAL

Other villages were told of the death. Each family had someone who took care of its dead and these came as soon as possible to take charge of everything and to determine the day of the funeral. The burial, usually on the third day, began with a feast, in order to feed the guests from other villages, to feed the deceased, and to provide an occasion for the exchange of food to console each other. At this feast, all the food that was not eaten was distributed (JR 10: 269).[47]

After the chief published throughout the village that the body was about to be borne to the cemetery, the village assembled and wept again.[48] The corpse was then put on a mat, covered with a beaver robe, and carried by four men to the cemetery [*agosayé* (S 75)], which was usually a harquebus-shot from the village. All followed in silence. At the cemetery had been constructed a tomb 8 to 10 feet high made of bark, supported on four posts, and somewhat painted. Before the corpse was put into it and before the bark was arranged, the chief presented the gifts: kettles, axes, beaver robes, wampum collars, and the like. If the deceased had been a person of importance, the chiefs of the other villages also presented gifts. These gifts were not placed in the grave, however, but rather, sometimes, only a wampum collar, comb, gourd of oil, tomahawks, and two or three little loaves of bread would be left there, and the tomb closed. Most of the gifts were distributed among the relatives "to dry their tears"; the remainder went to those who directed the funeral ceremonies, as a reward for their trouble. These were distributed by an official standing on a tree trunk. Everything he received he lifted up to be seen by all and said, "Here is such-and-such, that so-and-so has given to dry the tears of so-and-so," and then put it into the hands of the deceased's widow or other nearest relative. Often, while this was

---

[46] Correspondingly, in present practice, after the meal and before the final rites, a speaker comes to the house and again consoles the mourners in a formal address (Shimony 1961 a : 243).

[47] Similarly, among modern Iroquois, a meal is served at noon to the gravediggers and mourners on the day of the burial (Shimony 1961 a : 243).

[48] See footnote 45, p. 129.

going on, two round sticks, each 1 foot long and not quite as thick as an arm, were thrown from the top of the bier. One on one side was for the young men, the other for the girls. [Perhaps, sometimes only one stick, for the boys, was used (cf. JR 10: 271).] A prize of some robes or some hatchets that had been set aside for the youth were offered to the person who could take the stick away: was able to lift it in the air in his hands. In the game which followed, the youths in a body fell on the one who had been given the stick by the chief, and much violence ensued in attempts to snatch it from one another's hands. It sometimes lasted an hour (JR 10: 269–271; S 207–208).[49]

During the entire ceremony, the mother or wife of the deceased man was at the foot of the grave calling to the dead man with singing or frequently complaining in a lugubrious voice (JR 10: 271).

Not all bodies were put into the tomb raised on four posts. A few bodies were buried in the ground, and over them a hut or shrine of bark was built (C 160–161; S 208). Around it was erected a hedge of stakes fixed in the ground, out of honor for the dead and to protect the burial house from dogs and wild animals (S 208).[50] If fire broke out in the village and in the cemetery, the fire in the cemetery was extinguished first (JR 39: 31; S 209).

The Huron were lavish in providing the dead with the proper clothing and the guests with gifts and food. Much time and effort were directed to this end (JR 10: 265; 23: 31). The Jesuits had seen several strip themselves of almost all their possessions by giving presents to the souls of several of their dead friends (JR 8: 121; cf. S 213). Gifts were also given to console a person; he did not consider himself comforted if he was given nothing but words (JR 14: 27).

---

[49] The distribution of the property of the deceased to relatives and friends and to those who helped during the wake, funeral, and 10-day feast, now occurs during the 10-day feast (see note 53, p. 133). Those who attend this ceremony usually contribute food for this feast (Shimony 1961 a: 247–250; Fenton 1953: 8). This method of distribution may be relatively recent. Jackson (1830 b: 30) records that the Iroquois said formerly when a distinguished man died, his possessions were not buried with him but kept for a year or more. Then at a council they were held up and those present told they were the goods of the deceased chief. Then any young man who wished could come forward and snatch the object away. In this fashion, the goods were distributed. Perhaps another comparable Iroquois custom is that of snatching cakes held up by some marchers as part of the 'ohgiwe ceremony (Fenton and Kurath 1951: 152). It also is possible that the game now played at the wake (Shimony 1961 a: 238–240) was once used to distribute the possessions of the deceased.

[50] The Iroquois also practiced scaffold burial (Morgan 1901(1): 166–167; Shimony 1961 a: 241) although now burial is interment in a grave, in a coffin. Beauchamp (1905: 116–117) thought that Morgan's statement, that the Iroquois had scaffold burial, referred to the Huron and to Huron influence on the Seneca. It also is said that Iroquois practice used to be to abandon the corpse in the house (Fenton 1946: 118 n.; Morgan 1901(1): 167) or in a shack (Shimony 1961 a: 241) or small bark house made for that purpose (Morgan 1901(1): 167; cf. also Curtin and Hewitt 1918: 458–460).

The use of the stockade around graves also seems to be older Iroquois practice (Beauchamp 1905: 117–118). Jackson (1830 b: 27) mentions that each grave had a separate covering of boards or clefts of wood.

If a man was killed in war, his relatives made presents to their patrons to encourage them to organize a group of warriors to avenge the death (JR 10:271-273).

Some unusual modes of death were treated in different ways.[51] If a person died by drowning or by freezing, the neighboring villages gathered and feasted. Many presents, double the usual number, were given. The corpse was stretched out on a mat at the cemetery, between a ditch on one side and a fire on the other. Some young men chosen by the deceased's relatives cut off the fleshy parts of the body which had been marked with a coal by the protector of the dead person. This flesh and the entrails were then thrown into the fire and the body, stripped of its flesh, was thrown into the ditch. Women walked several times around the men who were cutting up the body, encouraged them to render this good service to the whole country, and put wampum beads into their mouths. Sometimes the mother of the deceased, crying, joined the group and sang in a pitiful tone, lamenting the death of her son. The ceremony was performed to appease the Sky or the Lake who was believed to be angry. If it was not performed, disastrous changes of weather and accompanying accidents would follow as a result of its anger. In one instance, a man drowned at the beginning of November and was buried on the 17th without any ceremony. On that same day a heavy snow fell that stayed on the ground all winter: the result of the Indians not having performed the ceremony to cut up the body (JR 10 : 163-165, 273).

A Huron who died a violent death was burned or buried immediately, often while still half alive. His bones, as well as the bones of those who died from cold, were not removed from the grave and reburied at the Feast of the Dead, as the Huron believed that those who died in war, by shipwreck, etc., had no communication in the afterlife with other souls (JR 39:31).

If a person died outside of Huronia, the Indians burned the body and extracted the bones to take back with them (JR 11:131).[52]

If a young baby, less than a month or two old, died, it was buried by the road, in order that it might enter a woman's womb and be reborn (JR 10: 273; cf. JR 15: 183—"They believe that souls enter bodies after death").

For years, one woman kept in her house the body of her dead son (JR 39:29).

---

[51] These special modes of burial may be related to the Iroquois rites to expel from the houses the souls of murdered enemies, witches, or those who died unnatural, suicidal, or violent deaths as mentioned by Hewitt (1895 b : 107).

[52] Compare the present Iroquois belief that "death in a foreign land is considered punishment for past sins or an evil life" and the strong feeling that "the body should be brought home" (Shimony 1961 a : 234).

MOURNING

For 10 days after the funeral, the spouse of the deceased lay on mats, covered with furs with his face against the ground. He or she did not speak or answer except to say *cway* (cf. *chay* in Appendix 3) to those who came to visit them, did not warm himself even in winter, ate cold food, did not go to feasts, and went out only at night for necessities. During this time, a handful of hair was cut from the back of the head (JR 10: 273–275).[53] The women wailed, especially in the morning just before daybreak, for entire weeks. Widows, in addition to this wailing, did not adorn themselves or bathe or anoint themselves, had dishevelled hair, and observed a sullen silence (JR 39: 29).[54]

As fish did not like the dead, a Huron did not go fishing when one of his friends had died (JR 10: 167).

This period was followed by a year of lesser mourning. When the Huron went visiting, they did not make any salutation, not even saying *cway* and they did not grease their hair (JR 10: 275). When a woman was in mourning, she did not visit anyone, walked with head and eyes lowered, was ill-clad and ill-combed, and had a dirty face, sometimes further blackened with charcoal (JR 29: 285). However, her mother might say otherwise and command her to grease her hair and go to feasts. Remarriage did not take place for a year after the death; otherwise the person "would be talked about" (JR 10: 275).[55]

The women, especially, frequently went to mourn at the tombs of the dead outside the village (JR 39: 31).

The Huron believed that the soul did not immediately abandon the body after death. When the corpse was taken to the grave, the soul

---

[53] Ten days of deep mourning is still prescribed by the Iroquois. This mourning ends with the 10-day feast, although lesser mourning obligations remain on the spouse and ritual friends (Shimony 1961 a : 245). Until this feast, the spouse of the deceased is distraught and "untidy" and ought not to talk to anyone. To symbolize the end of the mourning, a matrilineal relative combs the hair of the mourner with a new comb and gives him material for new clothes, as he has been said to have rent his clothing (Shimony 1961 a : 248). The feast itself marks the final departure of the dead from the earth (Shimony 1961 a : 245 ; see note 63, p. 140). Mary Jemison said that a fire was built at the head of the grave for 10 nights, after which the deceased had reached the end of his journey (Seaver 1824 : 182 ; see also Beauchamp 1922 : 238 ; Jackson 1830 b : 27 ; Morgan 1901(1) : 168 for other early and similar references to such customs). The Wyandot also had a feast at the graves of the deceased (Finley 1840 : 52).

[54] At present, also, the spouse occasionally does not end his mourning at the 10-day feast (Shimony 1961 a : 248). It may have been against this extended mourning that Handsome Lake preached (Parker 1913 : 57 ; Shimony 1961 a : 245).

[55] This period of lesser mourning, during which the mourner should not participate in pleasurable social events, now lasts until the next long ceremonial, either Green Corn or Midwinter, or at the most half a year. During these ceremonials, the mourner is released in a special ritual and is free to remarry. There is still, however, a feast held on the anniversary of the death (Shimony 1961 a : 250–251). It is not unlikely that in the past the surviving spouse was free to remarry after this latter observance (cf. Curtin and Hewitt 1918 : 459–460).

walked in front and remained in the cemetery until the Feast of the Dead. At night, it walked through the villages and entered the houses. There it took part in the feasts and ate what was left at evening in the kettle.[56] For this reason, many did not eat the left-over food the following morning and some did not attend feasts given for the souls of the dead because they thought they would die if they ate of the food for the dead (JR 10: 143). Feasts to honor the dead were given from time to time throughout the village (JR 10: 275; S 84).[57] [For giving the name of the deceased to another, see above under "Chiefs".]

The greatest insult that could be said to a man was, "Your father, mother, or kinsmen are dead." Merely to say, "Your dead," was the most horrible of all curses and was capable of bringing one person to blows with another. As to speak a dead man's name was a cruel insult, if he had to be mentioned, "deceased" was added at the end. For this reason, when someone died in the village, the chiefs promptly announced the fact in a loud voice through the village, so that he might no longer be named without "the late." If anyone in the same village had the same name as the deceased, he changed it for some time in order not to irritate the wound of the afflicted relatives (JR 39:33).

FEAST OF THE DEAD [58]

The Feast of the Dead was given approximately every 8, 10, or 12 years (JR 10:143, 275; JR 39:31; C 161; S 211).[59] At this time the bodies of those that had died since the last Feast of the Dead were

---

[56] The dead among the Iroquois are supposed to attend dances and feasts, especially the *'ohgiwe* ceremonies given for them (Fenton and Kurath 1951: 161–162; Shimony 1961 a: 229); and Waugh (1916: 47–48) reports that food dropped during a meal is not picked up; it is for the dead.

[57] These feasts were probably the feasts for giving the name of the deceased to another. But it is also possible that a ceremonial similar to the present Iroquois *'ohgiwe* ceremony which is given annually or semiannually for the dead (Jackson 1830 b: 28; Fenton and Kurath 1951; Shimony 1961 a: 231–233) or to other rites for the dead (Shimony 1961 a: 279–281) is being referred to. The Wyandot also held feasts for the dead (Finley 1840: 58).

[58] The Feast of the Dead in connection with ossuary burial was a distinctively western Iroquoian (Huron and Neutral) custom and was not an eastern Iroquoian (the Iroquois proper) one. The best evidence for this distribution is archeological: ossuary burials are found in the territory occupied by the western Iroquoians and are not found in the territory formerly occupied by the Iroquois.

Various students of the Iroquois have suggested Iroquois ceremonials that are comparable to the Huron Feast of the Dead. Hale (1883: 73; see also Fenton and Kurath 1951: 143 for a similar suggestion by Simeon Gibson) states that the Iroquois Condolence Ceremony replaced the "wasteful" Huron ceremony, a contention that seems unlikely in view of the fact that the Huron apparently also had a Condolence Ceremony and that the two ceremonies were given for two different reasons. The object of the Condolence Ceremony is to "raise the dead," to transfer the title of a deceased person to his successor, and the purpose of the Feast of the Dead was to collect and rebury together the bones of those who had died since the last ceremonial. However, both rituals are concerned with the dead and they share certain symbols. For example, when the chiefs chant the Eulogy of the dead chiefs and the Roll Call of the Founders of the League in the Iroquois Condolence Ceremony,

(Footnote continued at bottom of next page.)

taken from the cemeteries and reburied in a common pit. Each chief made the feast for the souls of his village; the largest and most magnificent was given by the master of the feast. Usually each nation had its own ceremony, but at the one that the Jesuits attended five villages held a separate ceremony and put their dead into a separate pit (JR 10: 261, 279–281). It was held in the spring of 1636 (JR 10: 289). Neighboring tribes were notified so that those who wished that town to be the burying-place of their relatives' bones might bring them and those who wished might come to the festival (S 211). As all were welcomed and feasted during the ceremony, they came in very large numbers and there was continual feasting and dancing (C 161–162; S 211) for 10 days (C 162).

Although the ceremonial had many parts, the principal ceremony was that of the kettle. Thus, the Feast of the Dead was usually referred to as "the kettle" and the terms of cooking were used in

---

they are said to be symbolically carrying the bones of the dead chief on their backs (Fenton and Kurath 1951: 144). The cry *haii hai* also occurs in both (note 60, p. 137).

The other Iroquois ceremonial which has been identified with the Huron Feast of the Dead is the semiannual or annual *'ohgiwe* ceremony (Fenton and Kurath 1951: 143). As was the Huron Feast of the Dead, this Iroquois ceremonial is concerned with placating the decreased members of the community. But there are some differences: the *'ohgiwe* ceremony is concerned with all the dead, while the Feast of the Dead was concerned with the recent dead (i.e., those who had died since the last such ceremonial) and the *'ohgiwe* ceremony is given twice (or at least once) a year, while the Feast of the Dead was given at intervals of 8 to 12 years. Such differences may indicate that the two ceremonials are quite distinct.

The *'ohgiwe* ceremony is probably related to other annual feasts for the dead among North American Indians. Unfortunately, there has been no comprehensive study of the distribution of this trait (at least to my knowledge), and there are some intrinsic difficulties in making such a study. Not only is the data spotty and difficult to obtain, but often there is a question as to whether the ritual is pre-Columbian or whether it was derived from the Catholic observance of All Souls' Day (see, for example, Walker 1949 and Kurath 1950). It seems most likely, however, that the ritual is pre-Columbian in at least most instances. It is entirely possible that the Huron had such a ceremonial that the French did not happen to describe, although they may have alluded to it (see note 57, p. 134).

The Huron Feast of the Dead probably is an elaboration of certain Iroquoian ideas regarding the dead (this is Hale's and Fenton and Kurath's real point), and particularly a concern with the bones of the dead—a trait widespread in the Southeast. The timing of the Huron ceremonial, every 8, 10, or 12 years, suggests that it might have been held whenever a village was about to move and the people wished to tell their dead. At least, the lapse of time between Feasts of the Dead is approximately that indicated by the French for the length of time a village site was occupied and the Iroquois in recent times also have felt that a feast for the dead should be held to inform the dead when the village moved (Fenton and Kurath 1951: 143–144; cf. Morgan's (1901(1): 167) statement: "After the lapse of a number of years, or in a season of public insecurity, or on the eve of abandoning a settlement, it was customary to collect these skeletons from the whole community around, and consign them to a common resting place"). The Huron and Neutral probably elaborated this idea—that the dead should be informed—and combined it with ossuary burial, a trait, as that of concern for the bones of the dead, that is common in the Southeast. It is also possible that the Huron ceremonial became more elaborate after European contact (Fenton 1940 d: 176, 191).

The Feast of the Dead practiced by some Algonquians probably was modeled after the Huron ceremonial, as Hickerson (1960) suggests, and is not evidence that the Huron ceremonial had a northern origin.

[59] Hunter (1893: 228) has pointed out that too many ossuaries dating between 1615 and 1649 have been found in Huronia for the ceremony to have taken place this infrequently. However, it is possible that the French correctly state the interval between Feasts of the Dead, but incorrectly state that it was given by each nation. It may have been given by each village or group of related villages.

reference to it: in speaking of hastening or delaying, they spoke of scattering or of stirring up the fire beneath the kettle and, in speaking of holding no Feast of the Dead, they would say that "the kettle is overturned" (JR 10:279).

In order to decide on the time that the feast would be held and what other nations should be invited, the old and important men of the country assembled. After they had made these decisions, each family went to get the bodies so that they could bring them to the village where they were to be reburied in a common grave. In each village on a particular day, the people went to the cemetery where the *aiheonde* (those who took care of the graves) removed the bodies from the tombs and the relatives wept as they had on the day of the funeral. On some of these bodies, the flesh was gone and only skin remained on the bones; others looked as if they had been dried and smoked, and others were still swarming with worms. After the bodies had been exposed for a while, they were covered with quite new beaver robes. Next, the corpses were stripped of their flesh, and the flesh and skin, and the robes and mats in which the deceased had been buried were thrown into the fire. Recently dead bodies were left as they were and simply covered with new robes. If, while cleaning the bones, a charm (as, for example, a turtle's egg with a leather strap or a little turtle the size of a nut) was found, they said that the deceased had been bewitched (JR 10: 281–285; C 161).

After the bones had been well cleaned and washed by the women, they were wrapped in fine new beaver skins. Relatives and friends contributed glass beads and wampum necklaces to the bundle, saying, "Here, this is what I am giving for the bones of my father, my mother, my uncle, cousin, or other relative." The bundle was then put into a new bag decorated at the top with many little ornaments, with neck-laces, bracelets and other things, to carry on their backs. The whole bodies were carried on a type of litter. All these were taken back to the village where each family made a feast for its dead (JR 10: 283–287; S 211–212). Skins, tomahawks, kettles, and other valuable articles, and much food then were carried to the appointed place. The bags and skins were hung in the house of the hosts and the food put together to be used for the feasts on the day when all were to be buried (C 161; S 212). Fishing nets were not left in the houses, for they would be profaned by the corpses there during the Feast of the Dead (JR 10: 169).

A very large and deep grave, 10 fathoms square (C 162), capable of containing all the bones, furniture, and skins offered to the dead, was dug outside the village. A high scaffolding was erected along the edge and all the bags of bones carried to it. Then the grave was lined on the bottom and sides with new beaver skins and robes. On the skins and robes the chiefs made a bed of tomahawks, then kettles, beads, necklaces, and bracelets of wampum and other gifts (S 212), as knives and sword blades (C 163). When this had been done, the bags of bones were emptied into the grave from the top of the scaffold. The grave then was covered with more new skins, then with tree bark (S 212), and finally with earth and big pieces of wood. Wooden poles were sunk into the ground around the grave and a covering put over it (C 163; S 212). A feast followed, after which all returned to the places from which they came (S 212).

In the village in which the Jesuits were, the bones were brought to one of the largest houses a day or so before setting out for the Feast of the Dead. One portion was hung on the poles of house and the other spread out through it. The chief made a magnificient feast in the name of the deceased chief whose name he bore. At this feast, the chief sang the song of the deceased chief, as the latter had, before he died, expressed the desire to have it sung on this occasion. The presents (robes, wampum collars, and kettles) that the relatives brought were hung on poles on both sides of the house. All the guests shared with one another whatever good things they had, and even took these home, contrary to the usual custom at feasts. In order to compliment the host, at the end of the feast the people imitated the cry of souls and left the house crying *haéé, haé* (JR 10: 287–289).[60]

The 7 or 8 days before the Feast of the Dead were spent in assembling the souls, and in the arrival of strangers [foreigners]. During this time, presents were made to the youth in honor of the dead. The women shot with a bow for a prize—a porcupine girdle or a collar or string of wampum—and the young men shot at a stick to see who could hit it for a prize of an ax, some knives, or a beaver robe (JR 10: 289–291).

From day to day more souls arrived at the village where they were to be reburied. Some of these processions had 200 or 300 people in them, each with his souls (bones) in parcels under a robe on his back. Some had arranged their parcels in the form of a man, ornamented with wampum collars and elegant bands of long red fur. When the procession left their village, they cried out *haéé, haé* and repeated this cry of the souls along the way. If they did not do this, the burden would weigh heavily on their backs and cause them a backache for the rest of their lives. The procession moved slowly: the village in which the Jesuits lived took 3 days to go the 4 leagues to Ossossané where the ceremonies took place. When they came near a village, they cried *haéé, haé*. The entire village came out to meet them and gifts were given. Each person went to one of the houses while the chiefs held a

---

[60] Hewitt (1898; 1917: 325; 1918: 544; see also Beauchamp 1907: 353) thought that this cry was the same as the *haii hai* used in the present Iroquois Condolence ritual.

council and discussed how long the group should remain in the village (JR 10: 291).

After they had arrived in Ossossané and when they were about to begin the ceremony, they took down the packages of bones from the poles, opened them to say their last farewell and cried again. One woman, the daughter of an influential chief, combed her father's hair, caressed his bones one by one, and put his council sticks beside him. She put bracelets of wampum and glass beads on the arms of her deceased children and bathed their bones with tears (JR 10: 293).

After the last farewell, there was a procession [probably of the village] to the pit. The person who bore the bones of the above-mentioned chief walked at the head of the procession, followed by the men and then the women. The pit was about 10 feet deep and 5 brasses wide. Around it was a well-made scaffold, 9 to 10 brasses wide and from 9 to 10 feet high. Above this, a number of poles were laid across with crosspoles to which the packages of souls were hung and bound. The preceding day the whole bodies had been laid under the scaffold at the edge of the pit on bark or mats fastened to stakes about the height of a man; later in the feast they were put in the bottom of the pit (JR 10: 293–295).

The people arrived about 1 o'clock in the afternoon and grouped themselves by families and villages. They laid their parcels on the ground and, unfolding their parcels of robes and all the presents they had brought, hung them on the poles that were from 5 to 600 toises [60a] in length. As many as 1,200 presents remained on view for 2 hours so that the strangers could see the wealth of the country. Approximately 2,000 people were there. About 3 o'clock, everyone put away his articles and folded up his robes (JR 10: 295).

Each chief then gave a signal and all, loaded with their packages of souls, ascended to the scaffold by ladders and hung them on the crosspoles. That done, all the ladders were taken away. A few chiefs remained and spent the rest of the afternoon (until 7 o'clock) announcing the presents that had been made in the name of the dead to particular persons. "This," they said, "is what such and such a dead man gives to such and such a relative." About 5 or 6 o'clock, they lined the bottom and sides of the pit with fine large new robes, each of 10 beaver skins, in such a way that they extended more than a foot out of it. As they were doing this, some went to the bottom of the pit and brought up handfuls of sand so that they might be successful at play.[61] Of the 1,200 presents that had been displayed, 48 robes were used to

---

[60a] A toise is 6.396 feet. The figure of 600 toises would seem to contain a typographical error.

[61] Compare the recorded Iroquois belief that if a person dies holding a secret, one may discover it by sleeping on the ground with a handful of grave dirt beneath his head and the belief that a bone from the grave of some celebrated runner will help a man become a swift runner (Parker 1913: 30 n.).

line the bottom and sides of the pit. Each entire body was covered with one or two robes in addition to that in which it was wrapped (JR 10: 295–297).

At 7 o'clock, the whole bodies were put into the pit to the accompaniment of great confusion and a great din of voices. Ten or twelve were in the pit arranging the bodies all around it. Three large kettles were placed in the very middle of the pit; inasmuch as one had a hole in it, another had no handle, and the third kettle was of scarcely more value, they were of use only to souls. There were very few wampum collars (JR 10: 297).

Everyone spent the night near the pit. They lighted their fires and hung their kettles (JR 10: 299).

The bones were to be thrown into the pit at daybreak. However, one of the souls fell by itself into the pit and the noise awakened the crowd, which immediately ran and climbed onto the scaffold, emptying the packages into the pit, but keeping the robes in which the bones were wrapped. After a while, the noise ceased and the people began to sing in sorrowful voices (JR 10: 299).

Five or six in the pit arranged the bones with poles as they were thrown in. When the pit was full, to within about 2 feet, they turned back over the bones the robes which lined the edge of the pit and covered the remaining space with mats and bark. Then the pit was covered with sand, poles and wooden stakes, thrown in without any order. Some women brought dishes of corn to the pit. On that day and on succeeding days, several houses of the village brought nets full of corn which they threw on the pit (JR 10: 299–301).

The entire morning was spent giving gifts. The greater part of the robes in which the bones had been wrapped were cut into pieces and thrown from the scaffold into the crowd for any one who could get them. Two or three people would get hold of a beaver skin and, as none would give it away, it was cut into many pieces. One man did not trouble to run after the skins, but offered tobacco to those fighting over a skin and so settled the matter to his own advantage (JR 10: 301).

The 1,200 presents that had been displayed were distributed as follows. The pit lining consisted of 48 robes. Each whole body had its robe and some had two or three. The master of the feast received 20 to thank the nations which had participated. The dead distributed a number of them through the chiefs to their living friends. Some served only for show and were taken away by those who had exhibited them. The old and important men in the country who managed the feast secretly took possession of a number of the robes. The rest were cut into pieces and thrown to the crowd (JR 10: 303).

By means of this ceremony the Indians confirmed their friendships, saying that as the bones of their deceased relatives and friends were united in one place, so they would live together in the same unity and harmony (C 162; S 213–214).

The Huron believed in the immortality of the soul (cf. C 163) which they thought to be corporeal; this soul was a body as large as that which it animated and was divisible (JR 8:121; 10:141–143). Further, they felt that dogs, deer, fish, and other animals had immortal and reasonable souls (JR 8:121).

The Huron believed that souls entered other bodies after death (JR 15:183). After the Feast of the Dead, one of the two souls of the deceased person remained in the pit and did not leave it unless a woman bore it again as a child. A proof of this rebirth was the resemblance of some living persons to dead ones. This idea indicates why the bones of the dead were called *atisken*, 'the souls' (JR 10: 141, 287). The soul separated from the body was denoted *esken* (JR 10: 141).[62]

The Huron believed that the other of the two souls of an individual left the cemetery at the Feast of the Dead.[63] Some said that these souls changed into turtledoves which later were hunted with bow and arrow in the woods and then broiled and eaten (JR 10:143, 287; cf. C 163—some believed in the immortality of the soul while others said that after death they would go to a place where they would sing like crows).[64] The most common belief, however, was that after the ceremony they, covered with the robes and collars which had been put into the grave for them, went to a great village in the west (JR 10:143, 287 [*ahahabreti onaskenonteta*, the place where the souls of the dead went (JR 13:251)]). It was also said that the souls, which were immortal, left the body and went at once to *Iouskeha* and his grandmother *Aataentsic* [see below], by way of the Milky Way, which they designated *atiskein andahatey*, 'the path of the souls.'[65] The souls of dogs always went by the way of certain stars near the souls' path, called *gagnenon andahatey*, 'the path of the dogs' (S 172).

---

[62] Compare *eskanane*, 'land of the souls' (Beauchamp 1922: 158). This and the other words for soul given in Appendix 3 are discussed by Hewitt (1902: 44–45; see also Hewitt 1895 b : 112–115; Shimony 1961 a : 229).

[63] The Iroquois also believe that the ghost spirit remains around while the main soul goes to the land of the dead in the west (Speck 1949: 120; Fenton and Kurath 1951: 144–145), although this belief is not well formalized (Shimony 1961 a : 229). The soul does not leave until after the 10-day feast (Shimony 1961 a: 236–237; Parker 1913: 61 n.).

[64] Compare Morgan's (1901(1) : 168) statement that in ancient times, a captured bird was freed over the grave after burial to bear away the spirit.

[65] The Iroquois also believe that the souls travel along the Milky Way to the land of the dead (Morgan 1901(2) : 253; Parker 1913: 62 n.; Shimony 1961 a : 229).

Each nation had its own village. Thus, if a soul of an Algonquin was bold enough to present itself at the village of the Bear Nation's souls, it would not be well received. The old people and the little children, not having as strong legs as the others, did not make the journey (for old people cf. JR 14: 51), but remained in the country, where they had their own villages. Some said that they had heard the noise of their house doors and the voices of the children chasing birds in the fields. These souls sowed corn in the fields the living had abandoned and, if a village took fire, they collected the roasted corn and laid it in as part of their provisions (JR 10: 143–145).

The souls of those who had died in battle formed a band of themselves, for the others feared them and did not allow them into the village.[66] Suicides also were not allowed to enter the village (JR 10: 145).[67]

Some had seen souls going to their village in the west. The road to this village was broad and well-beaten and passed near a rock named *ecaregniondi*, which was often found marked with the paint they used on their faces (JR 10: 145). On this road was a house in which lived *oscotarach* ("Pierce-head"), who drew the brains out of the heads of the dead and kept them.[68] There was also a river across which the only bridge was a tree trunk; it was guarded by a dog who jumped at many souls and made them fall into the water and drown (JR 10: 147).[69]

The land of the dead was known to the Huron from the reports of those who had died and who had been brought back to life (JR 10: 147; 13: 153). They said that the village of the souls was like the village of the living; that the souls went hunting, fishing, and to the woods, and that axes, robes, and collars were highly valued there (JR 10: 147). The souls in the afterlife needed to drink, eat, clothe

---

[66] This may be related to the present Iroquois belief that death in a foreign land is considered punishment for past sins (see note 52, p. 132).

[67] Kirkland also said that the Iroquois who were suicides, as well as those who had been disobedient to the councils of the chiefs, and those who put away their wives because of pregnancy, were not admitted to the afterworld (Beauchamp 1922 : 158; cf. note 51, p. 132). The Iroquois today believe in a heaven and a hell, the one governed by the Great Spirit (Creator) and the other by the Evil Spirit (i.e., the Devil, in Western thought) (Morgan 1901(1) : 163), but it is difficult to know how much of these beliefs were introduced by Handsome Lake, who did make use of Christian elements (Shimony 1961 a: 204–205; Parker 1913: passim; Deardorff 1951). Jackson's (1830 b: 23) implication that one went to the land of the dead if one's conduct had been orderly and his mention of a Great Spirit and an Evil Spirit indicate that perhaps these basic dualistic ideas were already present in Iroquois culture, although there is always the question of how much of Christian beliefs Christians read into other eschatologies. The most probable interpretation on the basis of this material is that there was in Iroquoian cultures a belief that certain individuals did not go to the land of the dead (a belief indicated by the Jesuits and by Kirkland) and that more and more Christian ideas were added to this, culminating in the doctrine of Handsome Lake.

[68] This "Head-opener" who takes out brains and eats, according to some, or keeps, according to others, is also mentioned by Hewitt (1895 b: 112).

[69] Kirkland notes an Iroquois belief in a gloomy, fathomless gulf where a great dog (some say dragon) lives and into which guilty people fall and catch a disease (a great itch) of the dog (Beauchamp 1922 : 158).

themselves, and till the ground as they did while they were alive. In order that the souls of their relatives would not remain poor in the afterlife, they buried or enclosed bread, oil, skins, tomahawks, kettles, and other utensils. They thought that the souls of these objects departed to the next life to serve the souls of the dead (S 172).[70] The only difference between this village of souls and a village of the living was that the souls complained day and night; behavior that the chiefs from time to time tried to stop (JR 10: 147).

In one case, a woman went to the land of the dead and came back to report, "I was dead and had already passed through the cemetery to go directly to the village of the souls, when I came upon one of my dead relatives, who asked me where I was going and what I intended to do—saying that, if I did not change my mind, they would be lost, that there would be no more relatives to prepare food for the souls thereafter. That is what made me return and resolve to live" (JR 13: 153).

In another instance, a dying man wanted to find his deceased half sister who, he said, had been changed into a serpent (JR 13: 193).

On these trips to the land of the dead, the Huron had an opportunity to check on the Jesuits' account of the hereafter. For example, one sick woman said that she did not wish to go to the heaven where the Huron went after death, but rather to that where the French went; she had just come from there and had seen a vast number of Frenchmen, wonderfully dressed, and some Indians of her acquaintance who had been baptized, including her uncle and sister. Her uncle said to her, "Well, my niece, so you have come here." Her sister asked her if the Father Superior had not given her something at her departure to which she answered, "No." The sister replied, "As for me, here is the bead bracelet that he gave me." The woman then resolved to return and ask the Jesuits for the same. She came to and, after having related her dream, lost consciousness and died (JR 13: 149-151).

Not all reports of the land of the dead agreed with those of the Jesuits. One sick man, for example, reported, after returning from this land, that he had seen nothing of what the Jesuits talked about, but had met some of his relatives who welcomed him and said that they had been awaiting his arrival for a long time and would give him many dances and feasts (JR 17: 151-153). Some Hurons did not want to be baptized because they did not want to go to the French land of the dead, but rather wished to join their relatives (JR 8: 137-139; 13: 127, 151, 199; 14: 15, 31; 15: 71; 19: 189). On the other

---

[70] Food and many of the smaller personal, ceremonial, or medicinal artifacts are still buried with the dead person (Shimony 1961 a: 242-243), and in the past the bow and arrow, pipe and tobacco of the deceased, and food for the journey also were put in the grave (Morgan 1901 (1): 168).

hand, one man, after his return from the land of the souls, reported that they had all gone to heaven (JR 8: 147). A woman imparted that the French there had welcomed her as an Iroquois captive was welcomed at the villages, with firebrands and torches; that all the French wanted were converts so that they would have captives to torture (JR 30: 29). One man thought that the Jesuits should not baptize Iroquois prisoners, as they would drive them from Heaven when the Huron arrived (JR 13: 177–179). After he had returned from the land of the dead, another man said that he had met two Englishwomen. They told him that he would not die yet, but on his return should burn his robe to cure his disease. They also told him that the Jesuits had resolved not to return to France until they had killed all the Indians (JR 15: 51). One did not wish to go to Heaven because the French would not give him anything to eat (JR 13: 127). Others did not want to go as there were no fields, trading, fishing, or marriage (JR 13: 179).

Others gave different reasons. Some said that they could not make the long journey to Heaven as they had such weak legs. Some said that they were afraid that they might fall from so great a height. Some wanted to know if there was tobacco in Heaven because they said they could not do without it (JR 17: 127).

MYTHOLOGY

LAND OF THE DEAD

There were myths about the land of the dead. Two examples will illustrate this type of knowledge (JR 10: 147–149).

An Indian, having lost his favorite sister, decided to look for her. He traveled 12 days, without eating or drinking, toward the setting sun where he had heard the village of the souls was located. At the end of this time, his sister appeared to him at night, gave him a dish of meal cooked in water, and then, when he wished to put his hand on her and stop her, disappeared. He traveled for 3 months and each day she showed herself and gave him a little food. At the end of this time, he came to a very swift river that did not appear fordable. There were some fallen trees thrown across it, but this bridge was so shaky he did not trust it. On the other side was a piece of cleared land that indicated to him that there were some people nearby. Looking more closely, he saw a little house at the edge of the woods. He shouted several times and a man appeared, only to shut himself up again in his house. Seeing the man, he resolved to cross the river and did. He went to the house and, finding the door closed, beat on the door. The person inside told him to wait and, if he wanted to enter, to first pass in his arm. The keeper was astonished to see a living body. Opening the door, he asked what his purpose was, for

this country was only for souls. He answered, "I know that well and
that is why I came here to seek the soul of my sister." "Oh indeed,"
replied the other, "well and good. Come, take courage, you will be
presently in the village of souls, where you will find what you desire.
All the souls are now gathered in a cabin, where they are dancing to
heal *Aataentsic* [see below], who is sick. Don't be afraid to enter.
Here is a pumpkin, you can put into it the soul of your sister." He
took the pumpkin and bid good-bye to his host. But, before he left,
he asked his host his name. He replied, "Be satisfied that I am he
who keeps the brains of the dead." When he arrived at the village of
the souls, he entered the house of *Aataentsic* and found that they were
dancing to cure her. He could not see the soul of his sister, however,
for the souls were so startled to see the living man they vanished. In
the evening, as he was sitting by the fire, they returned. At first,
they appeared at a distance, but slowly they approached and began
to dance. He recognized his sister in the group and tried to seize her,
but she fled from him. He withdrew. Finally, he chose his time so
well that she could not escape his grasp. He struggled with her all
night and in the contest she grew so small that he put her into the
pumpkin without any difficulty. He immediately returned to the
house of his host, who gave him his sister's brains in another pumpkin
and told him what he should do in order to resuscitate her. "When
you reach home," he said, "go to the cemetery, take the body of your
sister, bear it to your house, and make a feast. When all your guests
are assembled, carry it on your shoulders, and take a walk through
the house holding the two pumpkins in your hands. You will no
sooner have resumed your place than your sister will come to life
again, provided you give orders that all keep their eyes lowered, and
that no one shall look at what you are doing, else everything will go
wrong." The man returned to his village. He took the body of his
sister, made a feast, and carried out the instructions that had been
given him. He felt motion in the half-decayed corpse, but when he
was two or three steps from his place, a curious person raised his eyes.
At that moment, the soul escaped. He could only take the corpse back
to her tomb (JR 10: 149–153).

In another of the Huron myths, a young man of highest standing
became ill. After much entreaty he said that his dream showed a bow
rolled in bark and that if anyone wanted to go with him, there was
but one man on earth who had such a bow. A group of resolute men
started on the journey with him to get it, but at the end of 10 days all
except six had turned back because of hunger. The six traveled with
him many days. Following the tracks of a little black animal, they
came upon the house of the man they sought. This man warned them
not to take what a woman who was there offered them the first time.
They obeyed him and found when they had upset the dishes on the

ground that they contained only venomous reptiles. After eating the second course, the men tried to bend the rolled bow, but none succeeded in doing it except the young man in whose behalf the journey had been undertaken. He received it as a gift from his host, who then invited him to take a sweat bath with him. After they had come from the sweat house, the host turned one of the companions into a pine tree. From there, they went to the village of souls. Only three returned alive, but frightened, to the house of their host. He encouraged them to return home with the help of a little meal of the kind that souls eat. He told them that on the way home they would pass through woods where deer, bears, and moose were as common as leaves on the trees and, as they had been provided with the marvelous bow, they had nothing to fear and would have successful hunting. When they reached their own village, there was much rejoicing (JR 10: 153–155).

CREATION MYTHS [71]

Some said that in the beginning the earth was entirely covered with water except for a little island on which lived one man and two companions: a fox (*tessandion*) and a little animal like a marten, which the Indians called *tsouhendaia*. The man sent Fox to plunge into the water to see if there was a bottom to it. But Fox, having wet his paws, drew back afraid to risk his life. The man, indignant, kicked him into the water where the animal drowned. The man then encouraged *tsouhendaia* to plunge in. This animal did not imagine that the water was so shallow and dived so violently against the bottom that he came back with his snout covered with slime. The man, pleased at this discovery, exhorted the animal to continue bringing up soil, a task that he performed so assiduously that he made the earth as we see it (JR 10: 131–133).

Another myth concerned the goddess *Aataentsic* (JR 10: 127) [*Ataentsic* (JR 10: 127; 14: 9), *Eataentsic* (JR 8: 117–119, 147), *Ataensiq* (S 169, 172)] who fell from the sky. She made earth and men. In the sky, people lived as on earth in a land like earth, with woods, lakes, rivers, and fields. There was some disagreement among the Huron as to the cause of *Aataentsic's* fall from the sky world. Some said that as she was working in her field, she saw a bear. Her dog began to pursue it and she followed him. The bear fell by accident into a hole and the dog followed him. *Aataentsic* approached this hole and seeing neither bear nor dog flung herself down it. When she fell, she was pregnant. After this, the waters dried up little by little and the earth appeared and became habitable (JR 8: 117–119, 147; 10: 127).

---

[71] See Appendix 2 : The Iroquoian Origin Myth Cycle, p. 151.

Others said that *Aataentsic*'s husband, who was sick, had dreamed that a certain tree from which they obtained their food should be cut down and that as soon as he ate of this fruit he would be healed. *Aataentsic* took his ax and went to cut down the tree. On the first blow, the tree split and fell to earth. She went back, told her husband this and then returned and threw herself after the tree. As she fell, Turtle raised her head and saw her. She called together the other aquatic animals, told them what she had seen, and asked what they thought should be done. Most referred the problem to Beaver, who in turn gave it to Turtle. Turtle said that they should all dive to the bottom of the water and bring up soil and put it on her back. This done, *Aataentsic* fell very gently on this island. Some time after this she gave birth to a daughter (JR 10: 127–129).

Aataentsic was the mother of him who made the earth (JR 14: 9) or the grandmother (S 169). She gave birth to two boys, *Tawiscaron* and *Iouskeha* (JR 10: 129, 163) [*Jouskeha* (JR 8: 117), *Yoscaha* (S 169, 172)]. When they grew up, they fought; *Iouskeha* using the horns of a stag as a weapon and *Tawiscaron*, some fruits of the wild rosebush. *Iouskeha* struck his brother so hard that his blood flowed abundantly and he fled. From his blood, a certain kind of stone [flint] sprang up, as that used in France to fire a gun, which the Indians called *tawiscara* after the name of the wounded brother (JR 10: 129–131).

The Huron believed that *Aataentsic* was the moon and *Iouskeha*, the sun (JR 10: 133). Both governed the world. *Iouskeha* had charge of the living, the animals, plants, and of the things that concern life, and gave good weather and everything else advantageous (JR 8: 117; S 169–170). He was considered good (JR 8: 117) and kind (S 169). *Aataentsic* was spiteful and often spoiled what the good *Iouskeha* did (S 170). She had charge of the souls and it was she who made men die; consequently, she was considered wicked. Some of the Hurons located the home of these two deities in the east [cf. JR 10: 133]; others, in the middle. They lived a life like the Indians; for example, made feasts as they did, but lived without famine (JR 8: 117–119). An Attiuoindaron told the Hurons that he had seen *Iouskeha* in a far-away place and his footprints on a rock in the river. His house was like theirs, with plenty of corn in it and everything else necessary for life. He sowed corn, worked, drank, ate, and slept like others (S 169). When *Iouskeha* grew old, he renewed his youth again in a moment and became a young man of 25 or 30; thus he never died (S 170).

Four young men once went on a journey to the land of *Aataentsic* and her son. They found *Iouskeha* alone in his house. He received them kindly and, after all had exchanged compliments, he told them to hide in a corner; otherwise he would not answer for their lives. Toward evening *Aataentsic* arrived and, perceiving that there were guests in the house, took the form of a beautiful young girl, handsomely adorned, with a beautiful necklace and bracelets of wampum. She asked her son where the guests were. He replied that he did not know what she meant. After she had left, *Iouskeha* told the men and thus allowed them to escape (JR 10: 135).

Although the house of *Aataentsic* and *Iouskeha* was very far away, they nevertheless attended the feasts and dances in the villages. There *Aataentsic* was often badly abused. *Iouskeha* threw the blame on a certain horned *oki* named *Tehonrressanden*. But at the end of the tale, it was *Iouskeha* who in this disguise insulted his mother (JR 10: 135).

In spite of this, *Iouskeha* was esteemed. Some said that the beginning of the earth was dry and all the waters were under the armpit of a large frog. *Iouskeha* could not have a drop of water except as was given by the frog. One day, he decided to change this and he made an incision under the frog's armpit. The waters flowed out in such abundance that they spread throughout the whole earth, creating the rivers, lakes, and seas. The Huron also believed that *Iouskeha* learned from the turtle the process of making fire. Were it not for him, the Indians would not have such good hunting or such ease in taking animals. In the beginning, the animals were shut up in a great cavern that *Iouskeha* guarded. One day he let them free so that they might multiply and he wounded them all in the foot with an arrow. The wolf, however, escaped the shot and this was why the Indian had such difficulty in catching him when hunting (JR 10: 135–137).

Iouskeha also made the corn grow. In 1636, *Iouskeha* was seen quite dejected and as thin as a skeleton and carrying a poor ear of corn in his hand. Some also said he was carrying a man's leg and tearing it with sharp teeth. All this was a sign that it would be a very bad year (JR 10: 137–139).[72]

In another case, the Mohawk and Andastoerrhonon had been brought one epidemic by *Aataentsic*. She had passed through all the

---

[72] Compare Connelley's (1899 b : 41) statement that the Wyandot twin brother—
   often manifested himself to them, being seen in the forests, fields, lakes and streams. If the stalk of corn seen in his hand was full-eared, well-grown, and perfectly grained, a bountiful harvest was indicated; but if it was blasted and withered, no corn was to be expected, and famine was imminent. If he carried in his hand the bare bone of fish or game, it was certain that none of either could be taken or killed for a season. If, pale and gaunt, he entered any village gnawing the shrunken, withered limb of a human being, he thereby foretold famine so dire that many Wyandots must perish from hunger and plague before it was stayed.

houses of two villages. At the second, they had asked her, "Now, after all, why is it that you make us die?" She answered, "Because my grandson, *Iouskeha*, is angry at men; they do nothing but make war and kill one another. He has now resolved, as a punishment for this inhumanity, to make them all die" (JR 14: 9). [For other mythological data see above passim.]

APPENDIX 1

NAMES AND PROBABLE TRIBAL AFFILIATIONS
OF HURON VILLAGES

[Compiled from Jones (1909:5–166). The following differs only slightly from Fenton's (1940 d:180–181) similar compilation.]

Attignawantan villages:

1. Ossossané, La Conception, La Rochelle (of the Jesuits), Tequeunoikuaye, Quieuindohian, St. Gabriel, La Rochelle (of Sagard). It was the capital village at the time of the Jesuits; at the time of Sagard, Quieunonascaran was the chief village of the Attignawantan (S 149).

2. Ihonatiria, St. Joseph I (of the Jesuits).

3. Khinonascarant (of the Jesuits), Quieunonascaran (of Sagard). This village apparently dwindled greatly after Sagard's time and split into three small villages sometime between 1623 and 1637 (Jones 1909:31).

4. Carhagouha, Carantouan (of Champlain), Arontaen (of the Jesuits), Taruentutunum (of Ducreux). It apparently dwindled to a hamlet between 1615 and 1623 (Jones 1909:39–40).

5a. Toanché I, Toanché (of the Jesuits), Toenchen, Troenchain (of Sagard), Toanchain, Tonachin (of Daillon), Otoüacha (of Champlain). It was abandoned before 1633 and its inhabitants moved to Toanché II.

5b. Toanché II, Teandeouiata (of the Jesuits).

6. Tondakhra (of the Jesuits), Tondakea (of Ducreux).

7. Carmaron (of Champlain), Karenhassa (of Ducreux).

8. Angoutenc, Ang8iens, Ang8tenc, Angouteus (of the Jesuits).

9. Arenté, Arentet, Auenté (of the Jesuits), Arenta (of (Ducreux).

10. Onnentisati (of the Jesuits).

11. Oënrio, Oüenrio, 8enrio, Ouenrio, Oenrio (of the Jesuits).

12. Anonatea, Anonatra, Aneatea, Anenatea (of the Jesuits).

13. Arendaonatia, Arendaonactia (of the Jesuits).

14. Iahenhouton (of the Jesuits). This village is mentioned only once by the Jesuits (Jones 1909:146).

Attignawantan villages—Continued
>15. Andiataé, Andiata, Andiatac (of the Jesuits).
>16. Taenhatentaron, St. Ignace I (of the Jesuits). It was later moved to St. Ignace II, nearer Ste. Marie I.
>17. Arethsi (of Ducreux). This village is not mentioned in the Jesuit Relations.

Attigneenongnahac villages:
>1. Teanaostaiaé, St. Joseph II (of the Jesuits). It was the chief village of the Cord Nation.
>2. Ekhiondaltsaan (i.e., Ekhiondastsaan), Khiondaësahan (of the Jesuits). Jones (1909: 149) thinks this was Cord village.

Arendahronon villages:
>1. Cahiagué (of Champlain), St. Jean-Baptiste (of the Jesuits). It may have been the chief village of the Rock Nation.
>2. Contarrea, Kontarea, Contareia (of the Jesuits).
>3. St. Joachim (of the Jesuits). Fenton (1940 d: 180–181) lists this village as belonging to the Bear Nation. However, it was, with the Algonquin (Jones 1909: 71–73) mission at Ste. Elizabeth, under the mission of St. Jean Baptiste "aux Arendaronons" (JR 20: 19–21). Ducreux's map seems to indicate that it was located at some distance from the other villages of the Rock Nation (Jones 1909: 152–153).

Tohontaenrat village:
>1. Scanonaenrat, St. Michael (of the Jesuits).

Ataronchronon villages:
>1. Ste. Marie I (of the Jesuits). This site has been excavated (Kidd 1949; Jury and Jury 1954).
>2. St. Jean (of the Jesuits).
>3. Ste. Anne (of the Jesuits).
>4. St. Denys (of the Jesuits).
>5. St. Louis (of the Jesuits).
>6. St. François-Xavier (of the Jesuits).

APPENDIX 2

THE IROQUOIAN ORIGIN MYTH CYCLE

The Huron creation myths recounted by the French are incidents from the Iroquoian origin myth cycle. This long myth recounts the adventures of the twin brothers and their grandmother. The name of this woman as it appears in the Relations, *Aatentsic*, *Ataentsic*, or *Eataentsic*, and her Iroquois name means 'old woman' or 'ancient bodied' (Hewitt 1910 f: 722; Converse 1908: 31 n.; Hewitt's 1895 a: 244-246, earlier etymology differs). She is also known among the Iroquois as Awĕⁿʰhā'i, 'Mature Flowers' or 'Mature (i.e., Fertile) Earth' (Hewitt 1910 f: 720, 722).

The name of the elder of the twin brothers, *Iouskeha* (or *Jouskeha*) in the Relations means in Wyandot 'the Good one' [Barbeau 1914: 292; Hale 1888: 181; Hewitt (1910 f: 719) analyzes it as meaning 'So it (is) again a dear little sprout'; Parker (in Converse 1908: 34 n.) gives the name as meaning 'the White One' and that of his brother as 'the Dark One']. His other Wyandot name means 'Man Made of Fire' (Barbeau 1915: 306; Connelley 1899 a: 123; 1899 b: 47, 74; Converse 1908: 34 n.). The Iroquois name for this brother, *Teharonhiawagon*, Hewitt (1910 f: 718–719) gives as meaning 'He is holding the sky in two places' or 'He, the Sky Holder' (Hewitt 1895 a: 241–244, in an earlier paper identifies this name as being that of the husband of *Aatentsic*). Hewitt (1910 f: 719) apparently thought that the early writers mistranslated the name of this brother as 'Sky.' Barbeau (1914: 301–302) would also identify the Huron deity 'Sky' with the elder twin brother on the basis of the importance of each in Wyandot and Huron religion and certain similarities between them (also see note 42, p. 81). The Wyandot equate this brother with the Christian God (Barbeau 1915: 49, 49 n., 51).

The younger brother's name, *Tawiscaron*, in the Jesuit and later accounts, both Iroquois and Wyandot, means 'Flint' (Barbeau 1914: 292; 1915: 306; Connelley 1899 a: 123; 1899 b: 47, 74; Converse 1908: 34 n.; Hale 1888: 181). Hewitt (1910 e: 707–708) would analyze this name as meaning 'He (is) ice in a double degree' or 'He (is) ice, cold in a double degree' as an alternative meaning and would associate him with winter. Most, however, use the translation of 'Flint.' The younger brother is equated with the Christian Devil by modern Wyandots (Barbeau 1915: 49, 49 n., 51).

In the longer Iroquois texts (Hewitt 1903: 141-169, 255-281; 1928: 470-479), the creation myth begins with an account of the birth and marriage of the woman who was to become the grandmother of the twin brothers. The basic plot of this episode is as follows: A man and a girl have been "down-fended" in different parts of the same longhouse. (The term "down-fended" refers to the seclusion of certain children until puberty, cattail down being scattered around the place of concealment such that any disturbance of it indicated an invasion of the seclusion. Children so isolated were thought to be especially endowed with power.) When the others in the house have left to perform their daily tasks, the girl goes every day to the man's part of the house to groom his hair. As a result, the girl becomes pregnant. The man (in one account, the uncle) dies and the girl gives birth to a baby girl. When this girl grows older, she cries and to end her depression she is taken to the place where her father's (in one account, uncle's) corpse is. After this, she goes frequently to her father's (uncle's) body and converses with him. He tells her that she is to be married to a chief, gives her directions for the trip to his house, and tells her what she is to do there. When she arrives at the house of the chief, she, naked, makes mush for him. When she has finished, the chief calls two dogs which so roughly lick off the mush that has splattered on her that she is covered with blood. She then dresses herself and stays with the man for a few days, becoming magically impregnated. She returns to her people and the chief magically sends a shower of corn to them. (This part of the story is somewhat different in Hewitt 1928: 471-479.) After this visit, she returns to the chief, to whom she is now married. [The girl's actions when she arrives at the house of the chief are in fulfillment of his dream (Hewitt 1928: 464; Cornplanter 1938: 19)—a motive that is not obvious to the non-Iroquois reader.]

The second episode in the longer versions is the core of the creation myth; it is found in all longer versions and forms the basis of the fragmentary ones. In the Iroquois versions (see Hewitt 1903: 171–178, 221–223, 281–285; 1928: 479–480), it begins with the chief falling ill. He is jealous as his wife has conceived magically and he believes that she has been unfaithful (Hewitt 1928: 464–465; Cornplanter 1938: 19–20). A number of people gather to suggest the cause of his illness. Finally, one suggests, or the chief suggests, that, in order to cure him (to fulfill his desire or dream), a certain tree must be uprooted. This is done and he pushes his wife down the hole.

Although the events and the motivations of the people involved are quite consistent in the longer Iroquois versions, they are not in the Huron and Wyandot versions (Barbeau 1914: 289). In one modern Wyandot version, a medicine man advised the girl to dig at the roots of the tree for the medicine to cure *her;* in another, the girl customarily gathered corn for her brothers, but she tired of this and as a punishment her brothers cast her down (Barbeau 1914: 289–290; 1915: 37, 47, 50); in still another version, the woman was pushed *by mischance* through the hole (Barbeau 1914: 290; Connelley 1899 b: 46, 67; Hale 1888: 180). The variability in the myth is apparently old; the Jesuits mention two versions of this incident. Barbeau (1914: 289) suggests that this variation in the accounts means that the reasons for the fall are of slight importance. However, the variability also may indicate a more heterogeneous origin of Huron culture than that of the Iroquois, and the apparent loss of the rather consistent Iroquois explanation that the woman fell in fulfillment of a dream to cure her husband may indicate a more recent loss of this method of curing among the Wyandot.

The second part of this major episode concerns the fall of the woman from the sky world to the underworld (i.e., the earth). In the Iroquois versions (Hewitt 1903: 179–182, 224–228, 285–289; 1928: 481–483) and in others (cf. the Jesuit version), she is seen falling by Turtle and some other animals. Turtle moves so that she lands on his back. Earth is made by the animals diving into the water and bringing up mud [also see Hewitt 1928: 465; in a Seneca version (Hewitt 1903: 226) earth is made by the handful of earth that the woman has brought with her]. A girl is either born or reborn to this woman. Essentially the same earth diver myth is told by the Wyandot (Barbeau 1915: 48, 50; Connelley 1899 a: 121–122; 1899 b: 68–69; Hale 1888: 180).

Although the earth diver myth in the Jesuit Relations is not tied to *Aataentsic's* fall, it is obviously a part of this myth. The reason for the Jesuit failure to connect these two myths is probably familiar to most anthropologists; often, when doing fieldwork, the ethnographer is told episodes from the creation myth and, because they are told as separate stories, it is not immediately apparent that they also form part of the creation myth until the entire myth is told.

The third episode in the Iroquois creation myth concerns this daughter of the woman who fell from the sky when she has grown up. A man appears and magically impregnates her and leaves. After a while, she gives birth to two boys, one (Sapling) is born first in the normal fashion and the other (Flint) comes out of her armpit, or navel in a Seneca version (Hewitt 1903: 231), and by so doing kills his mother. The grandmother asks the two which one killed his mother. Both deny it, but the grandmother believes Flint's denials, and so believes the wrong brother (Hewitt 1903: 184–186, 228–232, 290–295; 1928: 483–486).

In the Iroquois versions, it is the *grandmother* (mother's mother) of these twins who fell from the sky, but it is not in the Huron and Wyandot versions (Barbeau 1914: 291–292, 291 n.) with the exception of Sagard's. In one Wyandot version, the woman, when she fell from the sky, was pregnant with the twins and when she arrived on earth, one was born the usual way and the other came out through her side, killing her (Hale 1888: 180–181). In another, the woman gives birth to the twins after finding and living with another woman called "grandmother" (Barbeau 1915: 44, 306; Connelley 1899 a: 123; 1899 b: 47, 73–74). In another, the woman found the two boys on the island (earth) (Barbeau 1915: 48, 51). In these Wyandot versions and in one Seneca version, at least (Parker 1910 a: 478; see also Converse 1908: 34), as that in the Jesuit Relations, the twins' mother is the woman who fell from the sky, not their grandmother.

The variation in these versions may indicate Huron and Wyandot cultural disintegration and, specifically, a breakdown in matrilineal descent. That the twins were the children of the daughter of the woman who fell from the sky seems to emphasize matrilineal descent; that they are children of the woman who fell does not.

Following these first three episodes of the creation, the longer myths proceed to recount the exploits of the twin brothers. The theme of these events is that the older brother creates the world so that mankind will have an easy life, while the younger twin tries to thwart his actions. Perhaps the best illustration, at least to the non-Iroquoian reader, is the story in which the elder creates rivers so that one stream runs uphill and the other downhill (making canoe paddling easy), but the younger brother changes this so that rivers run only downhill and adds falls and rapids. The Jesuit statement that *Iouskeha* had charge of the living and of things that concern life is an obvious reference to the fact that he created the flora and fauna that was to be useful to man and tried to create the world so that man could live easily in it. (For the Wyandot descriptions of the works of the brothers see Barbeau 1915: 48, 51; Connelley 1899 b: 74–77; Hale 1888: 181.) The wickedness attributed to *Aataentsic* probably stems from her alliance in many of the Iroquois myths with *Tawiscaron*; both of them try to harm men.

The Jesuit statement that *Aataentsic* was the moon and *Iouskeha* the sun is difficult to substantiate; the Iroquois material is quite confused (Barbeau 1914: 303). Hewitt (1895 a: 245) thought this identification of *Aataentsic* with the moon was a confusion of *Aataentsic* with her daughter; in some Iroquois versions this daughter becomes the sun and moon (Hewitt 1903: 201, 295–296, 319).

The episodes that recount the adventures of the twin brothers are given in apparently random order in the Iroquois cycle. In one of them, Sapling (the elder brother) finds his father (sometimes he is Turtle) who gives him a bow and arrow, animals, and corn—the versions vary (Hewitt 1903: 188–190, 232–236, 297–301; 1928: 487–499).

The Jesuit statement that *Iouskeha* learned from the turtle the process of making fire would seem to be part of this episode.

In another, after Sapling creates the animals or is instrumental in their creation, Flint locks them up in a cave. Finding this out, Sapling goes and opens the cave, releasing the animals (Hewitt 1903: 194–197, 302–309; 1928: 499–503). The Jesuit statement that the animals were shut up in a great cavern that *Iouskeha* guarded and then let free would seem to be a variant on this episode.

The episode mentioned by the Jesuits in which *Iouskeha* cut open the frog to release the earth's waters is also mentioned in one Wyandot version: the brothers separated and while the good brother was creating the animals, the evil one made an immense toad, which drank up all the fresh water that was on the earth. Among the other animals he created, he made a partridge. This partridge led him to the land of his brother where he found snakes, insects, and other malevolent creatures and overcame them. Finally, he found the toad, which he cut open, releasing the waters (Hale 1888: 181). Hale (ibid.) in a note remarks that this is a widely diffused myth.

The fight between *Iouskeha* and *Tawiscaron* in which *Tawiscaron* is defeated is also mentioned in some Iroquois and Wyandot accounts. In three Wyandot versions, the good brother uses deer horns to defeat his brother (Barbeau 1915: 46; Connelley 1899 b: 81; Hale 1888: 182), while the good brother said that he could be destroyed only by being beaten to death with a bag full of agricultural food (Hale 1888: 182). In two Iroquois versions, Sapling uses flint and deer's horns (Hewitt 1903: 328-332; 1928: 499) and Flint uses the spike of the cattail flag (Hewitt 1903: 328). In a Seneca version, both brothers use the thorns of a giant crabapple tree (Converse 1908: 36) and in a Wyandot version, Flint uses the flowering branch of the wild apple (Connelley 1899 b: 81). A comparison of all these versions suggests that the Huron version in the Relations is perhaps the oldest. There are, of course, other variants of this tale: in a Seneca version, the elder twin is not responsible for his brother's death (Hewitt 1903: 241-243) and in an Onondaga version, the incident gets synthesized with Christian ideas and Flint is sent to where it is hot (Hell) (Hewitt 1903: 217-218).

APPENDIX 3

ADDITIONAL HURON WORDS AND PHRASES

FROM THE JESUIT RELATIONS

ho, ho, ho, outoécti, 'many thanks.' Said to acknowledge hospitality on leaving a house (JR 8 : 95 ; cf. JR 8 : 129).

yo eiouahaoua, 'Come, put on the kettle' (JR 8 : 113).

ca chia attwain aa arrihwaa, 'Certainly these are important matters, and worthy of being discussed in our councils; they speak the truth, they say nothing but what is to the purpose; we have never heard such discourse' (JR 10 : 17).

oniondechouten, 'Such is the custom of our country' (JR 10 : 19; cf. below).

ta arrihwaienstan sen, 'Teach me, I pray you' (JR 10 : 25).

enonche watiwareha, enonche watiátaté (a prayer that they might not be shipwrecked and might not suffer by fire) (JR 10 : 73).

(The following five refer to the soul :)

khiondhecwi, the soul in so far as it merely animates the body and gives it life (JR 10 : 141).

oki andaérandi, 'like a spirit, counterfeiting a spirit'; the soul in so far as it is possessed of reason (JR 10 : 141).

endionrra, the soul in so far as it thinks and deliberates (JR 10 : 141).

gonennoncwal, the soul in so far as it bears affection to any object (JR 10 : 141).

ondayee ihaton onennoncwat, 'That is what my heart says to me, that is what my appetite desires' (JR 10 : 141).

Aoutaerohi hechrio kihenkhon, '*Aoutaerohi,* ah, I pray thee that this one may know who you are, and that you will make him feel the ills that you make me suffer' (JR 10 : 183). (This was said by a sick woman to a Jesuit after he had assigned another cause of her sickness and laughed at her *Aoutaerohi.*)

aiendawasti, a polite person (JR 10 : 213).

Jesus taïtenr, 'Jesus, have pity on me' (JR 13 : 53). Also written :
> *Jesous, taïtenr* (JR 23 : 71, 131)
> *Jesus taitenr* (JR 30 : 49)
> *Jesous taitenr* (JR 30 : 101 ; 33 : 177)

chieske, 'What do I know ?' (JR 13 : 125).

teouastato, ' I do not wish it' (JR 13 : 141) ; 'I am not willing' (JR 19 : 189).

156

rihouiosta, 'I believe' (JR 13:191).

oniondechanonkhron, 'Our countries are different,' 'You have your
ways of doing and we have ours' (JR 13:213; cf. above).

onanonharatan, 'What will you have? Our brains are disordered'
(JR 13:235).

ho, ho, ho, echiongnix et sagon achitec, 'Ah, my nephew, I thank you;
be of good heart for the morrow' (JR 13:255).

theandihar, the Polar Star (JR 14:83).

etsagon ihouaten etsagon taouacaratat, 'Courage, nephew, courage,
take care of us' (JR 14:95). This phrase was used in speaking to
the Lord and was the usual phrase by which the old men addressed
the young men (JR 14:95–97).

ho, ho, ho, said when they accepted the conclusion of a chief (JR 15:
117; cf. S below).

chay, 'Good day' (used as the usual greeting) (JR 15:161–163); cf.
kwai (JR 10:183) and *cway* (JR 10:275) and *quoye* (S below).

aronhiac eskenonteta, 'I'm going to Heaven, then' (JR 17:109).

aondechichiai taitene, 'You have made the earth, have pity on me'
(JR 18:27).

taouskeheati iatacan, 'It is a strange thing, my brother' (JR 19:147).

*io sakhrihotat de sarakounentai, onne ichien aihei aronhiae eeth de
eihei,* 'Sun, who are witness of my torments, listen to my words; I
am at the point of death; but after this death, Heaven shall be my
dwelling' (said by an Iroquois prisoner after having ascended the
scaffold) (JR 21:171).

quio ackwe, 'Come, let us go away together' (JR 21:205).

onhoua etsitenroutaoua, 'We will tear you out of the earth as a poisonous root' (an expression used to threaten those suspected of
being sorcerers when they wished to kill them) (JR 23:135).

ao! an audience expression of approval (on giving gifts to a chief
being raised up) (JR 23:169).

FROM SAGARD

quoye, greeting (S 74) with approximately the meaning of 'What is
it, what do you say.' It was used with friends and enemies. The
reply was *quoye* or more courteously, *yatoro* (my friend), *attaquen*
(my brother), etc. (S 85).

agnonha, 'the French' (literally, "iron people" because before the
French arrived the Indians did not know what iron was (S 79–80)).

anderoqua, 'birch bark bucket' (S 83).

ho, ho, ho, salutation of joy; the sound *ho, ho, ho* made as if laughing
(S 85).

agochin, 'feast' (S 110).

sascoinronte, 'bearded,' 'you have a beard' (S 137).

téondion or *tescaondion,* 'You have no sense' (S 138).

atache, 'ill balanced' (S 138).

cachia otindion, 'You are very clever' (S 138).

hoüandate daustan téhondion, 'And the Hurons are not [very clever]' (S 138).

arondiuhanne or *ahondiuoyissa*, 'You are people who understand matters on high and supernatural' (S 138; cf. words for medicine man).

saracogna, 'Make me shoes' (S 146).

tintian, woodpeckers (S 218).

stinondoa (purple finch) (S 218).

oüaiera (red-headed woodpecker) (S 219).

sondaqua, eagle (S 219).

ahoüatantaque, a kind of bird of prey (S 219).

ondettontaque, wild turkey (S 220).

ahonque, bustards or wild goose (Canada goose) (S 220).

tochingo, crane (Great Blue heron) (S 220).

oraquan, crow (S 220).

acoissan, white and gray partridges (S 221).

orittey, turtledoves (passenger pigeon) (S 221).

taron, ducks (S 221).

horhey, swan (S 221).

yachiey, midges (S 221).

hahyuha, a kind of fox with black fur (S 222).

tsinantononq, a kind of fox with red fur and a stripe of black fur along back (S 222).

andasatey, common fox (S 222).

sahoüesquanta, flying squirrel (S 222).

ohihoin, a species of squirrel, striped (S 223).

aroussen, a species of squirrel, like those in France (S 223).

queutonmalisia (*quieuronmalisia*), rabbit or hare (S 223, 188).

toutsitsoute, lynx (S 223).

anarisqua, common wolf (S 223–224).

tiron, a kind of leopard or wild cat (S 224).

otay, an animal as large as a small rabbit with very black soft, smooth, and handsome fur (probably one of the moles). The Indians valued these furs and made them into robes, with the heads and tails around the edge (S 224).

scangaresse, skunk (S 224).

sondareinta, moose (S 225).

ausquoy, caribou (S 225).

sconoton, deer (probably the Wapiti) (S 225).

tackro, a species of large mouse (S 227).

touhauc, fleas (S 227).

tsiouy, lice (S 227–228).

assihendo, a species of fish, see above (S 230).

ahouyoche, trout (S 230).

soruissan, pike (S 230).

hixrahon, sturgeon (S 230).

einchataon, a species of fish rather like the barbel in France, about a foot and a half long (S 230).

auhaitsiq, a species of fish like herring but smaller (probably the lake herring) (S 231).

tsoutaye, Canadian beaver (S 232).

ondathra, muskrat (S 234).

angyahouiche, turtle (S 235).

tioointsiq, snake (S 235).

kiotoutsiche, a species of frog (S 235).

oüraon, a species of frog, green and twice or three times the size of common ones (S 235–236).

ohentaqué, blueberries (S 237).

hahique, small fruits in general (S 237).

tichionte, strawberries (S 237).

toca (cranberries) (S 238).

tonestes, plums (S 238).

poires, pears (fruit of the shadbush) (S 238).

orasqueinta (Jerusalem artichoke) (S 239).

sondhratates (ground nuts or cowparsnip) (S 108, 239).

anonque, little onions (chives) (S 239).

ongnehon, a small herb, in taste and shape like wild sweet marjoram (probably American pennyroyal) (S 239).

asquata, cedar (S 240).

atti (probably basswood) (S 240).

ononhasquara (Indian hemp) (S 240).

angyahouiche orichya (pitcher plant) (S 241).

eindauhatayon, roses (S 241).

Huron song (S 119):

Ongyata éuhaha ho ho ho ho ho
Eguyoronuhaton on on on on on
Eyontara éientet onnet onnet onnet
Eyontara éientet à à à onnet, onnet, ho ho ho.

APPENDIX 4

AUTHORS OF THE DOCUMENTS CONTAINED IN "THE JESUIT RELATIONS AND ALLIED DOCUMENTS"

Volume and pages	Author	Document and date written
8: 68–155	Jean de Brébeuf	Relation, 1635
10: entire vol	____do	Relation, 1636
11: 6–21	____do	Letter, ca. 1636
13: entire vol	François Joseph le Mercier	Relation, 1637
14: 5–111	____do	Do.
15: 9–141	____do	Relation, 1638
15: 147–189	François du Peron	Letter, 1639
15: 191–195	Simon le Moyne	Do.
15: 197–201	Joseph-Marie Chaumonot	Do.
16: 221–253	Hierosme Lalemant	Relation, 1639
17: 7–215	____do	Do.
17: 217–231	____do	Letters, 1640
18: 10–45	Joseph-Marie Chaumonot	Do.
19: 75–267	Hierosme Lalemant	Relation, 1640
20: 17–85	____do	Do.
20: 88–101	Charles Garnier	Letter, 1641
20: 102–105	Jean de Brébeuf	Do.
21: 126–265	Hierosme Lalemant	Relation, 1641
21: 268–273	Charles Lalemant	Letter, 1642
21: 274–291	Charles Garnier	Do.
21: 292–307	Hierosme Lalemant	Do.
22: 299–311	____do	Relation, 1642
23: 17–233	____do	Do.
23: 236–245	Charles Garnier	Letter, 1643
23: 246–253	Jean de Brébeuf	Do.
25: 81–87	Charles Garnier	Letter, 1644
26: 164–313	Hierosme Lalemant	Relation, 1643
27: 19–71	____do	Do.
28: 38–101	____do	Relation, 1645
29: 240–291	Paul Ragueneau	Relation, 1646
30: 17–143	____do	Do.
30: 146–151	Charles Garnier	Letter, 1647
32: 58–65	Jean de Brébeuf	Letter, 1648
33: 57–249	Paul Ragueneau	Relation, 1648
33: 251–269	____do	Letter, 1649
34: 67–235	____do	Relation, 1649
35: 18–29	____do	Letter, 1650
38: 203–287	Francesco Gioseppe Bressani	Relation, 1653
39: entire vol	____do	Do.
40: 13–65	____do	Do.

REFERENCES

BAILEY, ALFRED GOLDSWORTHY.

1933. The significance of the identity and disappearance of the Laurentian Iroquois. Proc. and Trans. Roy. Soc. Canada, ser. 3, vol. 27, sec. 2, pp. 97–107.

BARBEAU, CHARLES M.

1912. On Huron work, 1911. Summary Rep. Geol. Surv. Canada, Anthrop. Div., 1910–1911, pp. 381–386.

1913. On Iroquoian field-work, 1912. Summary Rep. Geol. Surv. Canada, Anthrop. Div., 1912, pp. 454–460.

1914. Supernatural beings of the Huron and Wyandot. Amer. Anthrop., n.s., vol. 16, pp. 288–313.

1915. Huron and Wyandot mythology. Canada Dept. Mines, Geol. Surv., Mem. 80.

1917. Iroquoian clans and phratries. Amer. Anthrop., n.s., vol. 19, pp. 392–402.

1949. How the Huron-Wyandot language was saved from oblivion. Proc. Amer. Philos. Soc., vol. 93, No. 3, pp. 226–232.

BEAUCHAMP, WILLIAM M.

1886. Permanency of Iroquois clans and sachemships. Amer. Antiq., vol. 8, No. 2, pp. 82–91.

1888. Onondaga customs. Journ. Amer. Folklore, vol. 1, pp. 195–203.

1891 a. Hi-a-wat-ha. Journ. Amer. Folklore, vol. 4, pp. 295–306.

1891 b. Iroquois notes. Journ. Amer. Folklore, vol. 4, pp. 39–46.

1892. Iroquois notes. Journ. Amer. Folklore, vol. 5, pp. 223–229.

1893. Notes on Onondaga dances. Journ. Amer. Folklore, vol. 6, pp. 181–184.

1895. Onondaga notes. Journ. Amer. Folklore, vol. 8, pp. 209–216.

1896. Iroquois games. Journ. Amer. Folklore, vol. 9, pp. 269–277.

1898. Wampum used in council and as currency. Amer. Antiq., vol. 20, No. 1, pp. 1–13.

1900. Iroquois women. Journ. Amer. Folklore, vol. 13, pp. 81–91.

1901 a. The Good Hunter and the Iroquois medicine. Journ. Amer. Folklore, vol. 14, pp. 153–159.

1901 b. Wampum and shell articles used by the New York Indians. New York State Mus. Bull. No. 41, pp. 319–480.

1905. Aboriginal use of wood in New York. New York State Mus. Bull. No. 89, pp. 87–272.

1907. Civil, religious and mourning councils and ceremonies of adoption of the New York Indians. New York State Mus. Bull. No. 113, pp. 341–451.

1922. Iroquois folk lore, gathered from the Six Nations of New York. Syracuse.

BIGGAR, H. P., EDITOR.

1929. The works of Samuel de Champlain. 6 vols. Toronto. [Cited in text as: C.]

C = The works of Samuel de Champlain. See Biggar, H. P., Editor.

CHAFE, WALLACE L.

1961 a. Comment on Anthony F. C. Wallace's "Cultural composition of the Handsome Lake religion." Bur. Amer. Ethnol. Bull. 180, No. 15, pp. 153–157.

1961 b. Seneca thanksgiving rituals. Bur. Amer. Ethnol. Bull. 183.

CLARKE, PETER DOOYENTATE.
 1870. Origin and traditional history of the Wyandots, and sketches of other
         Indian tribes of North America. Toronto.
CONNELLEY, WILLIAM E.
 1899 a. Notes on the folk-lore of the Wyandots. Journ. Amer. Folklore,
         vol. 12, pp. 116-125.
 1899 b. Wyandot folk-lore. Topeka.
 1899 c. The Wyandots. Rep. of the Minister of Education, Ontario, 1899,
         Appendix, Ann, Archaeol. Rep., pp. 92-123.
CONVERSE, HARRIET MAXWELL.
 1908. Myths and legends of the New York State Iroquois. A. C. Parker,
         ed. New York State Mus. Bull, No. 125, pp. 5-195.
CORNPLANTER, JESSE J.
 1938. Legends of the longhouse. Philadelphia.
CULIN, STEWART.
 1907. Games of the North American Indians. 24th Ann. Rep. Bur. Amer.
         Ethnol. for 1902-03, pp. 1-846.
CURTIN, JEREMIAH, and HEWITT, J. N. B.
 1918. Seneca fiction, legends, and myths. 32d Ann. Rep. Bur. Amer.
         Ethnol. for 1910-11, pp. 37-189.
DEARDORFF, MERLE H.
 1951. The religion of Handsome Lake: its origin and development. Bur.
         Amer. Ethnol. Bull. 149, No. 5, pp. 77-107.
DESERONTYON, JOHN.
 1928. A Mohawk form of ritual of condolence, April 9, 1782. (J.N.B.
         Hewitt, trans.) Mus. Amer. Indian, Heye Foundation, Indian
         Notes and Monographs, vol. 10, No. 8, pp. 85-110.
DOCKSTADER, FREDERICK J.
 1961. Indian art in America. Greenwich, Conn.
FENTON, WILLIAM N.
 1936. An outline of Seneca ceremonies at Coldspring longhouse. Yale
         Univ. Publ. Anthrop. No. 9.
 1937. The Seneca society of faces. Scientific Monthly, vol. 44, pp. 215-238.
 1939. A further quest for Iroquois medicines. Explorations and Fieldwork
         of the Smithsonian Inst. in 1939, pp. 93-96.
 1940 a. An herbarium from the Allegheny Senecas. In Historical Annals of
         Southwestern New York (Doty, Congdon, and Thornton, editors),
         pp. 787-796. New York.
 1940 b. Masked medicine societies of the Iroquois. Ann. Rep. Smithsonian
         Inst. for 1940, pp. 397-430.
 1940 c. Museum and field studies of Iroquois masks and ritualism. Explo-
         rations and Fieldwork of the Smithsonian Inst. in 1940, pp. 95-100.
 1940 d. Problems arising from the historic northeastern position of the
         Iroquois. Smithsonian Misc. Coll., vol. 100, pp. 159-252.
 1941 a. Contacts between Iroquois herbalism and colonial medicine. Ann.
         Rep. Smithsonian Inst. for 1941, pp. 503-526.
 1941 b. Iroquois suicide: a study in the stability of a culture pattern. Bur.
         Amer. Ethnol. Bull. 128, No. 14, pp. 79-138.
 1941 c. Tonawanda longhouse ceremonies. Bur. Amer. Ethnol. Bull. 128,
         No. 15, pp. 139-166.
 1942 a. Fish drives among the Cornplanter Seneca. Pennsylvania Archaeol.,
         vol. 12, pp. 48-52.

1942 b. Songs from the Iroquois longhouse: program notes for an album of American Indian music from the eastern woodlands. Smithsonian Publ. 3691.

1946. An Iroquois condolence council for installing Cayuga chiefs in 1945. Journ. Washington Acad. Sci., vol. 36, pp. 110–127.

1949 a. Collecting materials for a political history of the Six Nations. Proc. Amer. Philos. Soc., vol. 93, No. 3, pp. 233–238.

1949 b. Medicinal plant lore of the Iroquois. Univ. State of New York Bull. to the Schools, vol. 35, No. 7, pp. 233–237.

1951 a. Introduction: the concept of locality and the program of Iroquois research. Bur. Amer. Ethnol. Bull. 149, No. 1, pp. 1–12.

1951 b. Locality as a basic factor in the development of Iroquois social structure. Bur. Amer. Ethnol. Bull. 149, No. 3, pp. 35–54.

1953. The Iroquois Eagle Dance, an offshoot of the Calumet Dance, Bur. Amer. Ethnol. Bull. 156, pp. 1–222.

1957. Long-term trends of change among the Iroquois. Proc. Spring Meeting Amer. Ethnol. Soc. 1957, pp. 30–35.

1961. Iroquoian culture history: a general evaluation. Bur. Amer. Ethnol. Bull. 180, No. 25, pp. 253–277.

FENTON, WILLIAM N., and DODGE, ERNEST S.
1949. An elm bark canoe in the Peabody Museum of Salem. Salem.

FENTON, WILLIAM N., and KURATH, GERTRUDE P.
1951. The Feast of the Dead, or Ghost Dance at Six Nations Reserve, Canada. Bur. Amer. Ethnol. Bull. 149, No. 7, pp. 139–165.

FINLEY, JAMES B.
1840. History of the Wyandot mission at Upper Sandusky, Ohio. Cincinnati.

GÉRIN, LÉON.
1900. The Hurons of Lorette. Rep. British Assoc. Adv. Sci., vol. 70, pp. 549–568.

GOLDENWEISER, ALEXANDER A.
1912. On Iroquois work, 1911. Summary Rep. Geol. Surv. Canada, Anthrop. Div., 1911, pp. 386–387.

1913. On Iroquois work, 1912. Summary Rep. Geol. Surv. Canada, Anthrop. Div., 1912, pp. 464–475.

1914. On Iroquois work, 1913–1914. Summary Rep. Geol. Surv. Canada, Anthrop. Div., 1913, pp. 365–372.

HALE, HORATIO.
1881. Hiawatha and the Iroquois confederation. Salem.

1883. The Iroquois book of rites. Philadelphia.

1888. Huron folk-lore. Journ. Amer. Folklore, vol. 1, pp. 177–183.

1894. The fall of Hochelaga, a study of popular tradition. Journ. Amer. Folklore, vol. 7, pp. 1–14.

HARRINGTON, MARK R.
1908. Some Seneca corn-foods and their preparation. Amer. Anthrop., n.s. vol. 10, pp. 575–590.

1909. Some unusual Iroquois specimens. Amer. Anthrop., n.s., vol. 11, pp. 85–91.

HEWITT, JOHN N. B.
1889. New fire among the Iroquois. Amer. Anthrop., vol. 2, p. 319.

1890. Iroquois superstitions. Amer. Anthrop., vol. 3, pp. 388–389.

1891. Kahastinens or the fire-dragon. Amer. Anthrop., vol. 4, p. 384.

1892. Iroquois game of la crosse.   Amer. Anthrop., vol. 5, pp. 189–191.

1894. Era of the formation of the historic league of the Iroquois.   Amer. Anthrop., vol. 7, pp. 61–67.

1895 a. The cosmogonic gods of the Iroquois.   Proc. Amer. Assoc. Adv. Sci., vol. 44, pp. 241–250.

1895 b. The Iroquoian concept of the soul.   Journ. Amer. Folklore, vol. 8, pp. 107–116.

1898. The term haii-haii of the Iroquoian mourning and condolence songs. Amer. Anthrop., vol. 11, pp. 286–287.

1902. Orenda and a definition of religion.   Amer. Anthrop., n.s., vol. 4, pp. 33–46.

1903. Iroquoian cosmology: first part.   21st Ann. Rep. Bur. Amer. Ethnol., pp. 127–339.

1907 a. Conestoga.   Bur. Amer. Ethnol. Bull. 30, vol. 1, pp. 335–337.

1907 b. Erie.   Bur. Amer. Ethnol. Bull. 30, vol. 1, pp. 430–432.

1907 c. Huron.   Bur. Amer. Ethnol. Bull. 30, vol. 1, pp. 584–591.

1910 a. Orenda.   Bur. Amer. Ethnol. Bull. 30, vol. 2, pp. 147–148.

1910 b. Otkon.   Bur. Amer. Ethnol. Bull. 30, vol. 2, p. 164.

1910 c. Oyaron.   Bur. Amer. Ethnol. Bull. 30, vol. 2, pp. 178–180.

1910 d. Susquehanna.   Bur. Amer. Ethnol. Bull. 30, vol. 2, pp. 653–659.

1910 e. Tawiskaron.   Bur. Amer. Ethnol. Bull. 30, vol. 2, pp. 707–711.

1910 f. Teharonhiawagon.   Bur. Amer. Ethnol. Bull. 30, vol. 2, pp. 718–723.

1910 g. White dog sacrifice.   Bur. Amer. Ethnol. Bull. 30, vol. 2, pp. 939–944.

1916. The requickening address of the league of the Iroquois.   Holmes Anniversary Volume, pp. 163–179.   Washington.

1917. Some esoteric aspects of the league of the Iroquois.   Proc. Int. Cong. Americanists 1915, pp. 322–326.

1918. A constitutional league of peace in the Stone Age of America: the league of the Iroquois and its constitution.   Ann. Rep. Smithsonian Inst. for 1918, pp. 527–545.

1928. Iroquoian cosmology: second part.   43d Ann. Rep. Bur. Amer. Ethnol., pp. 449–819.

1932. Status of women in Iroquois polity before 1784.   Ann. Rep. Smithsonian Inst. for 1932, pp. 475–488.

1933. Field work among the Iroquois Indians of New York and Canada. Explorations and Fieldwork of the Smithsonian Inst. in 1932, pp. 81–84.

1944. The requickening address of the Iroquois condolence council.   (William N. Fenton, ed.)   Journ. Washington Acad. Sci., vol. 34, pp. 65–85.

HEWITT, JOHN N. B., and FENTON, WILLIAM N.
1945. Some mnemonic pictographs relating to the Iroquois condolence council.   Journ. Washington Acad. Sci., vol. 35, pp. 301–315.

HICKERSON, HAROLD.
1960. The Feast of the Dead among the seventeenth century Algonkians of the upper Great Lakes.   Amer. Anthrop., n.s., vol. 62, pp. 81–107.

HUNT, GEORGE T.
1940. The wars of the Iroquois: a study in intertribal trade relations. Madison.

HUNTER, ANDREW F.
1893. National characteristics and migrations of the Hurons as indicated by their remains in North Simcoe.   Trans. Roy. Canadian Inst., vol. 3, pp. 225–228.

JACKSON, HALLIDAY.
  1830 a. Civilization of the Indian natives.   Philadelphia.
  1830 b. Sketch of the manners, customs, religion and government of the
          Seneca Indians in 1800.   Philadelphia.
JONES, ARTHUR EDWARD.
  1909. "Sendake ehen" or old Huronia.   5th Rep. Bur. Archives Province of
          Ontario, 1908.   Toronto.
  1910. Huron Indians.   Catholic Encyclopedia, vol. 7, pp. 565–583.
JR=The Jesuit Relations and allied documents.   See Thwaites, Reuben Gold,
          Editor.
JURY, WILFRID, and JURY, ELSE MCLEOD.
  1954. Sainte-Marie among the Hurons.   Toronto.
KENTON, EDNA, EDITOR.
  1927. The Indians of North America.   2 vols.   New York.
KEPPLER, JOSEPH.
  1941. Comments on certain Iroquois masks.   Mus. Amer. Ind., Heye Founda-
          tion, Contr. vol. 12, No. 4, pp. 1–40.
KIDD, KENNETH E.
  1949. The excavation of Ste. Marie I.   Toronto.
KINIETZ, W. VERNON.
  1940. The Indians of the western Great Lakes, 1615–1760.   Univ. Michigan
          Mus. Anthrop. Occ. Contr. No. 10.   Ann Arbor.
KNOWLES, NATHANIEL.
  1940. The torture of captives by the Indians of eastern North America.
          Proc. Amer. Philos. Soc., vol. 82, No. 2, pp. 151–225.
KURATH, GERTRUDE P.
  1950. The Iroquois ohigwe death feast.   Journ. Amer. Folklore, vol. 63,
          pp. 361–362.
  1951. Local diversity in Iroquois music and dance.   Bur. Amer. Ethnol. Bull.
          149, No. 6, pp. 109–137.
LIGHTHALL, W. D.
  1899. Hochelagans and Mohawks; a link in Iroquois history.   Proc. and
          Trans. Roy. Soc. Canada, ser. 2, vol. 5, sec. 2, pp. 199–211.
MOONEY, JAMES.
  1910. Tionontati.   Bur. Amer. Ethnol. Bull. 30, vol. 2, pp. 755–756.
MORGAN, LEWIS H.
  1850. Report to the Regents of the University upon the articles furnished
          the Indian collection.   Ann. Rep. Univ. State of New York, No. 3,
          pp. 65–97.
  1852. Reports on the fabrics, inventions, implements and utensils of the
          Iroquois.   Ann. Rep. Univ. State of New York, No. 5, pp. 67–117.
  1871. Systems of consanguinity and affinity.   Smithsonian Contr. Knowl-
          edge, No. 17.
  1881. Houses and House-life of the American aborigines.   U.S. Geogr. and
          Geol. Surv. Contr. North Amer. Ethnol., vol. 4.   Washington.
  1901. League of the Ho-de-no-sau-nee or Iroquois.   Herbert M. Lloyd, ed.
          New York.   (1st ed. 1851; Lloyd edition reprinted by Human Rela-
          tions Area Files, 1954, New Haven.)
  1959. The Indian journals, 1859–1862.   (Leslie A. White, ed.)   Ann Arbor.
PARKER, ARTHUR C.
  1909. Secret medicine societies of the Seneca.   Amer. Anthrop., n.s., vol. 11,
          pp. 161–185.
  1910 a. Iroquois sun myths.   Journ. Amer. Folklore, vol. 23, pp. 473–478.

1910 b. Iroquois uses of maize and other food plants.   New York State Mus.
        Bull. 144, pp. 5–119.

1913. The code of Handsome Lake, the Seneca prophet.   New York State
        Mus. Bull. 163, pp. 5–148.

1916. The constitution of the Five Nations.   New York State Mus. Bull.
        184, pp. 7–158.

1928. Indian medicine and medicine men.   Rep. of Minister of Education,
        Ontario, 1928, Appendix, Ann. Archaeol. Rep., pp. 9–17.

POWELL, J. W.
    1881. Wyandot government.   1st Ann. Rep. Bur. [Amer.] Ethnol., pp. 57–69.
QUAIN, BUELL H.
    1961. The Iroquois.   *In* Cooperation and competition among primitive peo-
        ples (Margaret Mead, ed.), pp. 240–281; 535–538.   New York.
RANDLE, MARTHA CHAMPION.
    1951. Iroquois women, then and now.   Bur. Amer. Ethnol. Bull. 149, No.
        8, pp. 167–180.
S=Father Gabriel Sagard: the long journey to the country of the Hurons.   See
        Wrong, G. M., Editor.
SEAVER, JAMES E.
    1824. A narrative of the life of Mrs. Mary Jemison.   (Republished Corinth,
        New York, 1961.)
SHIMONY, ANNEMARIE ANROD.
    1961 a. Conservatism among the Iroquois at the Six Nations Reserve.   Yale
        Univ. Publ. Anthrop. No. 65.
    1961 b. The Iroquois fortunetellers and their conservative influence.   Bur.
        Amer. Ethnol. Bull. 180, No. 20, pp. 205–211.
SKINNER, ALANSON.
    1925 a. Some Seneca masks and their uses.   Mus. Amer. Ind., Heye Founda-
        tion, Indian Notes, vol. 2, No. 3, pp. 191–207.
    1925 b. Some Seneca tobacco customs.   Mus. Amer. Ind., Heye Foundation,
        Indian Notes, vol. 2, No. 2, pp. 127–130.
    1926. Seneca charm canoes.   Mus. Amer. Ind., Heye Foundation, Indian
        Notes, vol. 3, No. 1, pp. 36–38.
SMITH, DE COST.
    1888. Witchcraft and demonism of the modern Iroquois.   Journ. Amer.
        Folklore, vol. 1, pp. 184–194.
    1889 a. Additional notes on Onondaga witchcraft and Ho^n-dó-ï.   Journ.
        Amer. Folklore, vol. 2, pp. 277–281.
    1889 b. Onondaga superstitions.   Journ. Amer. Folklore, vol. 2, pp. 282–283.
SMITH, ERMINNIE A.
    1883. Myths of the Iroquois.   2d Ann. Rep. Bur. Amer. Ethnol., pp. 47–116.
SNYDERMAN, GEORGE S.
    1949. The case of Daniel P.: an example of Seneca healing.   Journ. Wash-
        ington Acad. Sci., vol. 39, pp. 217–220.
SPECK, FRANK G.
    1949. Midwinter rites of the Cayuga long house.   Philadelphia.
TAFT, GRACE ELLIS.
    1914. An Onondaga festival.   Records of the Past, n.s., vol. 1, pp. 101–102.
THWAITES, REUBEN GOLD, EDITOR.
    1896–1901. Jesuit Relations and allied documents.   73 vols.   Cleveland.
        [Cited in text as: JR.]
TRELEASE, ALLEN W.
    1960. Indian affairs in colonial New York; the seventeenth century.   Ithaca.

TRIGGER, BRUCE GRAHAM.
 1959. The destruction of Huronia: a study in economic and cultural change, 1609–1650. Trans. Roy. Canadian Inst., vol. 33, No. 68, pt. 1, pp. 14–45.

WALKER, LOUISE J.
 1949. Indian feast of the dead. Journ. Amer. Folklore, vol. 62, p. 428.

WALLACE, ANTHONY F. C.
 1958. Dreams and the wishes of the soul: a type of psychoanalytic theory among the seventeenth century Iroquois. Amer. Anthrop., n.s., vol. 60, pp. 234–248.

WAUGH, FREDERICK W.
 1916. Iroquois foods and food preparation. Canada Dept. Mines, Geol. Surv., Mem. 86.

WILSON, DANIEL.
 1885. The Huron-Iroquois of Canada, a typical race of American aborigines. Proc. and Trans. Roy. Soc. Canada, ser. 1, vol. 2, sec. 2, pp. 55–106.

WITTHOFT, JOHN, and HADLOCK, WENDELL S.
 1946. Cherokee-Iroquois little people. Journ. Amer. Folklore, vol. 59, pp. 413–422.

WRONG, G. M., EDITOR.
 1939. Father Gabriel Sagard: the long journey to the country of the Hurons. Toronto. [Cited in text as: S.]

INDEX

Aaskouandy, charms, 120
Aaskwandiks, charms, 120
Aataentsic (mythical grandmother), 140, 144, 145, 146, 147, 151, **153**, 154
Achirigouans, Algonquin tribe, 19
Acointa (corn hulls), 69
Aconite, used for suicide, 56
Acorns, 61, 62
Acwentonch (manner of speech at meetings), 50
Adónwe' Ceremony, 72, 75
Adoption into a nation, 11
Aescara (straw game), 115
Agnée, see Mohawk Indians.
Agneronons, see Mohawk Indians.
Agnieeronons, see Mohawk Indians.
Agnichenon, see Mohawk Indians.
Agnierhonon, see Mohawk Indians.
Agnierrhonons, see Mohawk Indians.
Agnierronons, see Mohawk Indians.
Agnietironons, see Mohawk Indians.
Agnonra (snowshoes), 23
Agochin atiskein (feast of souls), 129
Agosayé (cemetery), 130
Agriculture, 58, 60–62, 71
    knowledge of, 25
    land owned by women, 60
    taken up by men, 124
    use of plow in, 58
    work done by women, 58, 71
Ahareti onaskenonteta (place of the dead), 140
Ahouenrochrhonons, see *Wenrôhronon* Indians.
Ahrendaronons, see *Arendahronon*.
Aiheonde (caretakers of the graves), 136
Aireskouy soutanditenr (spirit), 82
Akhiataendista (rich present), 54
Akhrendoiaen (ceremony), 98
Akwanake (strangers), 13
Algonquian tribes, 3, 7, 8, 9, 12, 17, 19, 25, 52, 58
    eastern, 3
    language of, 8, 12, 14
Algonquin Indians, 18, 19, 23, 25, 27, 28, 52, 73, 80, 84, 94, 122, 135, 141, 150
Allies of the Huron, 19
All Souls' Day, Catholic observance, 135
American Revolution, results of, 58
Amikouek, Algonquin tribe, 19
Amulet, 91
Amusements, 83, 124
    See also Games.
Anastohé, people of, *see* Andastoerrhonon Indians.
Andachienrra (poisonous root), 56
Andacwander (curing ceremony), 101, 106–107, 113

Andastoé, see Andastoerrhonon Indians.
Andastoerhonons, see Andastoerrhonon Indians.
Andastoeronnons, see Andastoerrhonon Indians.
Andastoëronnons, see Andastoerrhonon Indians.
Andastoerrhonon Indians, Iroquoian-speaking group, 16, 147
Andataroni (breads), 70, 87
Andiataé, Huron village, 150
Andichons (benches), 41
Anenkhiondic, principal chief of Bear Nation, 44
Angont (monstrous serpent), 117
Angoutenc, Huron village, 149
Angwiens, village, 98
Aniencuny (logs), 41
Animals:
    bones of, used in witchcraft, 117
    bones of, not to be burned, 67
    claws of, used in witchcraft, 117, 118
    drives of, 65
    fur-bearing, 9
    guts used for bow strings, 30
    heads given as presents, 72
    skins of, 25, 49
    souls of, 140
Annieronnons, see Mohawk Indians.
Annierronnons, see Mohawk Indians.
Anonatea, Huron village, 149
Anondahoin (tobacco), 73
Aondironnon, Neutral tribe, 14
Aouasanik, Algonquin tribe, 19
Apothecary, assistant to medicine man, 84, 91
Apples, wild, 15, 62, 155
Apricots, 116
Aquientor (armor), 30
Arendaenronnons, see *Arendahronon*.
Arendahronon (Rock People), Huron tribe, 3, 9, 10, 11, 26, 34, 44, 150
Arendaonatia, Huron village, 149
Arendarhonos, see *Arendahronon*.
Ardendaronnons, see *Arendahronon*.
Arendarrhonons, see *Arendahronon*.
Arendiwane (medicine man), 92–97, 114, 117
Arenté, Huron village, 149
Arethsi, Huron village, 150
Aretsan, see *Ontetsans*.
Armor (*aquientor*), 30, 89
Armorial bearings, 109, 128
Arms, coat of, village, 24
Arocha (sledge), 23
Arrows, 29, 30, 79, 86, 95, 122, 124, 140
    points of iron, 26, 30
    points of stone or bone, 30

Ascwandics, see *Ascwandies*.
Ascwandies (charms), 120
Ash bark, 40, 108
Askikwanehronons, see Nipissirinien Indians.
Asqua (companions, not wives), 127
Ass, wild, 93
Assemblies, general, 49
Assihendo (large fish), 63, 64, 108
Assitagueronon, see Nation of Fire.
Astataion, see *Athataion*.
Ataconchronons, see *Ataronchronon*.
Ataentsic, see *Aataentsic*.
Ataronchronon (People of the Fens), 10, 37, 150
Atchougue, Algonquin tribe, 19
Aténonha (wives), 127
Athataion, farewell feast, 36, 75
Athistaëronnon, see Nation of Fire.
Atigagnongueha, see *Attigneenongnahac*.
Atignaouantan, see *Attignawantan*.
Atignenonahac, see *Attigneenongnahac*.
Atignenongach, see *Attigneenongnahac*.
Atingueennonniahak, see *Attigneenongnahac*.
Atingyahointan, see *Attignawantan*.
Atinniawentan, see *Attignawantan*.
Atiouandaronks, 13
Atiouendaronk, see Neutral Indians.
Atirenda (brethren), 99
Atironta, Chief of Arendahronons, 44
Atiskein andahatey (path of souls), 140
Atisken (souls), 140
Atiwanens, see *Atiwarontas*.
Atiwarontas (elders), 44
Atouront aochien (singing feast), 75
Atsataion, see *Athataion*.
Atsatonewei (council sticks), 47
Atsihiendo, see *Assihendo*.
Atsirond, chief of the Montagnet, 51
Atsistaehronons, 14
Attignaouentan, see *Attignawantan*.
Attignawantan (Bear Nation), Huron tribe, 9, 10, 11, 34, 44, 50, 51, 99, 141, 150
Attigneenongnahac (Cord People), Huron tribe, 9, 10, 11, 34, 150
Attigouautan, see *Attignawantan*.
Attigueenongnahac, see *Attigneenongnahac*.
Attingueenongnahak, see *Attigneenongnahac*.
Attinguenongnahac, see *Attigneenongnahac*.
Attiouandarons, see Neutral Indians.
Attiouendaronk, see Neutral Indians.
Attiuoïndaron, see Neutral Indians.
Attiwandaeons, see Neutral Indians.
Attiwandaronk, Huron name for Neutral Indians, 13
Auhaitsique, boiled with corn, 68
Auoindaon (principal chief of Bear Nation), 26, 44
Awataerohi (curing ceremony), 75, 97, 103, 104, 105, 106
Awenrehronon, see *Wenrôhronon* Indians.

Awls, 26, 110, 123
    used in tattooing, 15
Axes, 19, 27, 51, 110, 130, 137, 141, 145
Bags, 136
    basswood bark, 60
    birchbark, 24
Bailey, Alfred Goldsworthy, 3
Balls, wooden, used in games, 124
Baptism, 88, 126
Barbeau, Charles M., 3, 21, 45, 55, 59, 78, 79, 100, 151, 152, 153, 154, 155
Bark, 60, 103, 104, 107, 109, 113, 119, 129, 130, 137, 138, 139
    medicinal use of, 84, 104, 108
    prepared by women, 59
Barrels, bark, 61
Baskets, 68
    birchbark, 59
    pack, 58, 127
    reed, 59
Basswood, 60
Bathing, 86, 133
    of hands, 57
Beads, 116
    glass, 26, 51, 112, 113, 136, 138
    wampum, 26, 35, 53, 54, 55, 57, 116, 121, 123, 132, 137
Beans (*ogaressa*), 15, 58, 59, 60, 68, 69, 70, 121
    as game tallies, 115
    wild, 62
Bear, 39, 65, 66, 73, 76, 101, 120, 126, 145
    bites of, treatment for, 85
    claws, 99
    fat, 21, 100, 101
    fattening of, 66
    hunting of, use of dogs, 67
    spirit, 100
Bear clan, 100
Bear Nation, see *Attignawantan*.
Bearskins, 78, 110
    covering of, 77, 107
    moccasins of, 20
Bear Society, 107
Bear tribe, see *Attignawantan*.
Beauchamp, William M., 4, 16, 18, 21, 23, 24, 30, 39, 41, 42, 43, 45, 46, 54, 58, 62, 71, 82, 87, 91, 102, 108, 110, 114, 115, 117, 120, 131, 133, 137, 140, 141
Beaver, 9, 15, 25, 65, 83, 87
    catching, 67
    eating of, 67
    mythical being, 146
    nets, 67
    tooth, used as knife, 24, 67
Beaver skins, 59, 67, 110, 121, 136, 139
    clothing of, 20, 99
    moccasins of, 20
    robe of, 26, 35, 51, 57, 114, 121, 126, 130, 136, 137, 138
    trade in, 21, 57, 67, 116
Beds, tree bark, 40
Beeches, 12, 23
Belts, 54, 113, 128
    porcupine quill, 21, 111
Benches, tree bark, 41, 77

Berries, 60, 62
  juice of, 62
Betting, *see* Gambling.
Biggar, H. P., editor, 8
Birchbark, bags of, 24
  bowls, 23, 59
  canoes, 22
  shelters, 23
Bird, supernatural (*ohguione*), 121
Birds, 109, 129, 140
Biscuits, 87
Bissiriniens, 19, 28
Blackberries, 62, 70
Blackberry Feast, 79
Blankets, 26, 27, 89, 112, 113, 116
  of skin, 16
Blood, used as glue, 60
Bloodroot, 84
Blueberries, 70
Boars, 22
Body paint, 21, 98
Bowl Game, 72, 109, 114, 115–116
  played to cure sick, 115
  players, 115
Bowls, 68, 69, 74
  bark, 59
  birchbark, 23, 59
  tree knot, 67
  wooden, used for bowl game, 115
Bows, 23, 103, 124, 137, 140, 144, 145
Bows and arrows, 30, 65, 66, 142, 154
Bowstrings, from animal guts, 30
Boys, 122, 124
Bracelets, 59, 77, 136, 142
  wampum, 20, 21, 126, 138, 147
Bread, 70, 73, 87
  buried with dead, 130, 142
  chewed, 70
  green corn leaf, 70
Brébeuf, Jean de, 5, 6, 160
  martyrdom of, 39
  Relation of, 5, 6
Breechcloth, 15, 20, 76, 77, 111
Bressani, Francesco Gioseppe, 55, 160
Buffalo Society, 107
Burial, 130–132
  ceremony, 132
  customs, 15, 130–132
  ground, 15, 60, 130
  house, 131
  ossuary, 134, 135
  scaffold, 131
Bustard, 66
Butternut bark, used for canoes, 23

Cache pits, 24, 41, 42, 61
Cahiagué, Huron village, 150
Cakes, 62, 131
  bran, 73
Canoes, 22, 23, 26, 56, 59, 63, 65, 86, 87, 93, 110, 112
  birchbark, 22
  descriptions of, 22
  dugout, 23
  slippery elm or butternut, 23

Captives, eaten by Indians, 29, 90
  killing of, 31
Carantouans, Iroquoian-speaking tribe, 16
Carhagouha, Huron village, 149
Carmaron, Huron village, 149
Cartier, Jacques, 3, 16
Casks, storage, 61
Cat, present of, 87
Catarrh, treatment for, 85
Catholicism, Roman, 88
Cat Nation (Erie Indians), 10, 14, 16, 17
Cattail, 155
  down, 152
Cattaraugus Reservation, 79, 122
Cayuga Indians, 10, 17, 18, 121
  See also Iroquois Indians.
Cedar, 12, 40
  bark, 40
  ribs of, used in canoes, 22
  shields of, 30
  white, 23
Cemetery (*agosayé*), 130, 131, 132, 135, 136, 144
Ceremonies:
  Adónwe', 72, 75
  Akhrendoiaen, 98
  Awataerohi, 75, 97, 104, 105, 106
  burial, 43, 130–132, 133
  calendric, 12, 13, 79, 87
  curing, 75, 93, 101–102, 106, 107, 108
  death, 139
  Four Sacred, 39, 72
  Green Corn, 133
  Iroquois Condolence, 45, 46, 54, 75, 134, 137
  marriage, 47, 126–127
  mating, 101, 106–107, 113
  Midewiwin, 99
  Midwinter, 39, 65, 67, 72, 80, 103, 109, 110, 133
  moon, 79
  Raspberry, 62
  resuscitation, 45
  Strawberry, 62
  Thunder, 103, 115
  War, 36, 43, 75
    See also Dances; False Faces.
Chafe, Wallace L., 1, 75, 81, 91
Champlain, Samuel de, 3, 5, 6, 7, 8, 11, 13, 16, 20, 21, 22, 23, 25, 29, 40, 41, 42, 47, 48, 58, 59, 60, 61, 62, 63, 65, 69, 70, 71, 72, 91, 92, 104, 105, 107, 108, 109, 110, 111, 123, 124, 125, 127, 128, 129, 131, 134, 136, 140
Chant, personal, 39
Charcoal, used in making fire, 24
  powdered, used in tattooing, 15
Charms, 91, 92, 99, 115, 116, 120–122, 136
  change in shape of, 121
  extraction of, 117–118
  hunting, 74, 121
  inheritance of, 121
  love, 121
  trade in, 122
  witchcraft, 121

Chaumonot, Joseph-Marie, 160
Cherries, 62, 108
Chestnuts, 15
Chickens, 73
Chiefs, 8, 38, 42–48, 49, 76, 77, 87, 89,
    101, 102, 103, 105, 106, 109, 112,
    114, 119, 129, 130, 131, 134, 135,
    137, 138, 139, 142, 152
    appointed by clan mother, 18
    as country treasurers, 51
    assistant to, 44
    authority of, 29, 35, 47
    corruption of, 48
    duties of, during war, 31
    federal, 46
    qualities for being, 43, 44
    raising up of, 45
    speeches of, 48, 50
    titles of, 44
    tribal, 45, 111, 115
Chieftainship, election to, 46
    inheritance of, 43, 46, 47
    refusal of, 47
    succession to, 47
    tribal, 43
Children, 77
    adoption of, 31
    attitudes toward, 124
    captive, 31
    dances forbidden to, 109
    division of, in divorce, 125–126
    selling of, 61
    sleeping places for, 41
    suicide of, 57
    trade rights of, 25
    training of, 57, 124
    treatment of, 124
Chives, see Onions.
Christian converts, 10, 11
Christian cross, belief regarding, 95
Christian God, 151
Christians, 88, 89, 90, 119
Citation explanations, 8
Clans, 12, 43, 44, 45, 55, 126, 128
    councils of, 52, 56
    exogamous, 126
    matrilineal, 44
    mothers of, new chiefs appointed
        by, 18, 46
    possessions of, 51
    symbols of, 21, 109
    totems of, 60
Clarke, Peter Dooyentate, 10
Cloaks, 113
    skin, 59
Clothing, decorations for, 20, 59, 111
    effect of European contact on, 20, 21
    for death, 128
    fur, 20
    mourning, 133
    Plains type, 30
Clowns, 78
Clubs, 37
    wooden war, 30, 32
Coals, hot, used in medicine rites, 104,
    106
Coffin, adopted by Iroquois, 131
Coinkia (boiled bread), 70

Coldspring, 97
Colic, 120
Collars, 59, 77, 111, 116, 141
    wampum, 28, 32, 50, 57, 86, 93, 114,
        116, 121, 126, 130, 137, 138, 139
Combs, 130, 133
Condolence Ceremony, Iroquois, 45, 46,
    54, 75, 134, 137
Conestoga Indians, 16
Conkhandeenrhonons, Iroquoian-speak-
    ing tribe, 16
Connelley, William E., 3, 10, 28, 43, 45,
    55, 79, 81, 91, 147, 151, 153, 154,
    155
Contarrea, Huron village, 150
Contraception, 123
Controller (Great Spirit), 81
Converse, Harriet Maxwell, 75, 79, 100,
    122, 151, 154, 155
Converts, Indian, 20, 26, 27, 48, 89, 126
Cord, hemp, 64
Cord Nation, see Attigneenongnahac.
Corn, 3, 9, 12–15, 23, 25, 27, 31, 51, 58, 59,
    60, 95, 110, 113, 118, 121, 123, 147,
    151, 154
    boiled (sagamité), 23, 38, 62, 63, 68,
        70
    cached along trails, 24
    carried on trips, 70
    cooking of, 67–68
    dried, 41, 61, 69
    flint, 68
    grinding of, 68
    harvested by souls, 141
    offered to dead, 139
    parched, 69
    planting of, 61
    pounded (ottet), 68, 70
    prepared by women, 58, 67
    protection of, 61
    roasted, 68, 69
    rotten (leindohy), 68, 69
    soup, 70
    stored, 61
    trade in, 61
Cornbread, 70, 127
Cornmeal (eschionque), 27, 30, 51, 58,
    68, 69
Cornplanter, Indian chief, 42
Cornplanter, Jesse, 65, 100, 152
Cornstalks, 61, 70
Corpses, treatment of, 136, 138
    See also Dead.
Councils, 48–51, 101, 105, 138
    assistants to chief of, 31, 43, 44
    calling of, 49–50, 89, 90, 94, 111,
        113, 115, 120, 131
    decisions of, announced by chief, 49
    fires for, 48
    members of, 49
    peace (endionraondaoné), 43
    place of, 49
    secret, 49
    speech at (acwentonch), 50–51
Council sticks, 47, 138
Cousin, 128
Cow parsnips, 62
Cows, 15, 65

Crabapple tree, 155
Cradleboards, 123
    description of, 123–124
Cranberries (*toca*), 62
Cranes, 66
Creator, 81, 141
Cross-cousin, 128
Crows, 66, 109, 128, 140
Cuirass, 30
Culin, Stewart, 114, 115
Curing Ceremony, 75, 93, 101–102, 106, 107, 108
    example of, 111–113, 118
    preparation for, 110
Curtin, Jeremiah, and Hewitt, J. N. B., 74, 81, 131, 133

d'Aillon, Joseph de la Roche, Recollet missionary, 5, 6
Dancers, 73, 77, 97, 98, 102
    costumes of, 98, 107
    nakedness of, 77, 98, 107
Dances, 43, 49, 59, 86, 87, 91, 93, 101, 103, 135
    before death, 36
    body-paint for, 77, 98
    costumes in, 30
    Feather, 72, 77, 79
    forbidden to children, 109
    invitations to, 98–99
    Medicine Society, 106
    position of hands in, 77
    reasons for, 76
    round, 77
    spectators at, 77
    sponsor of, 73
    Thanksgiving, 30
    War, 30, 75, 79, 115
Dancing, 72, 76–78, 95, 103, 107
    positions of bodies in, 77
Dead, the, distribution of property of, 131
    disposal of bones of, 15, 132, 135
    flesh removed from body of, 132
    guarded by friends, 129, 132
    habits of, 134
    myths about, 142
    painting of, 129
    resurrections of, enacted by Hurons, 45
        Neutrals, 16
    scaffold used for, 15, 54, 131, 136, 137, 138, 139
Deardorff, Merle H., 141
Death, 39, 128–143
    causes of, 12, 132
    ceremony of, 139
    cold as cause of, 12
    customs, 44–45, 46, 128–143
    dreams, 129
    feasts, 45, 46, 80, 129–133
    freezing as cause of, 132
    preparation for, 129
    restitution for, 28
    shipwreck as cause of, 132
    sign, 129
    smallpox as cause of, 12, 120

Death—Continued
    speech, 129, 130
    starvation as cause of, 12
    unusual modes of, 132
Deer, 15, 23, 25, 39, 65, 66, 67, 74, 76, 101, 109, 121, 128, 140, 145
    drives, 65, 66
    fat used as butter, 66, 70
    horns, magic use of, 155
    meat, used for feasts, 66, 70
    skin, 66, 110
        clothing from, 20
Deer clan, 12
Delaware Bay, 17
de Noüe, Anne, Jesuit missionary, 5, 6
Deputies, 111, 112
Descent, 128
    inheritance through, 43, 47, 128
    matrilineal, 126, 127, 128, 154
Deserontyon, John, 45
Desires of the soul, 86, 87, 88, 92, 93, 101
    See also Sick, desires of the.
Devil, see Evil Spirit.
Dew Eagle, 82
Diagnosticians, consulted in sickness, 91, 92, 104, 106, 114, 117
Diapers, substitute for, 124
Digging stick, 61
Diseases, 82, 109
    European-introduced, 3
    Jesuit-introduced, 11, 119–120
Dish game, see Bowl game.
Divorce, 125, 126
Dockstader, Frederick J., 99
Dogs, 64, 79, 86, 89, 101, 110, 112, 118, 131, 140, 145
    eaten by Indians, 35, 39, 66, 67, 73, 74, 90, 114, 126
    feast of, 90, 93, 94, 96, 104, 105, 114
    killing of, 67, 78, 90, 114
    pet, 40, 89
    quivers from skin of, 30
    raising of, 66, 67
    sinews of, 99
    supernatural, 141
    used in hunting, 66, 67
Dolls, used in rituals, 99
Doorkeepers, 78
Dream-guessing, 87, 110, 112, 113
Dreams, 76, 83, 86, 87, 90, 106, 115, 117, 152, 153
    and the desires, 86–91, 92, 114
    death, 129
    influence of, 90–91, 92
    reenactment of, 90, 107
    visitation, 90
Dress of the Huron, 20–22
Drought, 95
Drowning, 12, 132
Drugs, 84
Drums, 79
Dutch, trade, 9, 16, 17, 27

Eagle Dance, 73, 75
Eagles, 66
    talons of, 99, 121
    wing and tail feathers of, used for arrows, 30

Eagle Society, 83
Earrings, 26, 77, 116, 126
Ears, bead ornaments for, 20
    piercing of, 123
    sticks passed through, 37
Earthquakes, beliefs about, 79
Eataentsic, see *Aataentsic*.
Ecaregniondi (supernatural rock), 141
Eclipse, 79
    beliefs regarding, 79
Eel, 108
    skin bands, worn on hair, 22
Ehonkeronons (Islanders), 111
Ehwae, Tobacco Nation village, 12
Eindichaguet (benches), 41
Ekhiondaltsaan, Huron village, 150
Elder trees, 85
Elk, 25
Elm trees, 12
    bark of, 40
    used for canoes, 23
Emetics, to extract charms, 117
    used for poison, 56, 83, 84, 85
Endahiaconc, chief of Teanaostahé,
    Huron village, 44
Endicha (benches), 41
Endionrra ondaon (house of the coun-
    cil), 43
Enditeuhwa (feast), 75
English, Quebec conquered by, 6
    trade, 16, 17, 27
Ensign or flag, 30, 89
    tree bark, 30
Entauaque, see *Endahiaconc*.
Entrails, removed from body and
    burned, 132
Epicerinys Indians, 19, 25
Epidemics, treatment for, 93, 94, 105,
    108, 114, 119, 147
Erie Indians, 10, 14, 16, 17
Eschionque (cornmeal), 69
Eskanane (land of the souls), 140
Esken (soul), 140
Estoqua (stirring paddle), 68, 69
Etiquette, 57
Eulogy of the dead chiefs, 134
Evil Spirit, governor of Hell, 141, 151
Explorers, professional, information
    from, 5

Face painting, 126, 129
Faithkeepers (deacons of longhouse),
    45
False Faces, 78, 80, 94, 97, 103, 108, 109
    masks, 60, 87, 97
    rites, 69
    sickness, 80
Familiars (*ascwandies*), 120
Familiar spirit, influence of, 92
Famine, prediction of, 147
Fans, tree bark, 70
Farewell Feast, 36, 75
Fasting, 100, 101
    preparation of medicine man for,
    97, 98
Feast of the Dead, 51, 129–132, 134–140
    reburial of dead at, 15, 132, 134, 135

Feasts, 39, 43, 47, 49, 59, 64, 72–76, 83,
    86, 88, 89, 90, 91, 93, 95, 97, 98,
    102, 103, 111, 115, 121, 133, 144
    customs of feast givers, 73, 74
    "eat-all," 74
    for the sick, 57, 74, 87, 101, 107, 108,
    118
    honoring the dead, 134, 137
    invitations to, 73, 109, 114, 115
    reasons for, 72, 74, 121
    regard for feast givers, 72
    10-day, 133, 140
Feather Dance, 72, 77, 79
Feathers, eagle, 30
    used in hair, 22
    worn for dance, 77, 98
Fenton, William N., 2, 3, 4, 10, 16, 17,
    18, 21, 24, 39, 42, 45, 46, 48, 49,
    54, 56, 57, 60, 62, 72, 73, 75, 76,
    77, 78, 79, 80, 82, 83, 84, 85, 86,
    87, 89, 90, 91, 92, 93, 96, 97, 99,
    102, 107, 108, 109, 110, 117, 124,
    126, 127, 131, 135, 149, 150
Fenton, William N., and Dodge, Ernest
    S., 23
Fenton, William N., and Kurath, Ger-
    trude P., 91, 131, 134, 135, 140
Festivals, 73
Fetishes, see Charms.
Finley, James B., 46, 52, 54, 56, 72, 74,
    78, 99, 103, 108, 117, 118, 121, 125,
    133, 134
Firearms, 17, 79
    not traded by French, 27
    obtained from the Dutch, 9, 27
Firebrands, 32, 33, 36, 37, 90, 143
Fire-dragon, 79
Fire-making, 24
Fires, 94, 96, 112, 131
    built at graves, 133, 138
    built in longhouse, 49
    community, 40
    extinguished during epidemics, 94
    jugglers of, 103, 109
    walking through, 112
Firs, 12, 40
Fish, 39, 56, 59, 69, 76, 87, 103, 107, 108,
    110, 111, 113, 126, 140
    armored, 122
    assihendo, 63, 64
    atsihiendo, 108
    aubaitsiq, 63
    catching of, 24
    cooked with corn, 68
    dried, 25, 29, 41, 64
    drives, held in summer, 62
    einchataon, 63
    glue, 30
    leinchataon, 41, 63
    nets, 24, 25, 56, 59, 62, 64, 136
    oil, making of, 64
    rituals, 64
    scarcity of, 65
    smoked, 64, 70
    spears, 62, 124
    storage of, 63
    taboos connected with, 133
    trade in, 25

Fishbones, not burned, 64, 67
uses of, 123
Fishhooks, 24, 26, 64
Fishing, 15, 58, 59, 62–64, 71, 75, 90, 91, 121, 127, 133, 141, 143
through ice, 63
Fish-preacher, 64
Five Nations, see Iroquois League.
Flint, origin of, 146
Younger Twin Brother, 151, 153, 155
Flour, 27, 101
Food, buried with dead, 142
carried to war, 30
presented to sick person, 107
served at death feast, 130, 136
trade for, 26
uneaten, 74
Fortunetellers, 83, 84, 85, 89, 91, 92, 94, 97
Four Beings, supernatural, 81
Four Sacred Ceremonies, 39, 72
Fox (tessandion), 145
Frames for drying fish, 64
France, Canada ceded to, 6
French, 1, 3, 7, 9, 10, 13, 27, 40, 52, 54, 55, 56, 62, 72, 90, 110, 115, 117, 119, 120, 135, 142, 143, 151
merchants, 57, 67
priests, behavior toward, 7, 95
trade, effect of, 5
traders, 5, 10, 11, 13, 17, 25, 26, 27, 40, 57, 67
Freshwater Sea (Lake Huron), 12
Freud, Sigmund, 86, 90
Friendships, dictated by dreams, 89
ritual, 89
Frog, supernatural, 147, 155
skin of, used as fish bait, 24
Frontlets, snakeskin, 20
Frosts, control of, 94, 95
Fruits, dried, 62, 70
stones of, used for bowl game, 115–116
wild, 15
Funeral ceremonies, 43, 130–132, 133
Furs, 51, 129, 133, 137
trade in, 9, 25, 27, 28, 61

Gagnenon andahatey (path of the dogs), 140
Gambling, results of, 56, 57, 116, 117
Game, leather bags for, 59
scarcity of, 65
Games, 43, 57, 59, 72, 109, 114–117, 124
dice, 116
football, 114
lacrosse, 43, 114, 115
peach stone, 79, 115
played by men and boys, 116, 124
played by women and girls, 116
players, 116
snowsnake, 87, 114
See also Amusements.
Gandougarse, Huron village, 10
Ganonchia (houses), 40, 66
Garihagueu (benches), 41
Garihoüa doutagueta (warrior), 44

Garments, skin, 15
See also Clothing.
Garnier, Charles, 160
Geese, 66
Georgian Bay, Ontario, Canada, 1
Gérin, Léon, 10
Ghost spirits, see Souls.
Giant, fictional, 76
Gibson, Simeon, 134
Gifts, 45, 46, 52, 53, 110, 130, 131
distribution of, 130–131, 137, 139
substitute, 87
Girdle, leather, worn by girls, 20
Girls, 125, 131
dress for dance, 77
newly married, 58
part in curing ceremonies, 106, 107, 108
positions in dancing, 77
preferred to boys, 122
pursuit of lovers by, 125
training of, 125
God, Christian Creator, 81
God of dreams, 91
Gods of war, ceremonials for, 36
Goldenweiser, Alexander A., 10, 21, 45, 47, 60, 85, 100, 102
Granaries, 14
Grapes, native, 62
Graves, 130, 133, 136, 138
common, skeletons buried in, 135, 136
covering of, 139
sand from, 138
Great Hunter, mythical person, 102
Great Lakes, home of spirits, 81
Great Spirit, 80, 81, 141
Green Corn Ceremony, 133
Ground nuts, 62
Guardian spirits, 90, 92
Guns, see Firearms.

Haau (expression of approval), 51
Haii hai, 135, 137
Hair, 116–118, 133
dyeing of, men and women, 22
oil, sunflower seed, 21
ornaments, bead, 20, 21
styles of dressing, 22
trimmings, feather, 20
Hale, Horatio, 3, 10, 18, 45, 52, 58, 134, 135, 151, 153, 154, 155
Half-pike, 66
Handsome Lake, 39, 42, 72, 81, 133, 141
Harrington, Mark R., 68, 69, 70, 87, 114
Hatchets, 26, 33, 37, 38, 52, 54, 110, 119, 131
metal, 58
stone, 58
war, 88
Hä-wen-né-yu (Great Spirit), 80, 81
Headbands, leather, 30
Heads, taken as trophies, 29, 31, 34, 38
Heaven, belief in, 141, 143
Hell, belief in, 141, 155
Hemlock bark, 108

Hemp, 9, 59, 95, 108
  gathering of, 59
Henarhonon, see *Arendahronon*.
Herbalists, 84
Herbs, not eaten by Indians, 62
  as remedies, 83, 84
Heron, great blue, 66
Herring (*aubaitsiq*), 63
Hewitt, John N. B., 3, 9, 10, 17, 28, 43, 44, 45, 46, 51, 52, 53, 54, 55, 60, 74, 78, 79, 83, 87, 91, 94, 100, 109, 110, 114, 132, 137, 140, 141, 151, 152, 154, 155
Hewitt, John N. B., and Fenton, William N., 10, 14, 16, 45, 46
Hickerson, Harold, 135
Hochelaga, 16
Hogs, boiled in soup, 73
Hominy (*sagamité*), 68
Honneha (cornstalks), 70
Honqueronons, Algonquin band, 27
Hooks, pruning, 110
Houses (*ganonchia*), 40, 66
  assigned to aliens, 28–29
  bark, 41, 42
  built in time of war, 31
  cabin, 8, 15
  community built, 42
  for fishing, 63
  log, 41
  made by men, 59
  occupied when snowing, 71
  ornaments for, 21
  owned by women, 60
  shape of, 40
  single-family, 41
  sweat, 86, 88, 93, 96, 105, 145
  trade for, 26
  used for ceremonies, 77
Hudson, Henry, 4
Hunt, George T., 9, 13, 27
Hunter, Andrew F., 135
Hunting, 15, 58, 59, 61, 65–67, 71, 74, 75, 90, 91, 121, 127, 141, 145
  charm, 74, 121
  season for, 65, 71
Huronia, 3, 5, 6, 12, 13, 14, 15, 16, 17, 19, 22, 25, 27, 34, 60, 62, 65, 80, 114, 122, 127, 132, 135
Huron League, 3, 9–12, 13, 44, 45, 49
Huron of Lorette, 10
Husk Faces, 78
  impersonators, 97
  masks of the, 97
  rituals of the, 109

Iahenhouton, Huron village, 149
Iannaoa (spirit), 81
Idos Society, 97, 99
Ihonatiria, Indian village, 11, 149
Infants, artificial feeding of, 123
  burial of, 132
  naming of, 123
  nursing of, 123
  transportation of, 124
  treatment of, 123
  weaning of, 123

Initiations, 99
Injuries, treatment for, 85
Insanity, 120
  cause of, 114
Insects, 155
Invisible Aids, supernatural beings, 80
Iouskeha (Elder Twin Brother), 81, 119, 140, 146, 147, 148, 151, 154, 155
Iron, 117
Iroquoian-speaking peoples, 3, 7, 13, 16, 17
  confederacies of, 4, 11, 17
  culture of, 1, 5, 80, 84, 86, 92, 100, 108, 141, 153
  language of, 14, 83
  religion of, 81
Iroquois Condolence Ceremony, 45, 46, 54, 75, 134, 137
Iroquois Indians, 3–4, 5–6, 9–10, 12–15, 17–19, 21, 23–24, 27–32, 34, 39, 41–43, 45–47, 51–52, 54–56, 58–61, 65, 67, 69, 70–75, 77–94, 96, 97, 99, 106, 108, 110, 114–117, 120–126, 128–132, 134–135, 137–138, 140–141, 143, 147, 153–155
  agriculture of, 3
  ceremonials, origin of, 76
  ceremonies, dress for, 76
  dress, similar to Huron, 20
  Huron defeated by, 9, 10
  mythology, 102
  territory, invaded by Hurons, 29
  tribes, 8
Iroquois League, 3, 4, 17–18, 28, 43, 46, 49, 52, 53
Island Indians, 26, 28, 111

Jack-in-the-pulpit, 85
Jackson, Halliday, 20, 24, 41, 42, 43, 56, 58, 65, 67, 69, 71, 84, 90, 94, 121, 123, 124, 125, 126, 127, 131, 133, 134, 141
Jaundice, 84
Javelins, 85
Jemison, Mary, 58, 125, 126, 127, 133
Jerusalem-artichoke (*orasqueinta*), 62
Jesters, 78
Jesuit Missionaries, 5, 6, 7, 11, 12, 13, 14, 15, 16, 17, 22, 25, 26, 27, 34, 39, 40, 42, 49, 50, 51, 52, 54, 55, 62, 65, 66, 71, 75, 79, 84, 85, 88, 91, 95, 97, 98, 99, 101, 106, 110, 119, 120, 122, 128, 131, 135, 137, 141, 142, 143, 153, 154, 155
Jesus Christ, identification with Indian God, 120
Johnson, Sir William, 54
Jones, Arthur Edward, 10, 149, 150
Jouskeha, see *Iouskeha*.

Kenton, Edna, 5
Keppler, Joseph, 87, 108
Kettles, 23, 24, 26, 27, 29, 52, 79, 103, 104, 110, 112, 113, 127, 130, 134, 135, 136, 137, 139, 142
  iron, 59

Khinonascarant, Huron village, 149
Khionontateronons, see *Khionontater-rhonon*.
Khionontaterons, see *Khionontater-rhonon*.
Khionontaterrhonon, *s e e* T o b a c c o League.
Kichesperini, see *Honqueronon*.
Kichkagoneiak, allies of Huron, 19
Kinietz, W. Vernon, 5, 10, 36, 99
Kinship terms, 128
Kionontatehronon, see *Khionontater-rhonon*.
Kirkland, Samuel, 141
Knives, 24, 26, 30, 32, 38, 51, 110, 117, 137
Knowles, Nathaniel, 32
Kurath, Gertrude P., 77, 135

Lacrosse, game, 114, 115
    matches, 43
    sticks, 87
Ladders, 138
    to ascend palisades, 40
Lake, supernatural spirit of, 132
Lake Huron, 12, 19, 25, 63
Lake of the Iroquois, *see* Lake Ontario.
Lake Ontario, 14, 34, 96
Lake St. Louys, *see* Lake Ontario.
Lalemant, Charles, 39, 160
Lalemant, Hierosme, 39, 160
Land, clearing of, 61
    name signs on, 60
    use ownership of, 60
Land of the dead, tales of, 142, 143–145
Language of the Huron, written by missionaries, 71
Lard, uses of, 60
Laurentian Iroquois, 3, 16
Leather, 110, 117, 118
    girdle worn by women, 20
Le Caron, Joseph, 5
Leggings, 111, 113, 116, 128
    skin, 20
    with shoes attached, 19
Leindohy (stinking corn), 68, 69
Lent, observance of, 65
Lice, 22
Lighthall, W. D., 3
Lightning, 82
Little People (Pygmies), 121
Little Water Medicine, 122
Lizards, giant, 82
Longhouses, 40, 41, 42, 73, 122, 127
    members of, 85
    use of as ceremonial places, 42, 48, 152
Longnose masks, 97
Lorette Huron, 10
Love charms, 121
Lynx skins, 110

Magical treatments, 84
Magic power (*orenda*), 78, 91
Maize, *see* Corn.
Maples, 12
Maple sugar, 69

Marriage, 125–127, 143
    announcement of, 127
    arranged by mothers, 126
    ceremonies, 126
    children not impediment to, 125
    feast, 126, 127
    matrilocal, 127
    patrilateral cross-cousin, 47
    rules on, 126
    thoughts regarding, 125, 126
Martenlike animal (*tsouhendaia*), 145
Mascot, 91
Maskers, 109
Masks, hung in doorways, 105, 109
    worn by dancers, 103, 108
Masqueraders, 120
Match, cotton, 24
Mating, ceremonial (*andacwander*), 101, 106–107, 113
Mats, 73, 77, 130, 132, 133, 138, 139
    maize leaf, 59
    reed, 23, 41, 48, 49, 59
    sleeping, 41, 99, 129
Mayapples, 62
Meat, 51, 59, 68, 69, 107, 117, 126, 127
Medicine, 60, 83, 92, 116, 120, 122
    bundle, 84, 99, 121
    complex of, 72
    French, 84
    herbs used in, 80, 84
    Indian, 84
    water, 120
Medicine man, 7, 19, 76, 78, 83, 84, 85, 87, 89, 91–97, 99, 102, 103, 115, 118, 122, 152
    powers of, 97–101, 109, 117, 118
    rules laid down by, 87, 107, 108, 114
Medicine societies, 39, 72, 75, 80, 88, 91, 99, 102, 106, 107, 109
    membership in, 109
    dances of, 106
Melons, 60
Men, dreams of, 91
    dress for dance, 77
    feasts of, women not admitted to, 59
    grieving of, 130
    ground cleared by, 58
    head, 48
    old, 36, 42, 47, 48, 49, 57, 76, 77, 101, 112, 115–116, 119, 136, 139
    positions of, in dancing, 77
    price for murder of, 52
    young, 36, 48, 76, 116, 120, 125, 131, 137
Menstrual periods, rules regarding, 125
Mercier, François Joseph le, 160
Messengers, volunteer, 50
Metal, 116
Mice, 64
Michisaguek, Algonquin tribe, 19
Midé Society, 99
Midewiwin ceremonies, 99
Midwinter ceremonial, 39, 65, 67, 72, 80, 103, 109, 110, 133
Midwives, 123
Migan (boiled corn), 68, 108
Milky Way, beliefs regarding, 140

Miniatures, made as gifts, 87
Missionaries, information from, 5, 65
Moccasins, skin, 20, 128
Mohawk Indians, 4, 10, 17, 18, 27, 73, 89, 116, 147
    See also Iroquois Indians.
Monogamy, practice of, 125
Montagnais Indians, 8, 17, 25, 27, 51
Moon, *Aataentsic* as, 146, 154
    ceremony, 79
    supernatural being, 79
    used to count time, 71
Mooney, James, 12
Moose, 67, 73, 126, 145
    sinews used as thread, 60
    skins, 59
Morgan, Lewis H., 3, 10, 20, 21, 23, 28, 30, 39, 41, 43, 44, 45, 49, 52, 55, 56, 60, 61, 62, 65, 67, 68, 69, 75, 77, 80, 81, 90, 91, 94, 110, 114, 116, 118, 125, 126, 127, 128, 129, 131, 133, 135, 140, 141, 142
Mortar and pestle, wooden, 68, 70
Mosquitoes, 82
Mourning, 133–134
    customs, 129, 133
    duration of, 133
    of matrilineal relative, 133
Moyne, Simon le, 160
Mulberries, 62
Mummers, 109
Murder, as cause for war, 52
    punishment for, 52–56, 96, 128

Names, changing of, 44–45, 134
    giving of, 123, 134
Nanticoke Indians, 99
Nation of Fire, 14, 15, 19
Nation of the Bear, see *Attignawantan.*
Nation of the Cat (Erie Indians), 14, 16, 17
Nation of the Deer (Tobacco confederacy), 12
Nation of the Puants, 19
Nation of the Wolves (Tobacco confederacy), 12
Necklaces, 77, 113, 137
    bead, 20, 21
    wampum, 20, 32, 136, 147
Needles, 26
    used in tattooing, 15
Neintahouy (roasted corn and beans), 69
Nets, hemp, 95, 106
    made by men, 59
Neutral Indians, 9, 10, 13, 14, 15, 16, 17, 18, 23, 61, 65, 134, 135
Neutral Nation, 9–10, 13–17, 23, 61, 65, 111, 134–135
New France, 5
New Sweden, 16
Niagara Falls, 17
Niagara River, 14, 17
Nigouaouichirinik, Huron allies, 19
Nikikouek, Algonquin tribe, 19
Nipissing Indians, 8
Nipissirinien Indians, 19, 25

North American Indians, 124
    cultures of, 5, 7
Northern Iroquoian cultures, 1
Nuts, 60, 62

Oaks, 12
Oatarra (small idol), 99
Ocata (diagnostician), 91
Ochelaga village (*minitik outen entagougiban*), Montreal, 16
Oënrio, Huron village, 149
'Ohgíwe Society (Singers for the Dead), 91, 133, 134, 135
Ohguione (bird), 121
Ohwachira (matrilocal extended family), 43
Oil, gourd of, 130, 142
Oki (spirit or medicine man), 78, 80, 81, 82, 92, 98, 99, 100, 120
Oklahoma Iroquois, 79
Oky, see *Oki.*
Oky ontatechiata (sorcerers), 118
Ondachienra (poisonous root), 56
Ondakhienhai, see *Atiwarontas.*
Ondatouatandy, part of Nation of Puants, 19
Onderha (the ground), 114
Ondessone, Indian tribe, 37
Ondinnock (desires of sick person), 82, 92, 112
Onditachiaé (Thunderbird), 82
Ondoutaehte (god of war), 89
Oneida Indians, 10, 17, 18, 73
    government of, 18
    village of the, 18
    See also Iroquois Indians.
Oneiochronons, see Oneida Indians.
Oneiouchronons, see Oneida Indians.
Onguiaahra (Niagara River), 14, 17
Onions (*anonque*), 62
Oniontcheronons, see Cayuga Indians.
Onneiochronnons, see Oneida Indians.
Onnentisati, Huron village, 149
Onnieoute, see *Ononjoté.*
Onniont (Algonquin charm), 122
Onnontaé, see Onondaga Indians.
Onnontaeronnons, see Onondaga Indians.
Onoiochrhonons, see Cayuga Indians.
Onondaga Indians, 4, 10, 17, 18, 28, 42, 73, 110, 155
    See also Iroquois Indians.
Ononharoia (war feasts), 76, 110, 111
Ononjoté, Mohawk village, 18
Onontaé, see Onondaga Indians.
Onontaerrhonons, see Onondaga Indians.
Onontagueronons, see Onondaga Indians.
Onontsira (scalps), 29
Onorotandi, brother of *Auoindaon*, 26
Ontaanak, allies of Huron, 19
Ontarraoura, mythical animal, 102
Ontetsans (curers), 117
Ooxrat (Indian turnip), 85
Oracles, received by medicine men, 19
Orenda (magic power), 78, 91
Orleans Island, 10

Ornaments, 116, 126
  silver, 20
Oscotarach (head-opener), 141
Ossosané, Huron village, 44, 137, 138, 149
Otakrendoiae (curing dance), 99
Otinontsiskiaj ondaon (house of cut-off heads), 43
Otkon (bad power), 78
Ottawa Indians, 8
Otters, 103
Otter Society, 103
Ottet (pounded corn), 68
Ouachaskesouek, allies of Huron, 19
Ouchaouanag, part of Nation of Fire, 19
Ouinipegong, part of Nation of Puants, 19
Oüioenrhonons, see Oneida Indians.
Ouionenronnons, see Cayuga Indians.
Outaouakamigouek (Algonquin tribe), 19
Outaouasinagouek, Algonquin tribe, 19
Outay robes, 111
Oven, for making pottery, 59
Overblouse, added to women's dress, 20
Owl, 102, 147
  claw of, 120
Oyaron (spirit), 78

Paddle, wooden, 59, 68
Paint, red or brown, 20, 21
Palisades, wooden, 39, 40, 41
Paouitagoung, Algonquin tribe, 19
Parker, Arthur C., 43, 46, 58, 60, 61, 62, 67, 68, 69, 70, 71, 75, 79, 80, 84, 85, 86, 91, 97, 99, 102, 103, 108, 117, 124, 126, 133, 138, 140, 141, 151, 154
Partridge, supernatural, 155
Peace treaty, 28
  between Huron and Seneca, 17
Peaches, 115
Peas, 59, 69
  wild, 62
Pensioners, functions of, 28
Periwinkles, wampum made from, 21
Peron, Francois du, 160
Petun, *see* Tobacco League.
Phratries, 52
Pigments, trade in, 25
Pig's head, ceremonial food, 73
Pike, 66
Pine trees, 39
Pipes, 21, 50, 110, 118, 142
  lighted, symbol of invitation, 57
Pit, *see* Cache pits; Graves.
Plants, medicinal, 84
Plates, wampum, worn on braids, 21
  wampum, worn over stomachs, 21
  wooden, 26
Plumes, moose hair, 30
  red, 111
  worn by Indians, 30
Plums (*tonestes*), 62
Plum stones, used for bowl game, 115, 116

Poison, administered by society members, 99
  See also Death.
Poisoner, 119
Poles (*ouaronta*), 41, 53, 61, 63, 64, 138
  with scalps attached, exposed in war, 29
Police chief, 44
Polygyny, 125
Porches, 41
Porcupine quill trimming, 20, 21, 59, 111
Portages, 26
Potawatomi Indians, 8
Pots, 113
  earthenware, 112
  firing of, 59
  making of, 59
Pouches, 115, 118, 121
Poultices, 83
Powell, J. W., 21, 28, 43, 45, 46, 52, 55, 56, 60, 89, 109, 118, 125, 126, 127, 128
Presents, 63, 107, 111, 112, 113
  exchange of, 49, 50, 57
  meaning of, 53–55
  presented at death, 132, 137, 138
  presented at marriages, 127
  presented for favors, 25, 26, 27, 28, 29, 47, 51, 52, 53, 74, 84, 94, 95, 96, 101, 106
  reparation for murders, 53, 54, 88
Preserves, fruit, 62
Prisoners, burning of, 33, 37, 38
  dress of, 34–35
  eating of, 29, 31, 38, 39
  escape of, 32, 34
  fattening of, 32
  female, 52
  mutilation of, 33–39
  platform used in torturing of, 34
  songs sung by, 32, 35, 37
  taunting of, 37–38
  torture of, 32–39
  treatment of, 15, 28, 29, 31
Proclamations, delivered by chiefs, 44
Procurers, 125
Protohistoric sites, 18
Puberty, fasting at, 100
  seclusion during, 85, 100
Pumpkins, 60, 61, 62, 68, 69, 71, 144
  wild, 62
Purgatives, 84
Purges, 86
Pygmies (Little People), 121
Pyrlaeus, —, 4

Quain, Buell H., 60, 65, 100
Quarrels, private, revenge for, 28
Quebec, 5, 6, 19, 25, 26, 27, 29, 81
  surrender of, 6
Quieunonascaran, Indian town, 24, 26, 44
Quivers, 23
  dog skin, 30

Rabbits, 66
Ragueneau, Paul, 160
Rain, 82, 94, 95, 115

Randle, Martha Champion, 42, 122, 124, 125, 126
Raspberries, 62, 70
Raspberry Ceremony, 62
Rattles, tortoise-shell, 77, 93, 98, 101, 102
Raven, 109
    charm from beak of, 121
Recollets, 4, 5, 19, 87, 124
Residence, matrilocal, 127
    patrilocal, 127
Resuscitation, ceremony of, 45
Rhiierrhonons (Nation of the Cat), 16
Riddles, guessed at ceremonies, 112
Rings, 26
River des Prairies, 26
Robes, 56, 86, 104, 111, 113, 116, 119, 128, 129, 131, 137, 138, 139, 141
    beaver, 35, 51, 57, 114, 121, 126, 130, 136, 137, 138
    outay (black squirrel?), 111
    skin, 16, 20
Rock, supernatural, 81, 82, 141
Rock Nation, *see Arendahronon.*
Roll Call of the Founders of League, 134
Roots
    poisonous, 56
    sondhratatte, 61, 62
Ropes, basswood bark, 60
Rosaries, worn by Indians, 26
Ruffs, down, worn around neck, 20
Ruptures, 99

Sacrifice, human, 32
    white dog, 32, 67
Sagamité (boiled corn), 23, 62, 63, 66, 68
Saguenay, Indians of the, 25, 26
St. Denys, Huron village, 150
St. François-Xavier, Huron village, 150
St. Jean, Huron village, 150
St. Joachim, Huron village, 150
St. Joseph (*Quieunonascaran*), 24, 26, 44
St. Lawrence River, 3, 16
St. Lawrence Valley, 3
St. Louis, Huron village, 150
Ste. Anne, Huron village, 150
Ste. Marie I, Huron village, 10, 14, 150
Sakahiganiriouik, Algonquin tribe, 19
Salmon, 68
Salt, 71
Santweronons, see Seneca Indians.
Sapling (Elder Twin Brother), 153, 154, 155
Sashes, 59
Saulteux Midé Society, 99
Scabs, treatment for, 84
Scahentoarrhonons, Iroquoian-speaking tribe, 16, 17
Scalps (*onontsira*), beliefs regarding, 34
    exposed in war, 29
    taken as trophies, 29, 31, 34
Scanonaerat, Huron village, 10, 11, 150
Scarecrows, hung to scare spirits, 106, 108, 109
Scarification, as medicinal measure, 83
Seashells, wampum made from, 21
Seaver, James E., 58, 79, 125, 126, 127, 133

Seine, supernatural spirit, 80
Seine nets, 63, 79
Seneca Indians, 4, 10, 14, 16, 17, 27, **43**, 75, 79, 91, 131, 153, 154, 155
    See also Iroquois Indians.
Senontouerhonons, see Seneca Indians.
Serpent (*onniont*), 122
    monstrous (*angont*), 117
    skin of, 120
Sex relations, abstinence from, 97, 115, 123
    premarital, 127
Shaman, 78, 84, 92
    See also Medicine man.
Shells, 55
    See also Wampum.
Shields, boiled leather, 30
    cedar, 30
Shimony, Annemarie Anrod, 10, 20, **43**, 45, 48, 58, 60, 61, 62, 68, 69, 71, 72, 73, 74, 75, 79, 80, 81, 82, 83, 84, 85, 86, 87, 88, 89, 90, 91, 92, 93, 97, 100, 102, 103, 109, 110, 114, 115, 116, 117, 121, 122, 123, 124, 125, 126, 127, 129, 130, 131, 132, 133, **134**, 140, 141, 142
Shirts, 20
Shoes, 20, 110, 111, 113, 116
Sick, curing the, 77, 78, 82, 93, 101–102, 106–108, 110, 111–113
    desires of the, 82, 83, 85, 87, 91, 93, 101, 102, 111, 112, 114
Sickness, hereditary, 109
Simples, 84
Singers, 73
    for the dead, 91
Singing, 91, 93, 102, **103**, **111**, **117**
    feast, 75, 76
Sioux Indians, 75
Six Nations Reservation, 71, 79, 110, 121, 122
Skeletons, buried in common grave, 135
    See also Dead.
Skenchiosronons, Indian tribe, 16
Skinner, Alanson, 80, 87, 108
Skins, 113, 136, 137, 142
    dressing of, 15
    garments of, 15
Sky, home of the gods, 145
    home of Thunderbird, 82
    spirit, 80, 81, 95, 132
Sled, 58
Sledge (*arocha*), 23
Slings and slingstones, 121
Smith, De C., 65, 87, 117, 121
Smith, Erminnie A., 117
Smoke holes, 40
Smoking, 24
Snakes, 109, 121, 128, 155
    magic, 81, 82, 120
Snares, hemp, 59, 66
Sneezing, 57
Snowshoes (*agnonra*), 23, 98
Snyderman, George S., 117
Society of Mystic Animals, 97
Sondhratates (Jerusalem-artichoke), 62
Songs, 91, 93, 115, 137
    sung by prisoners, 34, 35

Sonnontouan, see Seneca Indians.
Sonnontoueronnions, see Seneca Indians.
Sonnontoueronnons, see Seneca Indians.
Sonontoen, Seneca town, 17
Sonontoüan, see Seneca Indians.
Sonontrerrhonons, see Seneca Indians.
Sonontwaëronons, see Seneca Indians.
Sonontwehronons, see Seneca Indians.
Sorcerers, 19, 83, 85, 99, 111, 117, 118, 119
    killing of, 118
    oky ontatechiata, 118
Souls, 137
    beliefs regarding, 133–34, 140, 141
    expelling of, 39, 132
    migration of, 91, 140
    of animals, 140
    rebirth of, 132, 140
Spade, wooden, 61
Spatula (*estoqua*), 69
Spears, 30, 88
    fish, 62
Speck, Frank G., 39, 60, 71, 72, 75, 77, 79, 81, 87, 91, 93, 108, 110, 114, 115, 117, 121, 140
Spells, 117, 118
Spirits, 78, 80–82, 88
    guardian, 90
Spoons, 23, 74
Spring Festival, 78
Spruces, 12, 40, 108
Squash, 15, 58, 60, 71
Squirrels, 64
    black, 111
    robe from skin of, 93, 111
Steel, for firemaking, 23
Sticks, as mnemonic devices, 46
Stockades, 39
Stones, 110
    red hot, juggled by medicine men, 104, 106
    red hot, used for sweating, 86, 105
    used as charms, 117, 120, 121
Storage, *see* Cache pits.
Strawberries, 62, 70
    dried, 62, 105
Strawberry Ceremony, 62
Straws, game, 57, 114, 115
Sturgeon, 64, 73
Sturtevant, William C., 2, 79
Sucking, as curing treatment, 84, 117
Suicide, 56–57
    beliefs regarding, 141
Suitor, rejection of, 126
    requirements of, 127
Sun, *Iouskehaas,* 146, 154
    supernatural being, 36, 38, 79
Sun Dance, 79
Sunflowers, 60
Sunflower seed oil, 60, 68
    used in tattooing, 21
    used on hair, 21
Supernatural beings, *see* Spirits.
Susquehanna Indians, 16, 17
Susquehanna River, 16
Sweat baths, 85, 86, 93, 104, 108, 118, 145

Sweat houses, 86, 88, 93, 96, 105, 145
Sword blades, 137
Sycamore bark, 84

Taenhatentaron, Huron village, 150
Taft, Grace Ellis, 94
Tahontaenrat, see *Tohontaenrat.*
Tamales, 70
Tattooing, 15, 21
Tawiscaron (Younger Twin Brother), 146, 151, 154, 155
Teanaostahé, Indian village, 44
Teanaostaiaé, Huron village, 150
Teharonhiawagon, Iroquois name for *Iouskeha,* 151
Thanksgiving Address, 73, 81
    dance, 30, 72, 75
    feast, 75
Thieves, 52
    discovery of, 97
    punishment of, 56
Thorn, used in tattooing, 15
Three Rivers, 5, 18, 27
Thunder, 128
    supernatural being, 75, 80, 82, 95, 115
Thunderbird, 82, 109
Thunder Ceremony, 103, 115
Ticks, wood, 82
Time, counted by the moon, 71
Toad, supernatural, 155
Toanché I, Huron village, 149
Toanché II, Huron village, 149
Tobacco, 9, 13, 15, 23, 26, 50, 60, 73, 80, 83, 86, 87, 98, 110, 111, 112, 139, 142, 143
    Anondahoin, 73
    burned as invocation, 64, 80, 93, 95, 109, 118
    distribution of, 50
    invocation, 79, 80
    offering of, 64, 74, 80, 81, 82, 94
    pouch, 20, 59, 116, 118
    rituals, 80
Tobacco League, 5, 9, 10, 12–13, 15, 21, 27, 66, 82, 111, 117
Tobacco Nation. *See* Tobacco League.
Tohontaenras, see *Tohontaenrat.*
Tohontaenrat (White-eared or Deer People), 3, 10, 11, 36, 150
Tomahawk, 76, 116, 130, 136, 137, 142
    red-hot, used in torture, 33
Tomb, bark, 130, 131
Tonawanda, 73
Tondakhra, Huron village, 149
Tools, European, 21
Torch, 90, 143
Tortoise shells, 77, 84, 106, 107
Torture, beliefs regarding, 33
    of prisoners, 31–39
    religious ceremonial, 32, 36
Trade, 15, 59, 71, 75, 90, 91, 121, 143
    and war, 25–31
    done by men, 58
    infringement of, 26
    private rights in, 25–26

Traders:
 Dutch, 9, 16, 17, 27
 effect of, on natives, 5, 115, 135
 English, 16, 17, 27
 European, 4, 17
 Flemish, 27
 French, 5, 10, 11, 13, 17, 25, 26, 27, 40, 57, 67
 King of Sweden as protector of, 16
 priests as, 26
 Swedish, 17
Traitors, 52, 56
Traps, 65, 66
Travelers, treatment of, 57
Trelease, Allen W., 9
Trigger, Bruce Graham, 9
Trout, 64, 66
Tumpline, use of, 59
Turkeys, wild, 15, 66
 wing of, 103
Turnip, Indian, 85
Turtle, 98
 cooking of, 66
 shells, 106
 supernatural being, 79, 146, 147, 153, 154, 155
Turtledoves, 140
Twin Brothers, supernational spirits, see *Iouskeha and Tawiscaron.*

Upper Algonquin, 18
Upper Great Lakes area, 10
Upper Great Lakes Indians, 99
Upper Iroquois, 18
Upper Sandusky, Ohio, 10
Urination, part of curing ceremony, 107

Vats, storage for corn, 61
Venison, cooked with corn, 68
Vessels, earthen, 59
 wooden, 59
Viel, Father Nicolas, 5, 6
Villages, 39–42
 defense of, 31
 elders of, 44
 fires in, as result of ceremonies, 112
 fortified, 18, 31
 moving of, 42
 palisaded, 11, 15, 39
 stationary, 16
 stockaded, 39
 unfortified, 40
Villages of the dead, 141, 142, 143, 145
Virginia, 16
Visions, 90, 97, 106
 quests for, 100
Vomiting, 87, 99, 117
Voting, method of, 48–49

Wage work, importance of, 58
Wake, *see* Death.
Walker, Louise J., 135
Wallace, Anthony F. C., 86
Walnuts, 62
Wampum (*onocoirota*), 47, 48, 50, 51, 52, 107, 110, 116
 beads (*hassaendista*), 26, 35, 53, 54, 55, 57, 116, 121, 123, 132, 137

Wampum—Continued
 belt, 52
 chains of, 21, 35, 46, 47, 51, 53, 126, 137
 collar of, 28, 32, 50, 57, 86, 93, 114, 116, 121, 126, 130, 137, 138, 139
 made from periwinkles, 21
 necklaces of, 20, 21, 32, 51, 126, 136, 137, 147
 trade in, 25
War, as cause of death, 132
 ceremonies, 43, 75
 chief, 36, 37, 43, 44, 73, 120
 council, 36, 43
 dance, 30, 75, 79, 115
 declaration of, 31, 52, 108
 exercises, 29
 feast, 29, 39, 73, 74, 76
 god, 89, 90
 lapse of, 58
 preparations for, 29, 31
 reasons for, 28, 91
 song, 39, 93, 129
 spoils, distributed by old men, 34
 victim, avenging of, 132
Warfare, 25–31, 71
Warriors, 11, 75, 78, 96, 97
 garihoniia doutagueta, 44
 scouts, 31
Wasáse' (War Dance), 75
Watch towers (*ondaqua*), 31, 39
Water, fetched by boys, 124
 myths relating to, 155
 soul of, 64
 stocked on palisades, 40
 substitutes for, 23
Water hemlock (*Cicuta maculata*), 56
Waugh, Frederick W., 24, 58, 60, 61, 62, 66, 67, 68, 69, 70, 71, 82, 94, 97, 100, 127, 134
Weanohronons, see *Wenrôhronon* Indians.
Weapons, 108, 137
 See also Firearms.
Weather, control of, 94
Webster, Ephraim, 4
Wedding bread, 127
Weirs, 62, 63
Wendat, native name for Huron, 9, 10
Wenrio, village, 98
Wenrôhronon Indians, 14, 86
Wenroronon, see *Wenrôhronon Indians.*
Wheat, 12
White, Marian E., 1
Whitefish (*assihendo*), 63
Widows, mourning customs of, 133
Wildcats, 15, 16
 robes made of skins of, 16
Willow, 24, 62
Wilson, Daniel, 3, 55
Wind, 82
Winter occupations, 71–72
Witchcraft, 74, 83, 84, 88, 90, 93, 117–120
Witches, 52, 84, 96, 120, 132
 killing of, 118–119
 torture of, 119
Wives (*aténonha*), 127
Wolf clan, 12

Wolves, 15, 102
  muzzle of, as ensign of war, 89
  supernatural, 147
  teeth of, 99
Women, 125
  as guards of clan supplies, 51
  as pottery makers, 59
  bones of dead cleaned by, 136
  chief selected by, 46
  dance of, 79
  dreams of, 91
  dress of, 15, 20
  household chores performed by, 49, 58
  in council meetings, 48, 59
  lamentations for dead by, 15–16, 133
  land owned by, 60
  menstruating, 108, 125
  mourning customs of, 133
  old, 77, 107
  participation in curing ceremonies by, 103, 104, 106, 107
  pastimes of, 59, 116
  planting by, 31, 58
  pregnant, 86, 122, 127
  price for murder of, 52, 53
Women—Continued
  remarriage of, 133
  returned from dead, 142
  torture of, 31
  treatment of, 31
Wood, used in witchcraft, 117, 118
  chopped by boys, 124
  collected by women, 58
  presented as gift, 89
  trade for, 26
  transportation of, 58
Worms, 82
Wounds, inflicted, payment for, 54
  treatment for, 85
Wrong, G. M., editor, 8
Wyandot Indians, 1, 10, 12, 13, 21, 43, 45, 46, 52, 54, 55, 56, 60, 72, 74, 78, 79, 81, 89, 91, 99, 103, 108, 109, 117, 118, 121, 125, 126, 127, 128, 133, 134, 147, 151, 152, 153, 154, 155

Yellow leaf cup (*Polymnia uvedalia*), 84
Yews, 12
Yoscaha, see *Iouskeha*.